EPERON'S FRENCH WINE TOUR

Arthur Eperon is one of the most experienced and best-known travel writers in Europe. Since leaving the RAF in 1945 he has worked as a journalist in various capacities, often involving travel. He has concentrated on travel writing for the past twenty-five years and contributed to many publications including *The Times*, *Daily Telegraph*, *New York Times*, *Woman's Own*, *Popular Motoring* and the *TV Times*. He has also appeared on radio and television and for five years was closely involved in Thames Television's programme *Wish You Were Here*. He has been wine writer to the RAC publications and a number of magazines.

He has an intimate and extensive knowledge of France and its food and wine, as a result of innumerable visits there over the last forty years. In 1974 he won the Prix des Provinces de France, the annual French award for travel writing.

D0566625

ARTHUR EPERON

EPERON'S FRENCH WINE TOUR

A traveller's guide to tasting and buying wine in France

Photographs by Patrick Eagar

PAN BOOKS

Also by Arthur Eperon in Pan Books

Travellers' France
Encore Travellers' France
Le Weekend
The French Selection
The British Selection
Travellers' Britain
Travellers' Italy (in association with the BBC)

First published 1986 by Pan Books Ltd,
Cavaye Place, London SW10 9PG

9 8 7 6 5 4 3 2 1

ISBN 0 330 29600 0
Designed by Peter Ward
Photoset by Rowland Phototypesetting Ltd,
Bury St Edmunds, Suffolk
Printed in Italy

CONTENTS

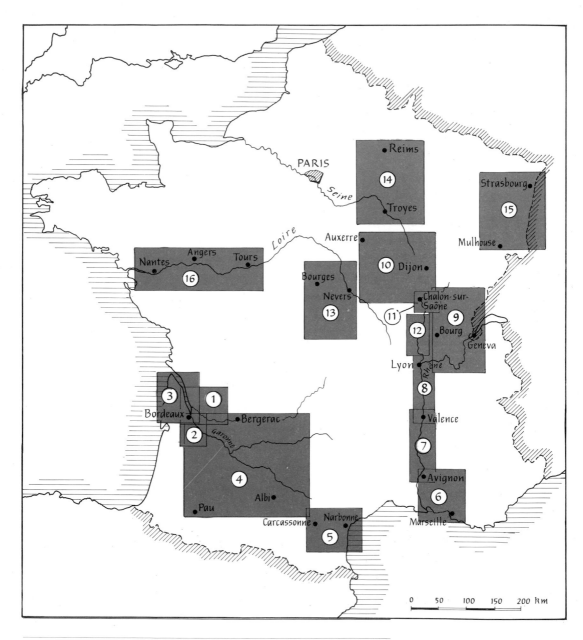

Map showing the wine-growing areas of France

INTRODUCTION

'Free booze all the way to the Med! Great!' said a radio presenter.

Please . . . no! I shall be banned from every wine cave from Bordeaux to Beaune, by way of Bergerac and Bandol. True, nearly all the tastings to which I shall point you are kindly offered free, but you can hardly blame the wine producers if they hope that the tasters are real wine drinkers, willing to buy a bottle or two; better still, that they will go on buying it when they get home.

This is not really a book for winesmen so dedicated that they can hardly enjoy their wine for analysing it. It is for people who enjoy drinking wine but who either cannot afford the grand old wines of Bordeaux and Burgundy or do not want to spend so much on one bottle and who would like to find a path through the bewildering number of 'lesser' wines of France. The choice is enormous. The problem is time and knowing where to look.

Bad weather and disease have hit many wine-producing areas over the last few years, including Champagne, Chablis, St-Emilion and some good Muscadet vineyards. Combined with high bidding from the Almighty Dollar and Unyielding Yen, this has forced up the price of many old favourites. The French themselves are seeking good substitute wines in the Rhône, South West, Dordogne and Provence. They are making new friends, and we must do the same. Happily, there are plenty of good wines about.

Unless you are a professional and have trade connections, you cannot taste or buy wines at most of the very grand top wine châteaux. You can visit a few if you make arrangements beforehand by writing. But, quite understandably, they do not have time to stop and receive passing travellers; their wine is too precious and expensive to give away, and they sell by contract through agents. The wines in this book are good or very good and there are even a few grand wines you can taste, especially in Champagne, but also in the Haut-Médoc of Bordeaux.

Like you, I am not a professional, although I have been drinking wine avidly for forty years. When I wrote about wine for the RAC they called me 'one of the world's greatest consumers'. Well, I have tried a few in my time and I have just completed a year of revision to bring me up to date. Alas, I had to do a lot of spitting-out rather than swallowing, not because I was playing the professional but because I was driving myself most of the time. I still do some stupid things in my late sixties but drinking and driving is not one of them.

I have compiled this list for all sorts of travellers — amateur enthusiasts looking for a choice of reasonably priced wine, people touring France who want to compare wines, and those driving through France, especially people in gîtes, villas or caravans. Above all, it is for people who want to bring wine home.

At present (late 1986), the duty-free allowance when you buy in EEC countries such as France (as opposed to duty-free shops) is 11 bottles (8 litres) of table wine if you take back no spirits, or 7 bottles (5 litres) if you take back 1½ litres of spirits. Instead of spirits, you can take back 4 bottles (3 litres) of Champagne or any fizzy wine up to twenty-two per cent volume alcohol.

But don't worry about taking back too much table wine if it is of good quality and you like it. Keep the receipts, declare the wine, and pay duty and VAT. You will still have a bargain, especially if you buy at the vineyard or tasting cave, where wine is invariably cheaper. You will still get your duty-free allowance. And remember that duty is only on volume and alcoholic content. The VAT is on price, so it is not worth paying duty on *vin de table* plonk. It is only worth paying on a wine with an AOC label (*see below*). The better the wine, the better the bargain. But that does *not* apply to the top wines, like *premier* or *deuxième cru* Médoc, *premier grand cru* St-Emilion or the best Burgundies, which are often as cheap in Britain or America, nor to real Champagne, which usually works

out much the same for the particular brand if you buy it in France and pay duty as if you buy it here.

If you find a wine you really like, buy a case of twelve bottles. If I find a younger wine which could do with a couple of years in bottle, I buy a *vrac* (strong plastic bottle) or *cubitainer* (square plastic container). When I get home, I let it rest for a fortnight or more, then bottle it. Use old bottles, washed with the disinfectant you can buy from a chemist/pharmacy or a Do-It-Yourself wine shop, and good new corks. You must buy (or borrow) a simple corking machine. Our old one looks like one of those two-handled bottle openers where you push down the handles, only it works the other way round, pushing the cork in.

Keeping wine so long without a cellar is a problem. Ideally wine should be kept lying flat at a temperature between 7–12°C (45–55°F). Keeping it at 15°C (59°F) may make the wine mature quicker. Better to keep it at a slightly higher but even temperature (say 60°F) than allow the temperature to rise and fall. Keep wine away from chemical fungicides or strong odours, which penetrate the cork and seal. Store it in the dark (especially if in clear glass bottles, like Sauternes) and try to avoid anywhere with vibration. Don't put it anywhere too dry where corks can dry out. The floor is better than the top of a cupboard (heat rises) and a wooden garden shed must be frost-proof and summer-heat proof. You can buy cold storage units if you mean to go on keeping wine over years, but be careful of those which are *too* cold.

Ask for a label (*étiquette*) of wines you taste and like. I ask also where I can buy them at home. I cannot put the answers in this book, alas, for many have long lists, but many also have a British or American agent. So ask for *Vos Agents en Angleterre* or *en Amérique* and write it down right away before you forget. Then write to the agent when you get home for a list of stockists. It is well worth taking this trouble, for it can be very frustrating to make a 'find' in France and be unable to get any more of it in Britain. If you are really stuck, try writing to the information

offices which I have given for each region of France or to Food and Wine from France, 41–46 Piccadilly, London W1V 9AJ.

Tasting to some is a great art, with its own mysteries and language. To others it is just a way of finding wines which you like and want to drink again. Basically, of course, it is a matter of smell and taste, with colour adding a touch of glamour.

First look at the wine in the glass to see if it is still or slightly fermenting (*pétillant*). Tilt the glass at about 45 degrees against a white background to see the true colour, which can actually tell you things. Most reds, for instance, get paler with age and, on the whole, a very deep colour means that wine is young; but colour varies enormously with grape varieties (the old 'black wine' of Cahors is made with a dark purple Auxerrois grape), and pale wine could come from a wet harvest. Colour depth in white wine usually means age.

Next swirl the wine round in your glass and smell it. The swirling releases vapour to the top of the wine and makes smells more definite. It can be fun trying to put words to what your nose is telling you. For one-upmanship, give another twirl and see if the wine sticks to the side of the glass, coming down slowly, or if it leaves little trace. If it sticks, it almost certainly has more 'body' – heavier, with more alcohol. Make rough notes for later.

Strong perfume or aftershave spoils tasting. Don't taste after a heavy meal – and certainly not with cheese. Almost all wine tastes splendid with cheese. Above all, don't let anyone smoke!

All this is elementary stuff to the great winesman, who studies every nuance of wine. But if you do want to know more, told simply and unpretentiously by the founder-editor of the *Which? Wine Guide*, read *Masterglass*, by Jancis Robinson (Pan).

There is, of course, a lot of nonsense talked about wine – and most of it by people who begin with that very sentence. There *are* wine snobs, of course, though not so many as food snobs. There are plenty of inverted snobs, too. If preferring Chambertin to the battery acid some folk bring back from supermarkets abroad is snobbery, then I am a snob. And people who tell me that 'the French I know just plonk a bottle of red on the stove to get hot' must surely have been staying with Normans, Bretons or Parisians. Any Bordelais or Burgundian will tell you that none of these have any palate or know very much about wine.

It really does pay to treat even the cheapest *Vin de Table* with some respect and serve it at the right temperature. It can do wonders for the flavour of the most humble red wine to bring it into the room a couple of hours or more before serving it and to remove the cork so that it gets aired or, better still, to decant it. Old wines long in bottle need decanting. It releases the flavour and character of the wine, apart from removing sediment. Though there are no strict rules about serving temperatures, the wine maker should know how best to serve his wines and is worth following. Basically, dry white wines like Muscadet and Sauvignon should be well chilled. Champagne, rosé and dry white Bordeaux not so long (half an hour in the fridge, perhaps, temperature around 7°C or 45°F). Serve Sancerre and Pouilly Fumé at about 10°C (50°F). Chablis, young red wines like Beaujolais, and other young red wines made from the Gamay grape at about 13°C (55°F). The French drink many young red wines at this temperature, including Bergerac, Provence, Gaillac and even Rhône wines, but it does depend where you are. What is coolly refreshing in the summer heat of Provence is no comfort on an English winter's day. Most reds, like Burgundy, Chinon, old Bandol and Cahors are served at 16°C (62–4°F). Red Rhône, and Bordeaux wines are served at real room temperature – about 19°C (68°F).

If you want to know more about serving temperatures, storage, and who produces what wines around the world, read my favourite wine writer Serena Sutcliffe's practical, down-to-earth paperback *The Wine Drinkers' Handbook* (Pan).

Don't take any notice of snobs who sneer at roadside wine tastings and call them 'tourist traps'. You don't have to buy.

Many are set up, even in markets, by good small growers and wine makers trying to make an honest bob and keep up the cash flow. Look at the name and credentials on the booth or cave. I have found some excellent little wines, like a good AOC Bourgueil in Langeais market and an excellent old Monbazillac (Vieil Curé) from a booth below the vineyards on a main road, with the owner's son explaining the wines expertly in excellent English.

The reason why French wines, from the *grand cru* downwards, remain so desirable is the strict controls both nationally and regionally of planting, types of grape used, methods of making and maturing. The secret is the classification AOC or AC (*Appellation d'Origine Contrôlée*) a legal definition which some well-known wines like Cahors had to wait until the 1970s to get and many more would dearly love to have. There were some deviations years ago, but rules are strictly applied now. VDQS (*Vins Délimités de Qualité Supérieure*) are good wines from a defined area, not quite AOC standard. *Vins de Pays* must be from recommended grape types, produced in the region indicated by the name. *Vins de Table* are blended wines with alcoholic content on the label – usually sold under brand names.

With Bordeaux and Burgundy prices rising, wine buyers have gone for more Rhône, Loire and other wines, pushing up their prices a bit too. Wine fashions of Paris have also affected availability and prices. A few years back Bourgueil red wines from the Loire were in vogue, then Cahors. Now red Chinon is 'in' and oddly, red Sancerre, which is fairly rare and not, to my mind, outstanding. Light young wines are fashionable, often drunk cold, and red wines are drunk as aperitifs. Some wine makers and wholesalers are positively encouraging this as, for them, it represents a quick cash flow, and less bother with warehousing and maturing in caves. But the old dedicated wine drinkers are too experienced to fall for it. Much of this young red wine drunk cold gives me indigestion, especially Nouveau or Primeur wines, a drinking fashion started as a stunt.

The French are very 'correct' in their manners and admire people who are *très gentils*, which means basically quiet and not pushy. That goes for French people in the vineyards and caves, too, even if they do often wear rough clothes and old flat hats while working because of the dirt and dust. Even if they do not speak English, they will try, if you, too, try to speak a little French. Most of them love to tell you about their wines, for they have put their hearts, labour and whole lives into them and they are proud of them. So they do not appreciate passing holidaymakers who breeze in and say something like 'Where's the wine, then?' Believe me, some do. *'Est-ce qu'il y a des dégustations, s'il vous plaît?'* or a simple 'Are there tastings, please?' said with a smile, will produce better results. The smile is important. As one grower said to me when I asked him if visitors needed any credentials for tasting: 'Only a big smile'.

Note

The caves are in business to sell wines, so do not be upset if they ask you if you would like to buy. You are not committed. Opening hours are normally for Monday to Friday unless otherwise stated but some of these caves may open on Saturdays and even Sundays in summer, especially in tourist areas.

Room and menu grades

C = cheap (approximately under 120 Francs for meals; under 250 Francs a night for a double room); M = medium prices (meals 120–200F; rooms 250–450F); E = expensive (meals 200–300F; rooms 450–600F); VE = very expensive (meals over 300F; rooms over 600F).

Prices are as quoted near the end of 1986.

GLOSSARY

(including some wine-tasting terms)

Appellation d'Origine Contrôlée (AC or AOC) classification of France's top wines, usually named after the place they are made

Acre bitter; too much tannin or acidity

Agressif aggressive; too much acidity/alcohol

Apre rough, harsh; too much tannin

Bouchonné wine gone mildewy, with disgusting smell, usually through a bad cork letting in disease. Corked.

Bref short; leaves no pleasant or lingering after-taste

Brûlant warm sensation from alcohol; burning if excess of alcohol

Brut very dry (especially Champagne and sparkling wines)

Cépage grape variety

Chais sheds for keeping wine above ground

Chambré wine brought to room temperature

Charnu fleshy; fills the mouth well

Charpenté well constituted; high in alcohol

Corsé full-bodied; high in alcohol

Crémant less sparkling than Champagne, more sparkling than *pétillant* wine

Cru raw, coarse, thin, under-developed

Crus vineyards classified by reputation

Cuvée wine from selected barrel or vat; in Champagne: first pressing

Décharné fleshless; gone thin, lost fruit and charm through old age

Dépouillé stripped; weakening of characteristics through age

Doucereuse rather unpleasant sweetness

Dur rough to swallow, usually caused by too much tartaric acid or tannin

Fade tasteless, weak, thin

Fin court short-finish; short-lived taste

Fleuri bouquet (smell) of flowers

Fondu well blended; well matured

Fort strong in alcohol

Franc clean, sound wine

Friand delicious; pleasant to drink

Gouleyant easy to drink, light, pleasant

Goût de terroir distinctive taste imparted by the soil and grape variety

Gras full-bodied, rich in alcohol, glycerine

Grossier dull, heavy, coarse, uninteresting

Jeune new young wine or wine which has kept its young character

Joyeux a wine that makes you cheerful

Léger light; low in alcohol

Liquoreux liqueur-like; rich, sweet, heady

Long long; wine with taste that lingers

Macération carbonique method of vinification in which whole grapes are put in vats to make them ferment quickly through their own natural gases. Produces fruity red wines for early drinking, like Nouveau Beaujolais

Mâche chewy; fills the mouth well

Mâché wine slightly oxidised by too much air; stale taste

Maigre thin; lacking in alcohol

Méthode Champenoise way of achieving sparkle by secondary fermentation in the bottle, as opposed to in cask or vat

Méthode Rurale (or Gaillacoise) old fashioned way of making sparkling wines by retarding fermentation, then letting it start again without adding any sugar

Mielleux honey-like, with too much sugar

Moelleux mellow wine; rich in sugar with little acidity; not always a sweet wine

Mou flabby, lacking in body and freshness

Négociant middleman between grower and retailer; not just a wholesaler, he may also blend, bottle, mature and ship wine

Onctueux not really 'unctuous' but mellow

Perlé very slightly sparkling

Pétillant semi-sparkling

Plein full, well balanced wine

Pourriture noble 'noble rot', the fungus which attacks white grapes, essential to making a great sweet white wine

Primeur nouveau wines; for drinking very young or bought young for keeping

Puissant powerful, rich, well balanced

Racé vital, lively

Raide stiff, acidic, lacking softness

Râpeux rough from too much tannin

Rassis well-balanced wine which has finished ageing

Rond well rounded, mellow, soft, full-bodied

Sec bone-dry wine except for sparkling, when it means a little less dry. For red wines it can also mean too dry in taste because of grape deterioration

Séché dried up; too old or deteriorated

Sur lie white wine bottled direct from lees

Souple soft; low tannin and acid; often applied to youthful reds expected to be sharper

Soyeaux silky texture

Tanique tannic – often used for wines with too much tannin, which can be unpleasant when a wine is young but is needed if a red wine is to keep well and mature

Tendre delicate, slightly sweet, non acidic

Terne uninteresting, lacking life, character

Terroir combination of soil and climate – main element in taste of wine together with grape variety

Usé worn out, lost its original qualities

Velouté velvety, soft in the mouth

Vendange tardive late picking of very ripe grapes, giving sugar and high alcohol

Vert young wine with too much acidity

Vif fresh light wines with the right alcohol and acid

Vin-de-garde a wine for keeping a long time

Vineux with good vinosity; high alcohol and warm to the taste!

Vin gris very light rosé, almost grey; fresh

Vin mousseux sparkling wine made by secondary fermentation or by addition of carbon dioxide

Vigneron grower of grapes for wine

Vignoble vineyard

AREA 1

BORDEAUX EAST

ST-EMILION · FRONSAC · POMEROL
BOURG · BLAYE

When we were young, the wine of St-Emilion was our Elixir of Life. Margaux and the great Médocs were too dear. Beaujolais was dubious. Cahors was hard to get. Corbières was mixed with Algerian as plonk to make you drunk. We sat on the terrace of St-Emilion's Hotel Plaisance beside the old Bell Tower looking over the crowded rooftops of the steep little mediaeval city to the vineyards beyond, sinking a bottle of *premier grand cru* St-Emilion and dreaming. When we were old, we thought, this was where we should like to die, in peace and quiet, after finishing the bottle.

I am now almost old and my dreams have changed with St-Emilion. Trees and shrubs block the view from the terrace. The

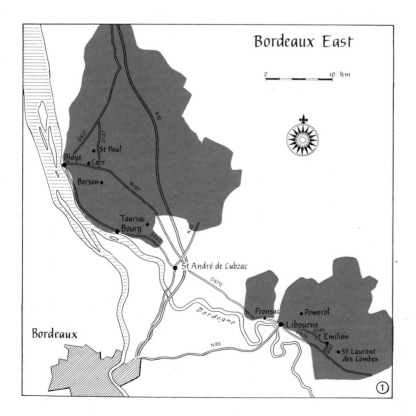

Plaisance is posher and charges higher prices for its wine for Parisians and Americans. From spring to autumn the streets are crammed with visitors on wine pilgrimages, just as they were once with religious pilgrims. Blessedly, the cave of the Union de Producteurs de Saint-Emilion is still in the tiny place du Clocher opposite the Plaisance and here you can taste good wine and buy a bottle or a plastic barrel to take home and bottle yourself, as I do, thus getting good St-Emilion at half the home market price or less. And I eat now at the little Logis de la Cadène (place Marché-au-Bois, tel. (57) 24.71.40) where the Mouliérac family serve great value traditional meals and their very own wine – Château la Clotte (*grand cru classé*).

St-Emilion has a Jurade (founded 1199 by King John of England) whose members control the quality of wine and classify it. The 1985 reclassification has caused fury! Wines are classified as *premier grand cru*, *grand cru classé*, *grand cru* and AOC St-Emilion, in descending order. Simple AOC St-Emilions vary greatly in quality and often it is worth paying extra for a *grand cru* wine. The wines should be rich, deep coloured, with concentrated fruit and so little tannin that they appeal even to people who prefer the sweeter white wines of Germany to claret. The wines can be drunk after three years, but are best left six–ten years.

There are about 1000 producers, most of which are small. In outlying villages a similar wine is produced and they are allowed to add St-Emilion to the village name (St-Georges, Puisseguin, Lussac and Montagne are the best of these). These wines are not so good as higher-grade St-Emilion but can be good value.

The key to St-Emilion is the Merlot grape, making up to eighty per cent of the juice, though only fifty per cent in many cases. Most of the rest is Cabernet Franc (called Bouchet here). Merlot vines were hit badly by a harsh winter, late frosts and disease in 1984, which forced up St-Emilion prices. But 1985 was prolific.

In the backyard of the old port of Libourne, which once rivalled Bordeaux for exporting wine, is Pomerol. Here Merlot is still the

top grape but clay soil gives a different wine. The area is small, growers many. Most have private clients, so the wine is not well known. It varies, but to my mind it is underestimated. Alas, I have found no growers with enough time to give tastings to passing travellers. But maybe you will be lucky enough to see the odd notice up announcing *Dégustations*. Please let me know! Otherwise phone the wine-tasting association Hospitaliers de Pomerol, Château de Tailhas (57) 51.26.02. Château Petrus is the best wine.

Fronsac, on the Dordogne bank north-east of Libourne, produces Canon Fronsac (usually the best vineyards) and Fronsac. Both are made, like St-Emilion and Pomerol, with Merlot (but only fifty per cent), Cabernet Sauvignon, Cabernet Franc and a few Malbec grapes. The Dutch buy most of the Fronsac wine. Do try it – excellent value and great with meat or cheese. Both are meaty wines, solid and robust. Both should be at least four years old. Canon Fronsac will even keep twenty years.

Across the Gironde river from Médoc, the Côtes de Blaye and de Bourg have long been poor relations to Margaux and the rest. In the fifteenth century, however, it was the other way round. Bourg and Blaye were considered the top Bordeaux wines and merchants would sell only if the buyer was prepared to take some of the 'rough stuff' from Médoc with them! Until the 'pieds noirs' growers arrived from Algeria in the '60s, oxen instead of tractors were still used for ploughing and carting. Picturesque but not competitive. Now red wines have improved enormously, rising prices in Médoc have attracted drinkers, and the trade has been forced to take notice. Premiers Côtes de Blaye wines are soft, fruity, have a most attractive smell, are lighter than Côtes de Bourg and usually drunk younger. Bourg wines last longer, can be kept six or even ten years and are much underrated by old-style wine snobs. They are certainly a good alternative to cheaper Médocs or St-Emilion.

Tastings

ST-EMILION

Union de Producteurs de Saint-Emilion

Place du Clocher, BP 27, 33330 St-Emilion, Gironde, tel.(57) 24.70.71. 9–12 hrs; 14–18 hrs. Shut Sundays.

Three hundred and eighty producers form this union, which makes AOC St-Emilion, and *grands crus* wine, plus the much-praised Château Berliquet, recently raised to *grand cru classé*. They have their own *marques* – Bois Royal (AOC Saint-Emilion) and four *grands crus* – Côtes Rocheuses, Royal Saint-Emilion, Haut Quercus (winner of the Trophy of Honour for St-Emilion wines in 1985) and Cuvée Galius (winner 1984). Very convenient place to taste. And possible to arrange vineyard visits. You won't get any *premier grand cru* wines, but few of those vineyards offer tastings to non-trade visitors anyway.

Château Pavie

33330 St-Emilion, Gironde, tel.(57) 24.72.02. D130 E St-Emilion to St-Laurent-des-Combes. 9.30–12 hrs; 14.30–17.30 hrs. Phone.

One of the few great wine producers of St-Emilion who offer visitors a tasting of their wine, but you should phone. And you cannot buy it there. You must use the trade. Pavie is *premier grand cru classé* at the top of the class – superbly vinified, full bodied, rich, with a plummy taste. The Valette family also make Château Pavie-Decesse (*grand cru classé* – more tannic than Pavie) part of the property since last century, and Château La Clusière, just south-west of Pavie, one of the oldest vineyards in St-Emilion (*grand cru classé*).

Château Vieux Clos (Michel Terras)

33330 St-Emilion, Gironde, tel.(57) 24.60.91. NW of St-Emilion off D243. Phone if possible.

One of the best of the *grand cru* wines, from the foot of the plateau where most *premier grand cru* wines are produced. Mouth-filling (*charnu*) and velvety.

Château Jean-Faure

Find it if you can. An elegant, full-bodied wine produced by old methods – hand picking, old press, nine rackings over two years into new wood barrels, fining with egg white – with a gorgeous bouquet and beautiful ruby colour. *Grand cru classé*.

33330 St-Emilion, tel.(57) 51.49.36. NW of city towards Pomerol, near Cheval Blanc (greatest St-Emilion – no visits). Daily 8–21 hrs. English spoken.

Château Canon (Eric Fournier)

Old Domaine de St Martin and marked as that on yellow Michelin. Phoning essential. *Premier grand cru* wine famous since 1770. Lovely old château well worth visiting. Most of the vineyard in a walled *clos*. Wine is kept long in the wood in oak barrels, half of which are replaced every year! A classic stylish wine with a lovely smell, silky smoothness and long-lasting flavour. It takes time to develop. One of my very favourites.

33330 St-Emilion, tel.(57) 24.70.79. Just outside city walls to west.

Château Soutard

The property has been in the Count des Ligneris' family for 200 years. *Grand cru classé* wine is made with sixty per cent Merlot grape – solid, traditional, vital. Takes time to mature. One of the best. Elegant château.

33330 St-Emilion, tel.(57) 24.72.23. NE of St-Emilion off D243. Phone – ask for Comte François des Ligneris who speaks English, or Jacques des Ligneris.

Château Canon La Gaffelière

33330 St-Emilion, tel.(57) 24.71.33. Off D172 into city from D670. 8–12 hrs; 14–18 hrs. English spoken. *Grand cru classé*.

Château Fonrazade

Traditional wine. *Grand cru*. Exceptional bouquet. Also produce Château Comte des Cordes wine.

33330 St-Emilion, tel.(57) 24.71.58. W of city, across railway from D670. Visits every day, all year. Tastings 5F. No English spoken.

Château Petit Gravet

Fruity, full-bodied wine. *Grand cru.* I like it.

33330 St-Emilion, tel.(57) 24.72.05. Convenient – just off D172 into city after junction with D670. Visits in working hours.

Further Information

Association de Propriétaires de Grands Crus Classés de St-Emilion, Les Templiers, rue Guadet, BP46, 33330 St-Emilion, tel.(57) 24.71.41 (visits to twenty-seven châteaux possible). Syndicat d'Initiative de St-Emilion, place des Crémaux, 33330 St-Emilion, Gironde, tel.(57) 24.72.03.

Jacques Borie, with Château de la Rivière in the background

FRONSAC · BLAYE · BOURG

Château de la Rivière

Jacques Borie is a passionate standard bearer of Fronsac wines. In a delightful castle high in the woods, with formidable towers, creepers reaching the blue-grey roof slates and an elegant terrace, he produces a wine which has forced respect from world experts who have rather patronised Fronsac. The praise which his wines received when he entered them for blind tastings made the most

La Rivière, 33145 St-Michel-de-Fronsac, tel.(57) 24.98.01. Take D670 NW from Libourne for 6km, just past St-Michel. Visits Monday–Friday 8–11 hrs; 14–17 hrs. English spoken.

experienced tasters sit up. In good years, the wines were rated with *premier cru* (first growth) Médocs, costing very much more. And prices for old wines at auctions show how surprisingly well his wines keep. He uses sixty per cent Merlot grapes, thirty per cent Cabernet Sauvignon, with a little Cabernet Franc and Pressac. The wines have a lot of fruity flavour, are rich in colour, full-bodied and *long* (the taste lasts a long time) because he waits very late to pick his grapes (one year recently he began on 22 October!). He ages them for months in oak and proposes a minimum of two–three years in bottle. The old cellars are huge and excellent. Wines have been grown here for 1300 years. A tower which Charlemagne built remains. 'Please come whatever the season and visit our cellars,' says Jacques Borie. 'We shall be pleased to show you the estate and let you taste our La Rivière, even if you buy nothing.'

Some of the 48,000 bottles in the cellars of Château de la Rivière

Château Brulesécaille

The Rodet's AOC Côtes de Bourg wine is fermented for three—four weeks, kept another eighteen months in small vats before bottling, should not really be drunk until four years old and, contrary to the belief of Frenchmen outside Bordeaux who think Bourg wines do not last, will keep a minimum of ten years. 1985 is a great year. 1981 and '82 both won important gold medals in Paris. Full-bodied and fruity, it becomes rounded (well balanced and mellow) and surprisingly smooth as it matures. Very good value.

Tauriac, 33710 Bourg, Gironde, tel.(57) 68.40.31. On D669 going E from Bourg, turn left at La Lustre turning. 9–12.30 hrs; 14–18.30 hrs. English spoken.

Château du Bouilh

A chance to visit the home of the Count de Feuilhade de Chauvin, a beautiful historic house with magnificent furniture and souvenirs of famous guests. You can see his monolithic caves, with wine in centuries-old oak barrels, taste the award-winning wine and buy it – with his name on the label.

33240 St-André-de-Cubzac, Gironde, tel.(57) 43.01.45. Just N of St- André on tiny D115 road; marked on yellow Michelin map. Tastings combined with visits to Château 1 May–1 October, Thursday, Saturday, Sunday, 14.30–18.30 hrs.

Château La Rivalerie

Very good Premiers Côtes de Blaye red and white wines from attractive property, very carefully made. Red has sixty-five per cent Cabernet Sauvignon, thirty per cent Merlot Noir, five per cent Cabernet – fruity bouquet, well constituted, mouth-filling, long lasting. Take home a double magnum or Imperial. Ten thousand bottles of Sauvignon white are also produced.

St Paul, 33390 Blaye, Gironde, tel.(57) 42.18.84. 7km from Blaye on D937, left on N137. 8–12 hrs; 14–18 hrs.

Château Sociondo

Michel Elie's family have lived here for four generations. Wine rather like a St-Emilion (sixty-two per cent Merlot grape). 1982 was outstanding. 1984 won a silver medal in Paris. Sold in bottles or *cubitainers* for bottling at home.

Ave Ferrand, Berson, 33390 Blaye, tel.(57) 64.33.61. D937 from Blaye, at meeting of N137. 8–12 hrs; 14–18 hrs.

Château Barbé

The Carreau family have been wine producers in Côtes de Blaye for eight generations and they have three other properties nearby. They sell most wine direct, so are not so well known in the trade. Château Barbé is an attractive eighteenth-century house. So is Château Pardaillan nearby. They have a Côtes de Bourg producing property, too – the seventeenth-century Château Eyquem, Bayon, 33710, which you can visit by phoning Château Barbé. It is at Bayon on D669 halfway between Blaye and Bourg.

Cars, 33390 Blaye, Gironde, tel.(57) 64.32.43. Take D937 for 4km E of Blaye. Monday–Friday 8–12 hrs; 14–18 hrs.

Château de Didonne

Château with superb old furniture and tapestries, farm, arboretum, fascinating museum of old agricultural equipment (worth seeing for the old tractors alone), tastings and sale of Charente white wine, Pineau (grape juice and brandy – a splendid aperitif) and Cognac. Owned by the local agricultural co-operative, it was, until 1980, an experimental model farm village which was totally self-supporting, even to its own water supply from wells to water-tower. The wine is very *ordinaire*, but the tastings are free and the whole set up is most interesting.

Semussac, 17120 Cozes, tel.(46) 05.05.91. Not in Bourg–Blaye; just off D730 W of Royan on Bordeaux road. 11–12.30 hrs; 15.30–19 hrs.

Hotels

Food *See* Area 3 (Médoc/Haut-Médoc)

St-Emilion

Auberge de la Commanderie, rue Cordeliers, St-Emilion 33330, Gironde, tel.(57) 24.70.19.

Old-style family hotel. Straightforward cooking. Good wine list. Meals and rooms M.

Hostellerie Plaisance, place du Clocher, 33330 St-Emilion, tel.(57) 24.71.40.

Excellent position, bedrooms much improved. Formal dining room. Very good wines but high mark up. Meals and rooms M.

Libourne

Hotel Loubat, 32 rue Chanzy, 33500 Libourne, Gironde, tel.(57) 51.17.58.

Old railway hotel renovated. I have not been lately but vignerons recommend it – probably because of its good wine list! Regional cooking. Meals C–E; rooms C–M.

Blaye

La Citadelle, place des Armes, Blaye 33390, Gironde, tel.(57) 42.17.10.

Comfortable, modern, uninteresting except for remarkable views across estuary. Useful. Meals and rooms C–M.

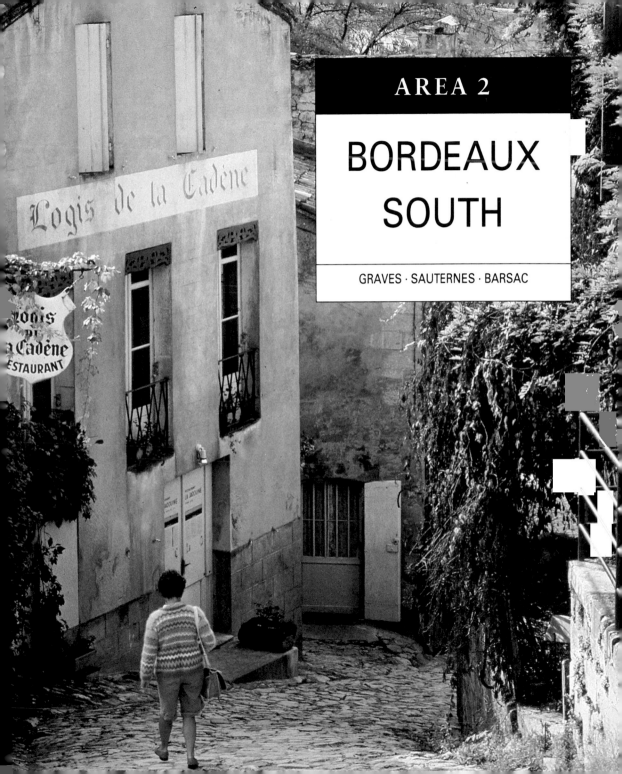

BORDEAUX SOUTH

GRAVES · SAUTERNES · BARSAC

Most Britons (and Americans) used to think of Graves as a slightly sweet white wine. If they knew the *premier grand cru* red of Haut-Brion, they regarded it as an eccentricity. Red Graves was something drunk by locals. We now import a lot of red Bordeaux AOC wines (which must come from Gironde Département and be made from certain grape varieties, mainly the Cabernets and Merlot) and Bordeaux Supérieur AOC (the same, but more alcoholic, which *is* superior in my view). Even today I am surprised if there is more than one red Graves on a wine list. Yet almost exactly the same amount of red and white wine is produced and locally the red is thought to be better, though the white is the best in the Bordeaux area.

The vineyard is not large – 8000 acres, from Bordeaux city to south of Langon. The name Graves comes from the gravelly soil

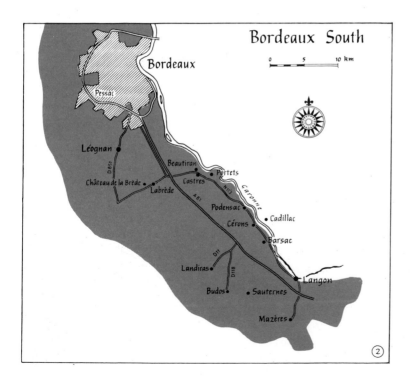

which suits the red wine grapes, not from burials, although the late Ronnie Delderfield, the novelist, would publicly and loudly demand 'a nice bottle of graves' to embarrass snobs. I often look at abandoned gravel pits in England and wonder if they would grow vines. The whites prefer sandy and clay soils.

Yield per acre and grape types are strictly controlled. The only grapes which can be used for red wines are Cabernet Sauvignon, Cabernet Franc, Merlot, Malbec and Petit Verdot, and for white wines Sémillon, Sauvignon and Muscadelle. Sémillon still dominates but Sauvignon is gaining. Red wines must have ten per cent alcohol, dry whites at least eleven per cent and sweet white wines twelve per cent. Red wines have a powerful, definite flavour, are not so delicate as good Médocs but have more body. Their bouquet improves with age and most can be kept for thirty years in good vintages but are usually drunk after five years. Whites are ready after two years, are better kept for five years and good ones last twenty years. Whites are served at 43–50°F, reds at 60–65°.

There are fifteen classified *grands crus* Graves. Locals say proudly 'Bordeaux is in Graves'. Sauternes and Barsac are from a very small area near Langon, producing strong, sweet wines from grapes picked at maximum concentration of sugar, even picking grape by grape. Sauternes is luscious, with an intense flavour, and should be kept ten–fifty years. The greatest is Château d'Yquem, one of the *grands premiers crus* wines. A famous Mayor of Bordeaux told me to drink it as elevenses. I wish I could afford it. Barsac is slightly lighter, with a lemony taste. Both are too precious to offer free tastings to passing amateurs.

Several lesser *appellations* in this area include Côtes de Castillon (on the Dordogne river W of St-Emilion), Cérons (N of Barsac), Saint-Macaire (across Garonne river from Langon), Entre Deux Mers (a light, fresh, fruity dry white, excellent with shellfish, which comes from a big triangle between the Garonne and Dordogne rivers – 'between the two waters' – but much replanted now with red grapes to give soft, fruity red Bordeaux

AOC which is good value). Also Loupiac (sweet wine from Garonne, opposite Barsac), Graves de Vayres (red, dry and *demi-sec* white from N of Entre Deux Mers), Sainte-Croix-du-Mont (across Garonne from Sauternes). Cadillac, opposite Cérons, produces sweet and semi-sweet whites – strange, for our family is supposed to have come from there and our belief has always been that a preference for sweet wines means an immature palate or galloping old age!

Bordeaux Clairet AOC is a very light red wine served cold, not iced – said to be the original 'Claret' when Bordeaux belonged to the English crown.

Tastings

BORDEAUX SOUTH

Château Pape Clément

Delightful historic château with tower. Given to Bertrand de Goth when he became Archbishop of Bordeaux in 1299 by his brother for bringing honour to the family. The Church owned it until the Revolution. Red wine sixty per cent Cabernet Sauvignon, forty per cent Merlot – beautifully constituted, natural, very distinguished, prized by French wine trade. 1978 and '82 were supreme. 1983 very good.

216 ave du Docteur-Nancel-Penard, 33600 Pessac, Gironde, tel.(56) 07.04.11. South suburb of Bordeaux, on N250 to Arcachon. 10–17 hrs.

Château Haut-Brion

Red Graves supreme – *premier grand cru* (one of only six). If you can get in, you will remember it for life. Elegant, perfectly balanced in tannin and fruit, it matures superbly. The first owner (who started the vineyard in 1533) lived to the age of 101 and survived three marriages 'with neither gout nor kidney stones, sound of mind, speech and understanding' (the wine, no doubt!). American banker Clarence Dillon bought it in 1934. It's president now is Dillon's granddaughter, the Duchesse de Mouchy. Nothing to do with the O'Brions – named after a river.

133 ave Jean-Jaurès, BP 24, 33602 Pessac, Gironde, tel.(56) 98.28.17. S and under railway from Pape Clément (above). Motorway sortie 13 Alouette – Pessac-Centre. You need an introduction from a good wine merchant in Britain. Or try writing direct or phoning 24 hours ahead.

Château Haut-Bailly

One of the best red Graves. Excellent bouquet, light colour, softish, with low tannin. Fine old manor house and farm.

33850 Léognan, Gironde, tel.(56) 21.75.11. 12km S Bordeaux by D651. 8–12 hrs; 14–18 hrs.

Château Magence

Red and white wines of good quality from a very old vineyard which has been in the same family since 1800. Replanting twenty years ago improved it greatly. The white wine is delicate, stylish, light-coloured, fruity with a flowery aroma, ideal with oysters, excellent with ham or cold chicken. I love it. The red has a velvety, grapey taste. Keep it at least five years. Wine also sold at a Co-op in Magence – SICA, tel.(56) 63.19.34. Open Monday–Friday same hours as Château.

St-Pierre-de-Mons, 33210 Langon, Gironde, tel.(56). 63.19.34. From Bordeaux N113 (or A62) to Langon, tiny D224 to St-Pierre-de-Mons. Monday–Friday 8.30–12.15 hrs; 13.30–17.30 hrs. Phone if possible. No English spoken.

Château Roquetaillade La Grange

Castle and vineyard dominate Brion river valley. Red and white wines. Red has intense colour, raspberry smell.

Mazères, 33210 Langon, tel.(56) 63.24.23. 7km from Langon by D222 or D932, then right on D125 (marked on yellow Michelin). Phone if possible.

Château de Mauves

Your chance to get a bargain to take home. Underestimated red wine – ruby colour, fine perfume, mellow (don't be put off by the French word *onctueux* – not unctuous!). Also white.

25 rue François Mauriac, 33720 Podensac, tel.(56) 27.17.05. N113 SE Bordeaux on Garonne river. 9–12 hrs; 14–18 hrs.

Maison des Vins de Graves (Syndicat Viticole de Graves)

If tasting, try to phone. English spoken. Extremely useful. Represents forty-four communes in Graves and you can buy a great many of the wines.

BP 51, 2 rue François Mauriac, 33720 Podensac, tel.(56) 27.09.25. Monday–Friday 8.30–17.30 hrs; July–August 8.30–19 hrs including Saturdays, Sundays.

Château de Chantegrive (Henri Lévèque)

Good quaffing white wine – deliciously fruity, fresh and slips down easily. Reds are pleasant, friendly and fruity and would appeal to people who are not sure that they like red very much.

33720 Podensac, Gironde, tel.(56) 27.17.38. At Podensac. 8–12 hrs; 14–18 hrs. Phone.

Château de Malle

The Domaine has been in the family of the Comtesse de Bournazel for 500 years. The seventeenth-century château with its magnificent décor, furnishings, fireplaces, ceilings, paintings and grounds is well worth visiting on its own. The vineyard is a bonus. It straddles Sauternes and Graves and produces both wines. Château de Malle is a vintage Sauternes of great finesse, gorgeous bouquet and fruitier than most Sauternes, so that it can be drunk chilled through every course from shellfish or pâté to white meats, soft cheese, desserts and fruit. Also an aromatic, fruity red Graves and a dry white light Sauvignon.

33210 Preignac, Gironde, tel.(56) 63.28.67. From N113, take right turn across VC4. Malle marked on yellow Michelin near A62. Château open Easter–15 October, 15–17 hrs. Wine chais visits by appointment on phone (ask for Secretaire). Tastings normally for professionals.

Château Méric (Pierre Baron)

Good wine produced naturally without chemicals, pesticides, or synthetics (*Nature et Progrès* system). White and red AOC Graves. Nearby is Château La Brède, a national monument in a lovely park, birthplace of the historian Montesquieu in 1689. It is open Mondays, Wednesdays, Thursdays, Fridays except January (admission fee).

33650 La Brède, Gironde, tel.(56) 20.20.53. Take D108 off N113 near Castres, to La Brède; left in village. Open working hours. Phone if possible.

Château Le Tuquet (Paul Ragon)

Attractive seventeenth-century manor; very old vineyards.

Beautiran, 33640 Portets, Gironde, tel.(56) 20.21.23. N113 SE from Bordeaux 25km. Monday–Friday 8–12 hrs; 14–18 hrs. Saturday 9–12 hrs.

Domaine l'Hermitage (Michel Courbin)

On borders of Graves–Sauternes. Wine AOC Graves white and red.

33720 Budos, Gironde, tel.(56) 62.51.58. D8 SW from Langon, right on D125 past Sauteprés. 10–12 hrs; 15–18 hrs.

Clos de la Perichère, Château Saint-Hilaire (Gabriel Guérin)

No chemical fertilisers or sprays used. *Culture Biologique* method, using seaweed, green compost, powdered rock. Aged in oak, cleared with egg whites. A highly praised *grand cru* Graves wine (white and red).

Castres, 33640 Portets, Gironde, tel.(56) 67.12.12. Edge of Castres, on N113, 24km SE Bordeaux. 8–21 hrs. To speak English, phone and ask for Mlle Hélène.

Château Saint-Agrèves

Vineyard in same family since eighteenth century producing red aged entirely in oak for eighteen months. Lively when young, mouth filling and subtle with age. Nice aromatic Graves dry white. Graves Supérieur sweeter wine (*moelleux*).

Landiras, 33720 Podensac, tel.(56) 62.50.85. N113 from Bordeaux, right on D117 at Cérons, D11 over A62 motorway. 9.30–12 hrs; 15–19 hrs. Phoning preferred, not essential. Mme Landry speaks English.

Château d'Arricaud (A. J. Bouyx)

Huge lovely old farm manor, built in 1783 by Count de Chalup. Very good red wine, light, perfumed, excellently made to tickle your taste buds. Whites range from very dry to sweet.

Landiras, 33720 Podensac, tel.(56) 62.51.29. For Landiras, *see* Château Saint-Agrèves above. 9–12 hrs; 15–18 hrs. Phoning preferred, not essential.

Further Information

Contact Maison des Vins de Graves, Podensac (*see* Tastings list); Conseil Interprofessionel de Vin de Bordeaux, 1 cours du 30 Juillet, 33000 Bordeaux.

Hotels

Food *see* Area 3 (Médoc/Haut-Médoc)

Langon

Claude Darroze, 95 cours Général-Leclerc, Langon, 33210 Gironde, tel.(56) 63.00.48.

Delightful food cooked by the son of the late great Jean Darroze of Villeneuve-de-Marsan. Michelin star. Meals M–E; rooms M. Shut Sunday evenings in winter; mid October–mid November.

Moderne, 3 place Général-de-Gaulle, Langon, 33210 Gironde, tel.(56) 63.06.65.

Recommended locally for cheap brasserie meals and rooms. Brasserie shut Wednesdays. Meals and rooms C.

Barsac

Hostellerie du Château du Rolland, Barsac, 33720 Podensac, Gironde, tel.(56) 27.15.27.

Fifteenth-century Chartreuse monastery converted into lovely little inn. Good regional cooking. Meals and rooms M. Shut part November. Restaurant shut Wednesdays in winter.

Cérons

Grappe d'Or, route St-Symphorien, Cérons, 33270 Podensac, Gironde, tel.(56) 27.11.61.

Local inn recommended to me by many vignerons. Meals and rooms C–M. Shut February.

Alouette, Pessac

(D650 S from Bordeaux, past Pessac; sortie 13 Alouette–Pessac from motorway)

La Reserve, 74 ave Bourgailh, l'Alouette, 33600 Pessac, Gironde, tel.(56) 07.13.28.

Modern Relais et Châteaux hotel with garden in quiet position. Near Château Haut-Brion and other vineyards. Excellent cooking, super wine list (Graves and Médoc). Meals E; rooms M–E. Open Easter–1 November.

MÉDOC
HAUT-MÉDOC

LISTRAC · MARGAUX · PAUILLAC

They say in Bordeaux there are three quick ways to bank-
ruptcy – keep race horses, an actress or a vineyard in Médoc. The
third is the quickest. I would add a fourth – drinking, not keeping,
grands premiers wines of Médoc. More truly great wines are made
along this Gironde estuary than anywhere in the world, and more
good quality wines, too. But many château owners have joined the
poor.

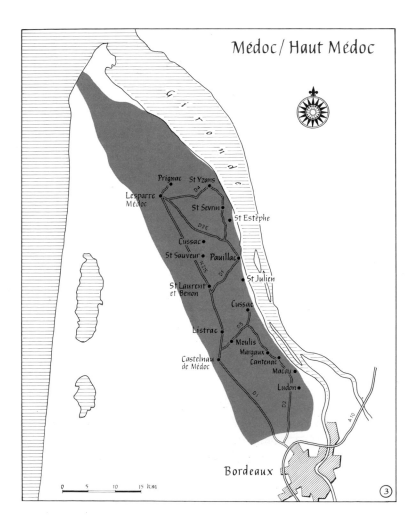

Médoc / Haut Médoc

Gironde

Prignac   St Yzans
Lesparre
Médoc
St Sevrin
St Estèphe
Cussac
St Sauveur   Pauillac
St Julien
St Laurent
et Benon
Cussac
Listrac
Moulis
Margaux
Castelnau   Cantenac
de Médoc
Macau
Ludon

Bordeaux

0   5   10   15 km

③

The vineyards were classified into five *crus* (growths) in 1855, and apart from promoting Château Mouton Rothschild in Pauillac to *premier cru*, to join Lafite, Château Margaux, Latour and Haut-Brion from Graves, nothing else has changed. Vineyards have got bigger, smaller, better and worse. The quality of the wines has likewise altered enormously, so the classification is now a very rough guide indeed, and it is time to change it. I prefer the personal classification of Alexis Lichine, vineyard owner and great wine writer, in his book *Guide to the Wines and Vineyards of France* (Papermac and Knopf).

Most of us simply cannot afford first, second or even third *cru* wines anyway. Blessedly, not only are some of the fourth and fifth *crus* very good value, but you can find wines from lesser classifications which are truly *excellent* value, such as *grand cru* Bourgeois Exceptionnel (only eighteen wines), *grand cru* Bourgeois and *cru* Bourgeois. Many of these deserve to join the *grands vins* classification. They are, after all, the wines which most of us drink most of the time if we love Médoc red, and it is mainly these vineyards to which I have directed you to taste the wine. Not many of the *grands* vineyards have time to receive amateur visitors, and their wines are certainly too valuable to give away. Apart from the cost of growing, picking, throwing out grapes not up to standard and making the wine, think of the capital tied up while the wine is in cask for two to three years and matures in bottle for anything from ten to twenty years. Château Latour has a million bottles maturing at a value of more than £20 a bottle (1986 prices). No wonder the wines are so costly and that Beaujolais growers in Burgundy delight to sell their wine 'Nouveau' for instant cash.

Good Bourgeois wines are best kept for six to twelve years. The French tend to drink them younger when the best are pure and harmonious but can be harsh (*austère*), which is probably why a lot of ordinary French drinkers prefer St-Emilion to Médoc and Burgundy to both. The English have always been the great Bordeaux drinkers (we owned the area for a long time).

Baron Philippe de Rothschild

Médoc is divided into two regions – Haut-Médoc, from Blanquefort to Saint-Seurin-de-Cadourne (including well-known appellations such as Margaux, St-Julien, St-Estèphe, Pauillac), and Médoc, north from St-Seurin. Haut-Médoc wines must have 10.5 degrees alcohol. They tend to have greater flavour and are more *élégant* than Médoc wines.

Cabernet Sauvignon grapes usually predominate in Médoc wines, giving a definite smell of blackcurrants, tannic when young but developing finesse and giving the wine ageing potential. The very similar Cabernet Franc are used rather less. They add perfume, make the wine a lighter colour, but bring softness to the tannin. Merlot grapes are used in varying amounts from around thirty per cent to forty-five per cent, with a few winemakers using over fifty per cent. They add deep colour and flavour, make the wine milder and make it mature faster. Very few Malbec grapes are used now but small amounts of Petit Verdot, which ripens late, add alcohol and tannin and make wines rounder for long keeping.

Listrac AOC wines can be a bit tough when young but are fine after four to five years. Not much snob value, so you can get bargains. Margaux AOC wines include Cantenac, a very good area, and the Bourgeois wines are often excellent – soft, smooth with strong flavour. Moulis AOC, like Listrac, are good value and mature fast. Pauillac AOC wines can be superb. They have intense colour, a strong bouquet and are full-bodied but smooth and long lasting. Don't drink them too young when they are harsh. Saint-Estèphe are beefy wines which age wonderfully, and the Bourgeois wines from around Pez could fool experts into believing they were grander. St-Julien AOC wines are favourites with a lot of amateurs, because they have the softness of Margaux and the full body of Pauillac. Called 'the claret for claret drinkers'.

A few white wines are made in Médoc from Sauvignon Blanc with Sémillon, which requires bottle age, so the wines should not be drunk too young. Château Margaux makes a super Pavillon

Blanc. Some growers add a little Muscadelle grape. I approve – it gives a beautiful flowery perfume and flavour.

Unless you spend a 'dégusting' holiday, just vineyard crawling, you will not have time to visit all these vineyards on one trip. If you have limited time and have not visited Médoc vineyards before, I suggest that you start with Château de Pez (St-Estèphe), Château Loudenne (St-Yzans), Château Hanteillan (Cissac), Prieuré-Lichine (Margaux) and Château Lynch-Bages (Pauillac) for variety, though some of their wines are not cheap.

Tastings

Château Loudenne

Bought by Gilbey Bros in 1875, who themselves now form part of Grand Met. A charming eighteenth-century château, called the Rose Pink Château, once famous for the Gilbeys' spectacular parties. A *cru grand* Bourgeois Médoc red wine, but one of the best – light in colour, with a lovely perfume and finesse. The white is crisp and delicious, young or older. The company markets the red and white wines branded La Cour Pavillon; also Château de Pez at St-Estèphe (*cru* Bourgeois) and Château Giscours from Margaux (*grand cru* – third growth with high reputation). Loudenne has an interesting wine museum.

St-Yzans de Médoc, 33340 Lesparre, tel.(56) 09.05.03. On D2 along Gironde estuary. Phoning preferable. Ask for Pamela Prior. April–October, Monday–Friday; 9.30–12 hrs; 14–16.30 hrs. English spoken.

Château Tour Haut Caussan (Philippe Courrian)

Medal-winning *cru* Bourgeois, eighty per cent sold direct to old customers, including good small restaurants. No chemical fertilisers, grapes hand picked, egg white used for clearing. Fruity aroma, long-lasting taste. Good proportion of Merlot (forty-five per cent) with Cabernet Sauvignon. A good buy. Restored windmill (1734) in vineyards.

33340 **Blaignan-Médoc**, tel.(56) 09.00.77. D3 NE then right from N215 at Lesparre-Médoc. Monday–Saturday office hours. No English spoken.

Château La Gorce (Henri Fabre)

'Just wear a large smile,' says Henri Fabre. 'We all speak very bad English.' Delightful vineyard, fine old manor house, a full-bodied red wine which 'seduces when young, delights when older'. That sounds like a girl I know.

Blaignan, 33340 Lesparre-Médoc, tel.(56) 09.01.22. 8–12 hrs; 14–18 hrs.

Société de Vinification

Makes Les Vieux Colombiers and Château de Bensse. Also AOC Médoc, sold in bottles or 22-litre *cubitainers* for home bottling.

Prignac-en-Médoc, 33340 Lesparre, tel.(56) 09.01.02. D3 NE from N215 at Lesparre-Médoc. 9–12 hrs; 14–18 hrs.

Château Coufran and Château Verdignan

Jean Miailhe is one of the leading *vignerons* of Médoc. His son Eric makes the *cru* Bourgeois wines. Coufran has eighty-five per cent Merlot grape – unique in Médoc. It is light, fruity, soft, with long-lasting taste and tempting to lap up in litres! Verdignan (attractive château) has forty-five per cent Merlot, the rest Cabernets. Aged in wood, it is well-made and solid, becomes strong flavoured but keeps its fruit. Eric Miailhe owns the nearby property of Château Soudars, producing award-winning *cru* Bourgeois wines.

St-Seurin-de-Cadourne, 33250 Pauillac, tel.(56) 44.90.84. (Bordeaux office) or (56) 59.31.02. Position, *see* Château Senilhac above. Visits in July, August 10–12.30 hrs; 14–18.30 hrs, except Sundays. At other times, phone.

Société Co-operative de Vinification

Light, fruity, full wines with superb colour – called Cru de la Paroisse.

St-Seurin-de-Cadourne, 33250 Pauillac, tel.(56) 59.31.28. For position, *see* Château Senilhac. 9.30–12 hrs; 14.30–17 hrs; Saturdays 9.30–11 hrs.

Château Haut-Marbuzet

Henri Duboscq makes superb St-Estèphe, unusually matured for two years in new oak barrels. A rare *cru grand* Bourgeois Exceptionnel. Deep colour, much fruit (fifty per cent Merlot) and a

33250 **St-Estèphe**, tel.(56) 59.30.54. At Marbuzet on D2 just before it joins D204. 8–11.30 hrs; 14–17 hrs.

subtle flavour all its own from the mixture of fruit and tannin from the wood. Can be drunk young or keeps well. Do try it. He has three other properties here, including Château MacCarthy-Moula, a livelier wine.

Château de Pez

St-Estèphe, 33250 Pauillac, tel.(56) 59.30.07. 8.30–12 hrs; 14.30–18 hrs; Saturdays 8.30–12 hrs. Shut Sundays.

I love it, and as a consumer I am happy that nearly all the experts agree. Most think it should be classified as a *grand cru* wine. The French call it a 'masculine' wine but I wouldn't dare in Britain. Has a lovely colour, its own distinctive and definite bouquet, and it fills the mouth with flavour which lingers. Robert Dousson makes it with utmost care. Kept in oak vats for six months, it is then transferred into casks to mature for eighteen months, racked every four months and fined with egg white. Distributed by Gilbeys of Château Loudenne. Fine old turreted château.

Marquis de St-Estèphe (Société de Vinification)

St-Estèphe, 33250 Pauillac, tel.(56) 59.32.05. 9–12 hrs; 14.30–18 hrs.

A modern co-op, founded in 1934 by forty-two producers, which makes an unusually good wine most years – full-bodied, tannic when young, best kept a long time. The 1981 should not be drunk until after 1988. Just right for red meat, game and cheese.

Société Viticole

Vertheuil en Médoc, 33250, tel.(56) 41.98.16. On D204 at turning off for St-Estèphe. 8.30–12.30 hrs; 14–18 hrs.

Co-op of eighty growers. Brand name wine Chatellenie is good value. Seven other châteaux wines made here.

Château Hanteillan

Cissac-Médoc, 33250 Pauillac, tel.(56) 59.35.37. On D204 between Lesparre and Pauillac; marked on yellow Michelin. 8–12 hrs; 14–18 hrs. Ask for M. Paquereau (cellar master).

One of the few houses run by a woman (Catherine Blasco, formerly a graphics designer, engineer, agronomist and sheep-farmer). *Cru grand* Bourgeois wine aiming to be classified as fourth or fifth *grand cru*. Experts like Alexis Lichine rate it high. Rather young large vineyard maturing splendidly. Also makes Tour de Vatican from young vines.

Château Vieux Braneyre

Georges-Claude Guges and his sons saved this 200-year-old château and vineyard which had fallen into 'a pitiful state' in 1979. The wine is getting a following among knowledgeable amateurs looking for value.

Les Gunes, Cissac-Médoc, 33250 Pauillac, tel.(56) 59.54.03. Little road W from Cissac. Weekdays 8–12 hrs; 14–18 hrs. Phone at weekends.

Château Liversan

Who would have thought to find the Prince and Princesse Guy de Polignac, whose family have been part of French history since the tenth century and more recently a large part of Pommery Champagne, producing a *cru* Bourgeois? But it is a superior, elegant Bourgeois, rich and strong. Since 1983 they have installed a new cuvier, started to age wines in wood, and are already producing one of the most attractive wines around here.

St-Sauveur, 33250 Pauillac, tel.(56) 59.57.07. W from Pauillac, 4km off N215. 9–12 hrs; 14–17 hrs. Preferable to phone for tastings (ask for Prince's secretary) but not vital. Not necessary for visits.

Château Lynch-Bages

A fifth *grand cru* wine which some of us would promote. The Cazes family, who also own Château les Ormes de Pez at St-Estèphe, have run it for three generations. Grandad lived until ninety-five. Father André Cazes is Mayor of Pauillac. Grandson Jean-Michel now lives in the big château and runs the vineyard. The wine has a strong Cabernet smell, a delightful blackcurrant fruity flavour balanced with a touch of wood from the tannin – cedar, perhaps? It's great. John Lynch fled here from Galway after the Battle of the Boyne in 1690. His son married an heiress who inherited Domaine de Bages. Their son became Mayor of Bordeaux and Count Lynch under Napoleon. The Lynches sold out in 1824.

33250 Pauillac, tel.(56) 59.19.19. At gates of Pauillac. 9.30–11.30 hrs; 14.30–17 hrs. Phoning not necessary but appreciated. English spoken.

Cave Co-operative La Rose

Makes a very good brand wine, 'La Rose Pauillac', soft, fruity and perfumed. Oldest co-op in Médoc (1933) with 125 growers. High reputation. Also makes several wines for single vineyards.

rue Maréchal-Joffre, 33250 Pauillac, tel.(56) 59.26.00. 8–12 hrs; 14–18 hrs.

Château Latour

One of the six *grand premier cru* wines. In certain years, the best. No wine goes on the market until ready for drinking, so you must be patient. 1976 was ready before 1966. The mouth-filling concentration of fruit and tannin are exquisite. The taste seems to last forever. One of my first moves when I returned from a prison camp in 1945 after four years with no wine and little food was to buy at auction a case of 1937 Latour. You may be invited to taste but you cannot buy at the Château. Owned now by Pearsons of London, under the control of Alan Hare. There are a million bottles maturing here!

33250 Pauillac, tel.(56) 59.00.51. 9–11.30 hrs; 14–17 hrs. Phone – but only if you are dedicated, knowledgeable or a professional.

Château Belgrave

A fifth *grand cru classé* wine, hopelessly run down when taken over by CVBG group in 1979 who have now modernised it. The wine is matured in new wooden barrels. Run by the famous oenologist Patrick Atteret, it is one to back in the future.

33112 **St-Laurent du Médoc**, tel.(56) 59.40.20. D101 between St-Laurent and St-Julien. 9–12 hrs; 14–17 hrs.

Château Balac

Luc Touchais, well known for his wines in Anjou, makes a wine of character which is good value.

33112 St-Laurent-Médoc, tel.(56) 59.41.76. Beside N215. 9–12 hrs; 14–18 hrs.

Château Clarke (Baron Edmond de Rothschild)

Huge estate of 170 hectares, originally planted by Cistercian monks in the twelfth century. It was neglected until Baron de Rothschild bought it in 1970 and started a costly operation of modern planting and most modern methods of vinification. Enormous strides have been made and are continuing, like altering the profile of the land. At present, the wines are light and easy to drink – wines of the future, I am told, for people in a hurry eating lighter meals. For me, wines to be taken with a snack! But it is early days. We shall see, taste and no doubt enjoy. They are not aiming at producing a Mouton-Rothschild, anyway.

Listrac, 33480 Castelnau de Médoc, tel.(56) 88.88.00. 2km SE Listrac on road to Moulis. Visits and tastings: 1 October–15 June: Monday–Friday 10–18 hrs. 15 June–30 September: best to go to Cercle Oenologique du Château Clarke at Moulis (2km – tel.(56) 88.84.29) to get a ticket for tasting and to join cellar visits each day at 11 hrs, 14.30 hrs, and 16.30 hrs. English spoken.

Château Fourcas-Dupré

Cru grand Bourgeois Exceptionnel – sappy, deep perfume, tannic strong in long-keeping years, easy to drink in lesser years. Guy Pages, alas, is dead but his son Patrice knows the business. Pretty château. Also owns Château Duplessis-Fabre at Moulis.

Listrac, 33480 Castelnau-Médoc, tel.(56) 58.01.07. Monday–Friday 8–12 hrs; 14–18 hrs.

Château Fonréaud et Château Lestage (Jean Chanfreau)

Fonréaud has a pretty château with bell tower, a local landmark, and is an attractive, fruity, easy to knock back wine which will keep well (forty-seven per cent Merlot). Lestage is more mouth-filling and complex (fifty-six per cent Merlot!). Rewarding visit.

Listrac, 33480 Castelnau-Médoc, tel.(56) 58.02.43. N215 S of Listrac. 8–12 hrs; 14–17 hrs.

Other Listrac caves to visit:
Château Lalande, tel.(56) 58.19.45. 9–12 hrs; 14–19 hrs.
Château Fourcas Hosten, tel.(56) 58.01.15. Monday–Friday 9–11.30 hrs; 14–17.30 hrs. World renowned wine.
Château Cap Léon Veyrin, Donissan, Listrac 33480, tel.(56) 58.07.28. Monday–Saturday 8–12 hrs; 14–18 hrs. Same family since 1810. Collection of vintages since 1929.

Chevaliers du Roi Soleil

Don't be discouraged by the 'barrel' architecture. Twenty-two good local growers work together to provide a reliable, strong and well-made wine.

Cussac Fort-Médoc (on D2 between St-Julien and Margaux), 33460 Margaux, tel.(56) 58.92.85. 15 June–15 September, 9–19 hrs. Other months phone.

Château Tour du Haut-Moulin

Traditional, well-constructed, fruity wine. *Cru grand* Bourgeois. Pleasant when young, but will keep twenty years. Said to have the vitality of a *grand cru* wine. Powerful, balanced, full of character. For red meat, game and cheese.

Cussac Fort-Médoc, 33460 Margaux, tel.(56) 58.91.10. 10–12 hrs; 14–18 hrs.

Château Aney

Very attractive château. Reliable *cru* Bourgeois.

Cussac Fort-Médoc, 33460 Margaux, tel.(56) 58.94.89. 9–13 hrs; 14–19 hrs.

Château Moulin à Vent (Dominique Hessel)

Has got much better. Lovely flavour, rich and smooth, and improving a lot with age.

Bouqueyran, **Moulis**, 33480 Castelnau de Médoc, tel.(56) 58.15.79. Beside N215. 8–12 hrs; 14–18 hrs.

Château Monbrison

Elisabeth Davis, the owner, is American. Her father bought the property in 1926. Her sons help her run it. Attractive, balanced wine.

Arsac (7km SW Margaux), 33460 Margaux, tel.(56) 88.34.52. 9–12 hrs; 14–19 hrs all week.

Château Citran

Big eighteenth-century château. Strong, smooth wine made mostly with Merlot.

Avensan, 33480 **Castelnau**, tel.(56) 58.21.01. 4km E Castelnau by D105. 9–12 hrs; 14–17 hrs.

Château Marquis de Terme

Old vines, long fermentation and fifteen to twenty-one months in the barrel produce a fourth *grand cru* wine that is attractive and solid, with much of the elegance of Margaux. Very pleasant château, named after the man who owned it in 1762.

33460 **Margaux**, tel.(56) 88.30.01. Monday–Friday 9–12 hrs; 14–17 hrs. English spoken.

Châteaux Boyd-Cantenac et Pouget

Boyd-Cantenac has had ups and downs, and disappeared as a name for forty years. Now made at Château Pouget. Some experts think it does not deserve its third *grand cru* status. As a consumer, I think that owner Pierre Guillemet and the great wine maker Emile Peynaud have brought it right back. I still have two cases of the excellent 1978! Pouget is a fourth *grand cru* wine and worthy of it.

Cantenac (4km SE of Margaux on D2), 33460 Margaux, tel.(56) 88.30.58. The tastings are at Château Pouget (the other was sold to Château Margaux). Monday–Friday 10–12 hrs; 15–18 hrs. Phone if possible.

Château Prieuré-Lichine

Alexis Lichine, who has been Russian, French and American in turn, and who is both a *vigneron* and writer on wine, built up Château Lascombes and sold it to Bass, the brewers, in 1971. He also bought Prieuré and has built it up from eleven hectares to fifty-five. The château was a Benedictine priory until the French Revolution and vineyard before that. A fourth *grand cru* wine, it has improved noticeably, but most years you must wait a very long time before you can drink it. The great 1982 vintage should not be touched before 1988, and will last long after that. But Alexis Lichine thinks that the 1984 wine will be ready by the winter of 1987–8. Superb collection of old firebacks adorns courtyard.

Cantenac, 33460 Margaux, tel.(56) 88.36.28. Visits 9–18 hrs weekdays; 10–18 hrs at weekends. Hostesses speak English. You will learn a lot about Médoc wines. For tastings, ask beforehand.

Château Giscours

Nicolas Tari and his son Pierre have performed wonders since they took over this vast property in 1952, not only with the wine but in restoring the château built under Napoleon III. Seventy out of 370 hectares are under vines and it takes 200 pickers to gather the grapes. A splendid Margaux, rated third *grand cru* but

Labarde (next to Cantenac on D2), 33460 Margaux, tel.(56) 88.34.02. 8–12 hrs; 14–18 hrs. Phone. Ask for Gudrun Frisch, public relations. English spoken.

deserving more. Deep coloured, with a strong scent, it is full-bodied yet often delicate, tasting of red berries. Distributed by Gilbeys of Loudenne.

Château La Lagune

Owned by Ayala Champagne house, the first *grand cru* property you reach coming out of Bordeaux. Immaculate, attractive château by Louis, the eighteenth-century architect, which has a delightful park and is as elegant and harmonious as the wine. Unusual modern methods of racking avoid oxidisation. All new barrels used each year. Another underclassed wine – third *grand cru*. It keeps longer than many pundits say – my 1973 will be good for a few years yet.

Ludon-Médoc (just off D2, 10km S Margaux), 33290 Blanquefort, tel.(56) 30.44.07. 9–12 hrs; 14–17 hrs. Phone if possible. Ask for Madame Boyrie, the director. No English spoken.

Other places to visit:
Château Lascombes, 33460 Margaux, tel.(56) 50.84.85. Normal business hours; lovely place, lovely second *grand cru*. Buying but not tastings.
Château Malescot St-Exupéry, 33460 Margaux, tel.(56) 88.70.68. Monday–Friday 9–12 hrs; 14–17 hrs; must phone; tastings by arrangement. Pretty château, third *grand cru* wine.
Château Poujeaux, 33480 Moulis-en-Médoc, tel.(56) 58.22.58. 9–12 hrs; 14–18 hrs. Must phone. Ask for tasting. *Cru grand* Bourgeois Exceptionnel, long lived; in barrel eighteen months. Wine has beaten *grand premier cru* wines in expert blind tastings. One to take home.
Château Maucaillou, 33480 Moulis-en-Médoc, tel.(56) 58.01.23. 9–12 hrs; 15–17.30 hrs. Welcoming. You can buy, but tastings 'offered to buyers'. Lovely château. Excellent value. Red and white wines.
Maison du Vin, Place La Tremoille, 33460 Margaux, tel.(56) 88.70.82. 9–12 hrs; 14–18 hrs. Sells twenty-seven different Margaux wines, all *grands crus* or *grands bourgeois*. No tastings.

Further Information

Conseil Interprofessionel du Vin de Bordeaux, 1, cours du 30 Juillet, 33000 Bordeaux.
Syndicat des Crus Bourgeois de Médoc, 24 cours du Verdun, 33000 Bordeaux.
Maison du Vin, quai Ferchaud, 33250 Pauillac. Also sells 150 wines.

Food

On the Bordeaux waterfront, they clean and open oysters outside the little restaurants to lure you inside. There the oysters will probably be served very cold with hot spicy little sausages called *crépinettes*, hunks of bread and dry white wine. You swallow an oyster, take a bite from the sausage, a bite of bread and a large draught of wine, then start again. In posher places the *crépinettes* may be truffled.

Fish is inevitably splendid round here, with the Gironde estuary down the wine road, the oyster beds of Arcachon not far away, the rivers of Charentes on the doorstep and the Dordogne and Garonne washing the vineyards of Entre Deux Mers and Graves.

Mussels are cooked in red wine and tomatoes or white wine and cream (*mouclade*). Little red mullet (*petits rougets*) is baked with chervil (*cerfeuil*). Sea bass is served in mushroom or even cèpes sauce (*bar aux cèpes*), whilst lampreys (little eels) are served with a leek, blood and red wine sauce (*lamproie aux poireaux et au vin rouge*). Leeks used to grow wild in the vineyards and were regarded as the wine workers' asparagus. Pesticides killed them off, so now they are cultivated. Wild mushrooms still abound in the woods and fields around the vineyards and in autumn cèpes, the most delicately flavoured of mushrooms, are gathered from

the woods, especially around Margaux. Many are canned to use later but when fresh they are superb simply stewed quickly in olive oil with parsley and garlic.

Some venison and pheasant comes from Les Landes. The Bordelais still eat more heartily than most city-dwellers of France and Nouvelle Cuisine has not made much headway. Basically, however, the wine is chosen first and the food to go with it, so tastes tend to be gentle and subtle. Butter is used for cooking – rare in the South West where pork fat is usual.

The lamb from the salt marshes of Pauillac is often eaten very young and breaded, so you need a delicate palate to appreciate it, although it is delightful when older.

Entrecôte Bordelaise is said to have been a cynical name from harder times when rats grown fat in wine warehouses were soaked in wine and grilled. Now it is grilled beef finished with shallots and beef marrow or, in the Parisian version, with a sauce of red wine scented with shallots. Gourmets insist on Bazas beef from Gironde cattle. All fine if you can find it.

Try *tourin Bordelaise* (onion soup thickened with egg yolks), trout stuffed with duck, and *mojettes* (broad beans with top skin removed, cooked in cream and delicious).

The Garonne gardens provide fruit from espaliered trees and Marmande gives its name to the best knobbly giant tomatoes. Watercress grows by the Garonne, too. Macau, south-east of Margaux, grows lovely globe artichokes, often, like carrots, served raw. Salad is served as a starter to meals. The Americans probably got the idea from here.

In Bordeaux shops you can buy gâteau Landais – folds of paper-thin pastry doused in brandy and baked with butter and sugar. With layers of apples or prunes, it is a *croustade*.

Several goat cheeses are made locally but oddly the Bordelais and many vineyard workers like Dutch Edam with their wine – a throwback to the days when boats came from Holland laden with cheese and took back wine.

Fruit is served in wine – not just sweet white but sharper reds such as clairette or chilled dry white. Do try it with strawberries.

Bordeaux has a great market every day except Sundays. Don't miss it if you are catering for yourself. St-Emilion's is on Sunday mornings, Blaye has markets on Wednesdays and Saturdays. Langon's is on Tuesdays and Fridays. Libourne has markets on Tuesdays, Fridays and Sunday mornings. Pauillac's are on Tuesdays and Saturday morning.

Hotels

Listrac

Hotel de France, Listrac, 33480 Castelnau, tel.(56) 58.03.68.

Recommended by vignerons for its food. Simple rooms. Meals and rooms C.

Margaux

Relais de Margaux (2km NE), Margaux, 33460 Gironde, tel.(56) 88.38.30.

Best hotel in this whole area, Bordeaux included. Nice grounds. New owner and chef in 1984. Michelin star. Try the Pauillac lamb and seabass (*loup*) in wine. Inevitably pricey. Meals and rooms E–VE. Shut 2–23 January.

Pauillac

France et Angleterre, 4 quai Pichon, 33250 Pauillac, tel.(56) 59.01.20.

Two-star hotel in nice position opposite Port de Plaisance. Meals and rooms C–M. Shut December, January.

St-Laurent-de-Médoc

La Renaissance, 33112 St-Laurent-de-Médoc, Gironde, tel.(56) 59.40.29.

Entirely renovated in 1984. Much used by local winesmen. Meals and rooms C. Shut Mondays.

St-Seurin-de-Cadourne

Du Midi, St-Seurin-de-Cadourne, 33250 Pauillac, tel. (56) 59.30.49.

'Not a palace but clean and comfortable.' Cheap.

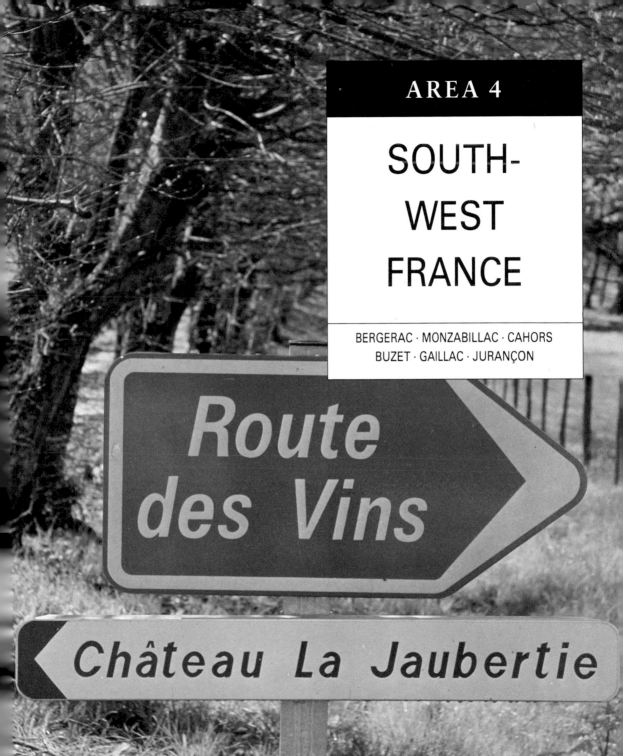

AREA 4

SOUTH-
WEST
FRANCE

BERGERAC · MONZABILLAC · CAHORS
BUZET · GAILLAC · JURANÇON

Route
des Vins

Château La Jaubertie

We sat on the lawns of Château La Jaubertie, built in the sixteenth century for Henry IV's mistress and now the home of Nicholas Ryman, sipping gorgeously perfumed, dry and fruity Bergerac white wine made from Muscadelle grapes. 'You know,' said Monsieur Ryman, 'if I had to choose between drinking red or white wine for the rest of my life, I should choose white. It is more subtle and has more variety.'

I agreed, but it's a difficult thought. I should miss Chambertin

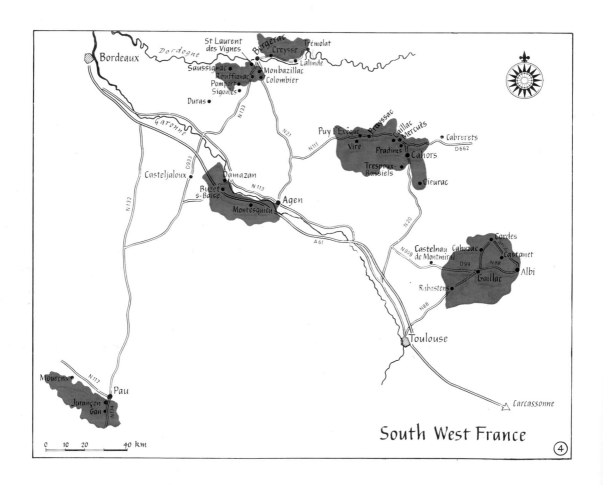

South West France

and Beaune, Margaux, Pauillac, St-Emilion – and Cahors. Please, St Peter, can I just skip the rosé?

The Bergerac area makes them all. A fruity white Blanc de Blancs, an exceptionally fruity and aromatic dry Bergerac blanc with all Sauvignon or Sauvignon with some Sémillon grapes, served cold, of course, as an aperitif, with hors d'oeuvres, fish or shellfish. A vivacious rosé; Bergerac and Côtes de Bergerac AOC red made from the same grapes as Bordeaux but lighter, with more fruit, quaffable slightly cold (57°F) with anything when young, pleasant with meat or cheese at 65°F (room temperature) when three to four years old. Red Pécharmant from gravelly hills, kept nearly three years in cask, then another three to ten years in bottle, full-bodied, beautifully balanced when well made, served with charcuterie, meat, game and cheese at 65°F. Côtes de Bergerac Moelleux, a soft, fruity sweet wine from Sémillon grapes, sometimes reaching 15 degrees alcohol. And Monbazillac, the great amber-gold sweet wine made from the same grapes as Sauternes and once passed off as Sauternes, though even richer – 14–15 degrees alcohol, which should be kept five to ten years and can be kept much longer. Usually drunk very cold as an aperitif, with pâté or with desserts, it can also be drunk through a meal.

All these wines are being improved by good wine makers, and, if you find the right one, you have a bargain. A few bad ones are still around, alas, and some are sent abroad – not worth the shelf-room except for cooking.

It is fortunate that at the moment when 'market forces' have made many favourite wines too dear for most of us, the wines of the South-West which our ancestors drank are either improving, like Bergerac, Buzet and Gaillac, or have improved, like Cahors.

Like Bergerac, Cahors was always popular with the English, who called it 'black wine' because of its purple colour when young. The Popes of Avignon were addicted, so were the Russians. They still make *Caorskoie* in the Crimea where Lot vines were planted. Later Bordeaux bought it to liven up pale, thin Bordeaux wines! But the dreaded phylloxera destroyed the vines last century, many hill vineyards were abandoned, and not until the 1950s did it begin to recover. After it was classified an AOC wine in 1971, improvement came fast. Made mostly from Auxerrois (Cot Noir or Malbec) grapes, with some Merlot, the Cahors we always knew, called Vieux or Vieux Réserve, has to mature in cask for three years and will keep many years after that. We drank it for years, congratulating ourselves on our secret bargain. Not long ago, Paris found out. A pity. The price went up. It has become something of a fashion in Paris, and, with the other vogue for light young wines, some growers are making lighter wines and selling them young, called Cahors Gouleyant (almost untranslatable, meaning something like 'easy to drink, light and pleasant'). Don't fall for it. The best growers are making the glorious, subtly perfumed refined wines again, even if it does tie up their capital. You needn't just drink them with red meat, game and cheese. They go with anything except shellfish or dessert.

Buzet red wines, with the Cabernets and Merlot grapes, have improved as much as any, and are justifiably becoming popular. We must thank the Cave Co-operative for their excellent care.

Gaillac wines have been produced for 1,000 years. Colette, who liked her wine, said of it: 'As an adolescent, I met a Prince – passionate, imperious, a deceiver like all seducers.' We know the dry white wine best, either still or *perlé* (slightly sparkling). They include two local grapes, Mauzac and L'En de L'El, with Sauvignon, Sémillon and Muscadelle, giving them aroma and a strong bouquet. But red wines are well worth investigating. Made from a variety of grapes, they vary, and some are just light and easy to drink with anything. But some good producers, blend the Bordeaux-style grapes with the local ancient Duras grape, giving body, colour and fruit, and Braucol, giving tannin for ageing power. This makes full-bodied, elegant wine which is worth keeping. Few of the old Gaillac sweet whites are made now, but I

have been most pleasantly surprised with the sparkling wines from good wine makers, especially those made by the natural local Gaillac method. They have fruity taste, delicate bouquet, softness and natural fizz. Worth considering for a wedding – or just romance.

Jurançon sweet white wines are risky for the growers, give a low yield and need keeping. They are becoming rare. But they are lovely. Dry wines replacing them are paler, have a clean taste with a touch of spice and are good for an aperitif or just thirst-quenching.

Tastings   BERGERAC AND MONBAZILLAC

Château La Jaubertie (Henry Ryman)

Nicholas Ryman sold his stationers' empire in England before he was forty to achieve his ambition to make wine in France. He bought this very charming sixteenth-century château which Henry IV of France, who loved women, wine and life, gave to his mistress Gabrielle d'Estrée, and started 'without knowing anything'. Now his wine is recognised by French experts such as Patrick Dussert-Gerber (adviser to the French trade) to be *the* Bergerac wine to buy. His white wine has won silver and bronze medals, his red wine two gold medals at the great Mâcon Wine Fair. Some French wine families spend generations trying to win just one. He has brought in fine modern cuves. And his son Hugh has studied wine making at the University of Bordeaux, in Burgundy, and especially in Australia with 'the man who makes the best white wine in the world'. (Don't be too surprised, many say that of the Aussies now.) Now Hugh makes the wine and I can only say that his dry white wine is captivating – a truly fruity and refreshing wine made mostly from Sémillon grapes, an extra fruity, perfumed Sauvignon with twenty per cent Sémillon

Colombier, 24560, tel.(53) 58.32.11. Take N21 SE from Bergerac just after crossing Dordogne river. 8km is sign on right to Colombier with vineyard name. 8–12 hrs; 14–18 hrs.

Nicholas Ryman

(Mirabelle) very much to most British tastes, and an absolutely delicious, fruity, highly perfumed, aromatic white made from old Muscadelle vines, not yet on the market but which I hope will be later. True to current fashion, the French praise his red wines. They are certainly fruity, mouth filling and well structured. Both are in a different world from Bergeracs I have drunk from French restaurant lists or our own supermarkets or most wine merchants.

Château de Tiregand (Comtesse de St-Exupéry)

In this beautiful château built in 1688, the St-Exupéry family, cousins of the airman-poet, make Pécharmant red wine which has been the flag-carrier for Bergerac. Kept to age in wood for twenty months, it matures in five to six years into a deep-coloured, full flavoured wine which any amateur could mistake for a high quality Bordeaux. I was disappointed recently to find how much tannin the wines were now keeping, even after five years. Too much for me. A *sommelier* suggested that the oak barrels in which they matured were too old. I am told that this will soon be altered. But do try for yourself. You may love the taste, as many do.

Creysse, 24100 Bergerac, tel.(53) 23.21.08. Take D660 E from Bergerac towards Lalinde. When board marking Creysse village appears, turn left under the railway bridge and the château is on left. 8–12 hrs; 14–18 hrs.

Domaine du Haut Pécharmant (Mme Roches)

Another really good Pécharmant wine which is allowed long fermentation, three years to mature, is racked regularly, allowed to clear naturally and bottled without filtering. Fruity, flowery, fairly powerful wine, with more Merlot than Cabernet grape. Some years are a bit tannic and need to be kept (1981 should not be drunk until 1988). Others are ready soon after bottling. Good value.

24100 Bergerac, tel.(53) 57.24.50. NE edge of Bergerac. 8–12 hrs; 14–19 hrs.

Château Corbiac (Bruno Durand de Corbiac)

Another good Pécharmant to taste and buy. Good value.

24100 Bergerac, tel.(53) 57.20.75. Take N21 N from Bergerac for 3km; right at Pombonne for 1km. 9–19 hrs.

Château de Monbazillac and Cave Co-operative de Monbazillac

The cave uses very modern methods of vinification. They produce Monbazillacs of three vineyards, including that of the château itself, and also Pécharmant from Château La Renaudie across the Dordogne, and Bergerac white, red and rosé. Also a Champagne-method *pétillant* (gently sparkling) white called Festival, and pure grape juice. Half-hour tours of cave, then tasting in the seventeenth-century chais (fee 12F). There is also a restaurant and shop for buying wine. The château was built in 1550 for pleasure

BP 2, Monbazillac, 24240 Sigoulés, Dordogne, tel. (53) 57.06.38. Take D933 S from Bergerac past St-Laurent. Caves on right, Château by tiny road left after Cave (D14). Both open 9–12 hrs; 14–18 hrs. Cave shut Saturdays, Sundays.

as well as defence but was a Protestant stronghold in the Wars of Religion. Very beautiful, with round towers and a superb entrance and courtyard. The chimneys and tapestry are delightful. In the sixteenth-century cellars is a Museum of Wine, with splendid old barrels and equipment, and old bottles in an ancient kitchen.

Unidor (Co-operative)

Co-op making wine for 2000 small growers in Dordogne. About eight million bottles are made each year and there are 11½ million maturing in the cellars. Reasonable prices, good value.

BP 1, Monbazillac, 24240 Sigoulés, tel.(53) 57.40.44. On D933 S of Bergerac before Monbazillac Co-op. Monday–Friday 8.30–12.30 hrs; 13.30–17.30 hrs.

Château Court Les Mûts (M. et Mme Sardoux)

Very interesting visit. Modern equipment, including laboratory. Pierre-Jean Sardoux is an oenologist from the Institute of Bordeaux. From old vines (forty per cent Merlot) red wine matures eighteen months in new oak barrels and keeps six to seven years. The tannin becomes softened and the wine beautifully full. A string of medals proves it. Also produces white (seventy per cent Sémillon), rosé, a Blanc de Blancs very dry sparkling wine and a delightful rare white Saussignac Moelleux (rich, sweet and strong – 12 degrees).

Ranzac-de-Saussignac, 24240 Sigoulés, tel.(53) 27.92.17. D936 W from Bergerac, left on D4 at Gardonne, right on D14, then lane left. 9–11.15 hrs; 14–17.15 hrs. English spoken.

Château de Panisseau

Go if only to see the delightful thirteenth-century château. In 1363, when the English owned Aquitaine, the Seigneur de Panisseau paid homage for his title to the Prince of Wales. Choice of two white wines – one Sauvignon, one half Sémillon. The red, which has twice won the Mâcon gold medal, has long-lasting flavour. Good value. Go for red '82 or '83. Very good rosé.

Thénac, 24240 Sigoulés, tel.(53) 58.40.03. Take D936 W from Bergerac towards Bordeaux for 5km, left on D16 to Cunèges, then sign to Panisseau (2km). 8.30–11.30 hrs; 14–18 hrs. No English spoken.

Jean Jouffreau inside the tasting room at Clos de Gamot

Domaine de l'Ancienne Curé

Very good Monbazillac. I have superb 1973 and 1982 to keep. Excellent value. Also quaffable red Bergerac in bottles or *cubitainers* (22 litres) for home bottling.

Colombier, 24560 Issigeac, Dordogne, tel.(53) 58.32.28. Just above N21, 10km from Bergerac towards Agen. Tasting booth on N21 open all year, mostly until dusk.

Other properties in Bergerac—Monbazillac to visit:
Domaine de La Lande (Jean Camus), Monbazillac, 24240 Sigoulés, tel.(53) 58.30.45. Open all year during working hours. No English spoken.
Michel Prouillac, Le Mayne, 24240 Sigoulés, tel.(53) 58.40.92. On D15 W from Sigoulés. 16–19 hrs in summer. Family of vignerons since 1756. Good value wines include Côtes-de-Bergerac white *moelleux* (sweet) which needs keeping (ten years).
Château Le Mayne, Le Mayne, 24240 Sigoulés, tel.(53) 58.40.01. D15 W from Sigoulés. 8–12 hrs; 14–17 hrs. Modern methods. Wines include a Côtes de Duras AOC from South of Bergerac (the white Sauvignon is very fruity and easy to lap up).
Cave Co-operative de Sigoulés, 24240 Sigoulés, tel.(53) 58.40.18. 2km SE of Sigoulés. Monday–Friday 9–12 hrs; 13.30–17.30 hrs. Wine

provided by 300 growers. Quality wines include good sparkling wine.

Le Poncet, St-Laurent des Vignes, 24100 Bergerac, tel.(53) 57.30.98. Visits afternoons. Meet Maurice Chevalier, respected wine maker! Family tradition.

Domaine de Haut-Montlong, Pomport, 24240 Sigoulés, tel.(53) 58.81.60. Pomport is N of Sigoulés on D17. Domaine is NE on D16 E across D16. Visits afternoons. Known especially for Monbazillac sweet (*liquoreux*) matured in cask.

CAHORS

Château du Cayrou (Jean Jouffreau)

Newer property of the great Jean Jouffreau (*see* Clos de Gamot, below), run by his daughter and son-in-law. Gorgeous twelfth- and fifteenth-century château in beautiful grounds where concerts are held sometimes. The Jouffreau family bought the château and the vineyard on gravelly Lot soil from Comte André de Montpezat in 1971 and have applied their expertise to it. The family have been vignerons for more than 300 years. Excellent modern equipment is used and a new underground cellar has been built. Each year, Jean Jouffreau decides how long the wine should age in wood. The result is a delight: *gras*, as the French say – rich in alcohol and content, full-bodied and fleshy, a great wine. 1979 and 1982 are both super. 1985 should be.

46700 Puy-l'Évêque, Lot, tel.(65) 36.43.03. Just N of river Lot in huge horseshoe. From Puy-l'Évêque go down to river bridge; just before it is a little road on left D28, marked to Château, which is marked on yellow Michelin 79. Visits 'at your convenience' (working hours, please!). English spoken.

Clos de Gamot (Jouffreau)

Jean Jouffreau's original property, producing Clos de Gamot from vines planted 100 years ago. Compares in all ways with Château de Cayrou; also a Blanc de Blancs dry and a rosé. No weedkillers allowed. A wonderful collection of old wine stocks,

46220 Prayssac, tel.(65) 22.40.26. D67 S to the Lot river. Marked on yellow Michelin 79. Visits in working hours.

with barrels, going back fifty years. You'll be lucky to taste those! My favourite Cahors and excellent value. Dr Roger Belcour, who runs a clinic in Cahors, is half-owner of La Pescalerie Hotel at Cabrerets (*see* Hotels), a true expert on Cahors wines, he recommends it passionately.

Clos Triguedina (Baldés Fils)

Another one which the Doctor (Belcour) recommends. The Baldés family are 'new boys' – only in the business for eight generations since 1830! A blend of modern and traditional methods produces a perfectly balanced wine which fills your mouth, satisfies your palate, brings out the best in duck, beef or game, and does not send you bankrupt. These Cahors wines are still wonderful value. The old vines, up to forty years old, are used to make a special cuvée Le Prince Probus, which must be hidden away for at least five years. The 1980, I am told, is a revelation. One French wine critic described it as having *un nez profond*, though that sounds more suitable to Bergerac and Cyrano himself.

46700 Puy-l'Évêque, tel.(65) 21.30.81. Just before Puy-l'Évêque on right of D911 going E. 9–12 hrs; 14–18.30 hrs.

Château La Haute Serre (Georges Vigouroux)

In 1971 Georges Vigouroux bought a hillside vineyard that had been abandoned for 100 years, cleared it of stones and tilled it. It now produces one of the best wines of Cahors – vital, balanced, fruity yet earthy. You may have tasted it on Brittany Ferries. His wines have the advantage of being pleasant drunk young (the fashionable French way) yet will keep and become heavier, polished and strong (the way we older English like them). Grapes are handpicked, fermentation is on the spot. Georges also raises wines (*éleveur*), ages them, is a wholesaler (*négociant*) and an exporter, besides owning Château de Mercuès, a magnificent hotel (*see* Hotels).

Cieurac, 46230 Lalbenque, tel.(65) 35.22.55; office (65) 38.70.30. Take N20 S from Cahors to airfield 12km; signboard points to Haute Serre on D149 left. Visits every day, including weekends, except 12.30–13.30 hrs. Audio-visual (English text) on wines (20 mins), tasting.

Les Côtes d'Olt

Group of 500 growers. Wines produced include Domaine des Landes (fruity wine for early drinking), Château les Bouysses (very good wine from the Cave's own land overlooking Lot at Mercuès), and Comte André de Montpezat (selected grapes from the best soil, then selected from the vats – an excellent wine for keeping).

Parnac, 46140 Luzech, tel.(65) 30.71.86. From Cahors go W on D8 (S of Lot river) to Luzech, then turn right. Monday–Friday 8–12 hrs; 13.30–17.30 hrs; also Saturdays 1 May– 1 September.

Domaine des Savarines

Local connoisseurs were keeping this to themselves until now! In a remote hillside vineyard, Mme Biesbroack makes and raises a true Cahors in oak barrels.

46090 Trespoux, tel.(65) 35.50.55. Take D24 Villesèque road from Valentré bridge in Cahors. Past Trespoux, turn right after a school. Then left fork to Domaine.

BUZET

Les Vignerons des Côtes-de-Buzet

Got AOC status as Côtes-de-Buzet in 1973, since when nearly all the AOC wine of the region from more than 500 growers is made in this co-op. Most of it is red, made Bordelais style. Elegance of Cabernets, soft fruit of Merlot, rounded, full-bodied but light. Can be drunk young, slightly chilled but better kept four to eight years and served at room temperature with meat. The huge effort to improve the wines has paid off. Increasingly popular in France, it is also catching on in Britain. Best and priciest wine is Cuvée Napoléon from best, ripest grapes, aged in new oak casks made at the cave and tasting like a good Médoc. Would be a good buy for keeping a few years. Château de Gueyze is excellent, too.

Buzet-sur-Baïse, 47160 Damazan, Lot-et-Garonne, tel.(53) 79.44.30. Buzet wine area is along left bank of river Garonne in a triangle Damazan, Nérac, Montesquieu, 104km SE Bordeaux, 32km NW of Agen. Buzet is between A61 motorway and river Garonne, on D962 on Baïse river. 9–12 hrs; 14–18 hrs.

GAILLAC

Domaine Jean Cros et Château Larroze

Well worth finding. Since Jean Cros, an agricultural engineer, took over from his father in 1945 and his sons joined him later to run the vineyards and wine-making, they have done much for Gaillac's reputation. Wines with their own definite character. A Gamay red is surprisingly mouth-filling for such a light fresh wine and so easy to drink. The Gaillac red of Larroze is full with a distinct flowery perfume. I felt I could drink it with any food. Larroze dry white has a powerful scent, is mellow and unusual. An interesting, refreshing, *perlé* (slightly fermenting) wine is made of two local grapes, Mausac (making it fruity) and Loin de l'Oeil or L'En de l'El (adding sap). I had a Domaine Jean Cros 1980 red which is light, spicy and has character. Red Gaillacs, made from a variety of grapes, are little known in Britain. Lance Edynbry, Jean Cros's son-in-law, a former Lancaster University lecturer, intends to alter that. He is the export manager. The sparkling Mousseux brut is delicious.

Cahuzac-sur-Vère, 81140 Tarn, tel.(63) 33.92.62. D922 N from Gaillac. Larroze down lane on right before Cahuzac, Domaine Jean Cros right 2km past. Both signposted; Domaine open for tastings; Larroze will be later. Tasting room being built. Ask for Génèvieve Edynbry. English spoken. Monday–Saturday 9–19 hrs; Sunday 15–18 hrs.

Other Gaillac area properties you can visit:
Cave de Técou, Técou, 81600 Gaillac, tel.(63) 33.00.80. 8km S Gaillac left off D964. 8–12 hrs; 14–18 hrs. Co-op. Makes charming, perfumed AOC red and fruity white, *Vin de Pays* Côtes du Tarn and *Vins de Table.*
Vignerons à Rabastens (Co-op), 33 route d'Albi, 81150 Rabastens, tel.(63) 33.73.00. N88 SW of Gaillac. Modern cave for 600 growers. Especially recommended for cheap, aromatic Gaillac white.
Domaine Labarthe (Jean Albert), Castanet, 81150 Marssac, tel.(63) 56.80.14. D600 NW from Albi, left to St Crois, Castanet; just past village. 8–12 hrs; 14–18 hrs. The Albert family has been here since the sixteenth century. Excellent fruity, earthy, honest dry white (half

Sauvignon, half Loin de l'Oeil); well made fruity red. Bottles, or 22-litre *vrac*.

Château Clarès, Florentin, 81150 Marssac, tel. (63) 55.40.12. S from N88 Gaillac–Albi road at Marssac by D30. Open business hours every day, even Sunday. Started 1964 by Jean Clarès. Reliable AOC wines.

Domaine de la Tour (Claude Fiault), Boisel, 81600 Gaillac, tel.(63) 57.06.05. Just off D922, 4km N of Gaillac. 8–12 hrs; 14–18 hrs. An old-established family vineyard that is very convenient for Gaillac and which has won many awards since 1893.

Manoir de l'Emmeille (Charles Poussou), Campagnac, 81140 Castelnau de Montmirail, tel.(63) 33.12.80. N from Gaillac D964, right for D15. 8–12 hrs; 14–18 or 19.30 hrs summer. English spoken. Good welcome. Fine old manor. Many enthusiastic French families and restaurants buy direct. Red and white.

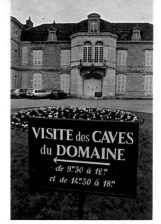

JURANÇON

Cave des Producteurs de Jurançon

The best place to buy this delightful, underestimated wine. Traditional moelleux sweet wines are rare because of the great risk in picking grapes late to get sugar and alcohol (minimum 12.5 degrees). The wine must also then be kept. Grapes (Gros and Petits Manseng) are often not picked until November. The wine is golden coloured, with an enormously rich bouquet – honey, a touch of nutmeg and cinnamon, and a fruity, almost lemon, taste. Nice when young, nectar if kept ten to twenty years. Here they make a great wine – Prestige d'Automne. The 1980 won the Grand Prix at Mâcon. They say that the '82 is even greater. I wonder how my '79 will last? They also bottle Château les Astous, made at an historic château with very old vines. And they make a fine Jurançon dry white, the majority wine these days. Three hundred growers belong to the Co-op.

53 ave Henri-IV, 64290 Gan, Pyrénées-Atlantiques, tel.(59) 21.57.03. 8km S Pau/Jurançon on N134. 9–12 hrs; 14–18 hrs; English spoken. They would like if possible two days' notice for serious tastings. Phone if you can. If not, apologise!

Château Larroze

Further Information

Bergerac: Comité Interprofessionel des Vins de Bergerac, 2 place du Docteur-Cayla, 24100 Bergerac, Dordogne.

Cahors: Union Interprofessionel du Vin de Cahors, ave Jean-Jaurès, 46004 Cahors, Lot.

Gaillac: Comité Interprofessionel des Vins de Gaillac, Abbaye Saint Michel, 81600 Gaillac, Tarn.

Food

I asked several chefs around the Dordogne what special dish suited a five–six-year-old Pécharmant red wine. The answers – *la feuilleté d'escargots aux cèpes* (snails in puff pastry with cèpes – the delicate fungi); *la côte de boeuf sauce moelle au vin* (grilled beef with beef marrow and wine sauce); *steack de canard au vin* (breast fillets of duck braised in wine); *contre-filet au roquefort* (sirloin steak in Roquefort cheese sauce); *pintades à la poitrine fumée et au vin* (smoked guinea fowl breasts cooked in wine); *lotte au Pécharmant* (burbot – freshwater river fish, poached in wine); *civet de langouste au Pécharmant* (lobster meat stewed in red wine, onions, tomatoes and garlic).

Quite a variety! But both red and white Bergerac wines are versatile and slightly cold red Bergerac (as opposed to Péchar-mant) can certainly be served through a meal, even with the inevitably popular Périgordian dishes.

Périgueux is only 47km away. Goose and duck are king here, too, and their fat is used for frying. *Confit de canard* or *d'oie* (duck or goose preserved in its own fat) is splendid simply fried in a little of the fat with the rest used for sauté potatoes. If self-catering, buy the confit in tins – not cheap but delicious. Cold meats, pâtés, and sausages cooked or dried, are as popular here as anywhere on the Dordogne. You may revolt against foie gras because geese are force fed or you may just find it too expensive. Certainly truffles are truly costlier than gold now, but the tiniest specks of this jet-black fungus in a terrine or a few pieces in an omelette make a marvellous starter.

Try *cèpes à la périgourdine* (cèpes mushrooms cooked with bacon, parsley, garlic and verjus – juice of unripe grapes), or *chou farci* (an old peasant dish still served in local restaurants consist-ing of whole cabbage stuffed with minced pork, veal and mushrooms and cooked in white wine for about five hours). Also *fricassé de volaille aux écrevisses* (chicken and river crayfish stewed in cream and white wine), *lièvre à la royale* (hare boned and marinaded, stuffed with veal and bacon, cooked in wine and brandy and served with a rich sauce of truffles or mushrooms), *ballotine de dinde* (white turkey meat stuffed with pâté de foie gras and encased in jelly), *sobronade* (thick soup of pork, ham, white beans, turnips, onions, garlic and herbs), and *tourin péri-gourdin* (onion soup with tomatoes, egg yolks, served over bread slices, often with grated cheese, and put under a grill).

Monbazillac goes beautifully with local strawberries. It's a land of walnuts, too, so dress salads with superb walnut oil and take some home. Bergerac and Périgueux markets are on Wednesdays and Saturdays.

They eat even more heartily in Cahors. In one restaurant in Quercy they proudly served me a Nouvelle Cuisine 'starter' of mousse of three salmons (fresh, marinaded and smoked) as a pre-meal snack with white wine. Another restaurant slipped in Nouvelle's *magret de canard* (duck's breasts in fruit vinegar) as an extra course, between fish and meat! The food goes with Cahors wines, whether young and light or old, strong and delicious.

Game is popular in season. But most of the dishes are very similar to those of Bergerac and Dordogne, including the peasant soup *oulade* of cabbage, potatoes, pork and bacon. From Rouer-gue just south they often borrow *mourtairol* (chicken broth or stew in a saffron sauce) and, like the rest of the world, Roquefort cheese, which goes nicely with an old Cahors wine (anyway, though they may mature it in Roquefort caves, the actual sheep's cheese comes from everywhere from the Pyrenees to Corsica). Cahors has its Quercy cheeses – excellent bleu de Quercy, blue cow's milk cheese carefully matured, and cabecou goat's cheese.

The Gaillac wine area adjoins Quercy, and meals can be similar. But there is an influence of Toulouse and Agen – chicken flambéed in Armagnac, jugged hare in Armagnac, roast pork with prunes, goose stuffed with prunes, long spicy Toulouse sausage, good local ham. And, of course, *cassoulet*, the stew based on white haricot beans, pork, sausage, herbs and garlic. When in the Toulouse area, confit of goose is a must. It should be simmered for twelve hours (or days!), must be ordered in a good restaurant or you will get a load of rubbish, and is the complete antithesis of Nouvelle Cuisine. Make sure you also order a full-bodied Gaillac red, like Château Larroze. Beware of *mouton en pistache* if you don't like garlic – the shoulder or leg of mutton is studded with anything up to fifty cloves of garlic, though most chefs are content with five to ten. It is then braised with wine and beans.

Albi, near to Gaillac, is fruit country – plums, peaches, cherries, apricots. Toulouse is famous for violets as well as sausages and violet-cream-filled chocolates are a speciality.

In Jurançon, the mountain influence starts – mountain lamb, ewe cheese (most of which is sent to Roquefort), fish from rivers and from the coast at St Jean de Luz, fine hams served cured and raw with a variety of other sausages and charcuterie. Try *garbure*, with pork, ham and a confit of chicken cooked with vegetables, including haricot and broad beans and cabbage, the meat served on one plate, the liquid poured over bread in a bowl, and the last of the juice mixed with wine, swilled round and drunk from the bowl (making *chabrot*). And try a genuine *piperade* of tomatoes, red peppers and onions, stewed in oil, then eggs stirred in and served with mountain ham.

Hotels

Bergerac

Le Vieux Logis, Trémolat, 24510 St-Alvère, Dordogne, tel.(53) 22.80.06. 34km E of Bergerac along Dordogne river.

A delightful country logis in a pretty walled garden turned into a superb little hotel with taste and understanding. Excellent cooking from a new chef and a sommelier who knows his wines. I love it. Meals and rooms M–E. Shut January. Restaurant, Tuesday and Wednesday.

La Panoramic, rte du Cingle de Trémolat, 24510 St-Alvère, Dordogne, tel.(53) 22.80.42. 3km Trémolat by D31.

Magnificent views. Meals C–M; rooms C. Shut January–February.

Relais de Saussignac, 24240 Sigoulés, Dordogne, tel. (53) 27.92.08. N136 W Bergerac, D4 left at Gardonne.

Comfortable, modern, attractive, peaceful. Regional and Périgordian cooking. Meals C–M; rooms C. Shut part November.

Manoir Grand Vignoble, St Julien de Crempse, 24140 Villamblard, Bergerac, tel.(53) 24.23.18. 12km N Bergerac by N21, D107, local lane.

Beautiful Louis XIV manor in park with pool, stables. Meals M–E; rooms C–M. Shut 6 January–2 February.

Le Cyrano, 2 boulevard Montaigne, Bergerac, 24100 Dordogne, tel. (53) 57.02.76.

Superb cooking with a choice of regional or very modern dishes. Excellent local wines. Menus outstanding value. Meals C–M; rooms C. Shut Mondays, Sunday evenings (except July–August) 26 June–11 July.

Bordeaux Hotel, Terroir Rest, 38 place Gambetta, Bergerac, 24100 Dordogne, tel.(53) 57.12.83. The cheap menus are excellent value.

Even Inspector Maigret lunched here (*Le Fou de Bergerac*). Run by the same family since 1855. Meals C–M; rooms C. Shut January; restaurant Saturdays from October–March.

La Diligence, 24240 Sigoulés, tel.(53) 58.30.48. Near Monbazillac, 6km S Bergerac on D933.

Magnificent terrace views over vineyards. Périgordian dishes. Meals C–E; rooms C. Shut 23 June–10 July. Restaurant shut Tuesday evenings, Wednesdays except mid July–mid September.

Cahors

La Pescalerie, Cabrerets, 46330 Lot, tel.(65) 31.22.55. At La Fontaine de la Pescalerie, E Cahors by D662, then D41, 34km.

Peaceful, informal old manor with elegant furnishings in lovely grounds. One of our favourite country hotels anywhere. Run by two doctors, one of whom, Dr Roger Belcour, is an expert on Cahors wines; super selection. Meals M; rooms M—E. Open 1 April—1 November.

Bellevue, Puy-l'Évêque, 46700 Lot, tel.(65) 21.30.70. 31km W Cahors on D911.

Glad I found it. Old-style inn, used by locals. Truly *belle vue* of Lot river from terrace and dining room. Meals good value. Simple, comfortable bedrooms. Meals C—M; rooms C. Hotel open 15 February—15 November, restaurant 15 March—15 October.

Château de Mercuès, Mercuès 46090 Cahors, Lot, tel.(65) 20.00.01. 9km N Cahors on D911.

Magnificent position, pricey. Wine producer Georges Vigouroux (*see* Tastings) restored this turreted, castellated mediaeval castle. Massive views from charming terrace. Pool. Rooms very comfortable. Meals M; rooms E. Open end March—end September.

Buzet

Cadets de Gascogne, place Gambetta, Casteljaloux, 47700 Lot-et-Garonne, tel.(53) 93.00.59. W from Damazan 20km on D8, D11.

Inn on market square; excellent regional and inventive cooking by Joël Malvaud, ex Prunier. Welcome from Martine Malvaud. Good value. Meals C—M; rooms C. Shut 15—30 November.

Hostellerie du Canal, Damazan, 47160 Lot-et-Garonne, tel.(53) 79.42.84.

On Blaïse river just N Buzet; 31km W Agen. Logis de France. Meals C—M; rooms C.

Gaillac

Grand Ecuyer, rue Voltaire, 81170 Cordes, Tarn, tel.(63) 56.01.03.

Attractive mediaeval village 24km N Gaillac on D922. In Gothic hunting lodge of Counts of Toulouse. Famous pastry cook Yves Thuriès, performs all his cooking with the same passion and perfectionism. Modern dishes. Good wine list. Excellent value, especially cheaper menus. Meals and rooms C—M. Shut Mondays, Tuesdays lunch in winter.

Hostellerie du Parc, Les Cabannes, route St-Antonin, 81170 Cordes, Tarn, Les Cabannes marked at Cordes on Michelin 79.

A little treasure, loved by *vignerons*; outstanding value in cheap regional meals. Has terrace and garden. Bargain weekday menu with wine. Meals and rooms C. Shut January—February; Sunday evening, Mondays out of season.

Pré-Vert, Promenade Lices, Rabastens, 81800 Tarn, tel.(63) 33.70.51. N88 15km SW Gaillac.

Recommended by local vignerons. Meals and rooms C. Shut Sundays out of season.

Hostellerie Saint-Antoine, 17 rue St-Antoine, Albi 81000 Tarn, tel.(63) 54.04.04.

In charming city 22km E of Gaillac (Toulouse-Lautrec was born here 1864 and you can see his original poster paintings in the Archbishop's Palace). Delightful, tasteful, quiet hotel in Rieux family 200 years. Fine traditional cooking. Meals and rooms C–M. Open 1 April–30 September.

The same family run La Réserve, at Fonvialane, 3km on Cordes road, tel.(63) 60.79.79; superb position with terrace overlooking Lot river. Lovely park with swimming pool. Relais et Châteaux hotel. Meals C–M; rooms M–E.

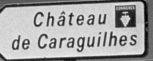

The wines of Languedoc are much maligned by people who seem not to have noticed the degree to which many of them have improved in the past few years. That is a good thing for bargain-hunters. And much of the gorgeous and wild Languedoc country-side is neglected by tourists, which is a good thing for travellers in France. I am not suggesting that the wines compare with those of Burgundy or Haut-Médoc, but nor do the prices. Gone are the days when played-out vineyards produced any old wine for mixing with Algerian as café plonk; long gone, too, are the post-war days when we thirsted for any wine and young Mark Gilbey filled redundant wartime water lorries with Corbières red, some mystery white, and pinkish Clairette, drove it to Britain and sold it in the shops for five shillings (25p) a bottle. A budget put up

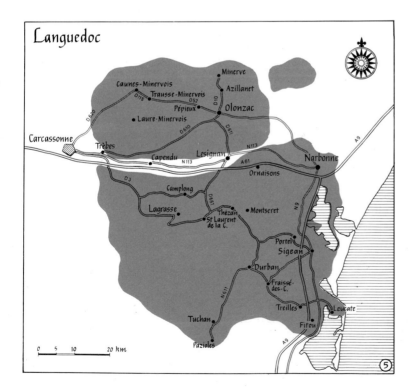

the price to 6s 9d and some wouldn't pay it. They had bought Château Talbot for that before the war.

Languedoc produces seventy-five per cent of France's *Vin de Pays*. Corbières alone produces seventy-five million bottles of VDQS wine, and, as Stephen Spurrier, the Englishman who has made himself 'Paris' wine merchant' says, the proportion of good to bad is high. The red has a minimum of 11 degrees alcohol, the Superior has 12 degrees. The red is normally drunk young, a year after the vintage, but good wines improve greatly up to five to six years. The young wine is useful, as it can be drunk with almost anything. White Corbières wines are rare and drunk little outside Languedoc but are light, fragrant and fruity. Corbières wines stand up well to travel.

Minervois wines have deservedly gained AOC recognition at last. I like the older wines best of Languedoc reds – deep colour, strong spicy smell and taste, and smooth as they slip down the throat. Mind you, if you really want to know you are drinking wine, the AOC Fitou reds are splendid – very dark red, slightly rough, powerful flavour and a touch of iron and tannin mixed with the fruit. Fitou spends eighteen months at least in wood before bottling and should be kept about five years. I don't understand how so many Frenchmen I know, especially younger ones, will drink wines like this young and say that they are overpriced or rough. More expensive than most Corbières but worth the money.

Val d'Orbieu produces very good *Vins de Pays* – red, dry white and rosé. The red is fruity and not too heavy – good for drinking in summer sun.

Blanquette de Limoux sparkling white (the blanket is a white dust which forms on the vine leaves) is made either by the Champagne method or *rurale* (*see* glossary) – soft, easy to drink, leaving a fruity dry taste. Going through one of its periodic 'fashions' in France.

Tastings

MINERVOIS

Lauran-Cabaret

The village was once a stronghold of the Albigeois religious sect and the strong, full-bodied red wine, aged in oak casks, is named after the local Lord Cabaret de Lauran who defended his village, people and vines against the cruel persecution of Simon de Montfort. My favourite from Minervois. Definitely for roast beef, stews, game and local *cassoulet*. There's a younger, lighter red, too, and dry white and rosé.

Laure-Minervois, 11800 Trèbes, Aude, tel.(68) 78.12.12. N113 E from Carcassonne, left at Trèbes on D136. 8–10 hrs; 14–18 hrs.

Cave des Vignerons 'Les Coeaux'

Outstanding red 'Ancien Comte' from old vines, kept a year in wood; at its best six–seven years old. Worth taking home.

Pouzols-Minervois, 11120 Aude, tel.(68) 46.13.76. N113, D610, then D11, D5 from Carcassonne towards Béziers. Monday–Saturday 8–12 hrs; 14–18 hrs. Sundays in summer.

Other Minervois caves to visit:

Cave Co-operative les Vignerons du Haut Minervois, Azillanet, 34210 Olonzac, Hérault, tel.(68) 91.22.61. 4km S of Minerve on D10. 8–12 hrs; 14–18 hrs. Phone if possible. Wines of three communes. Good red.

Cave Co-operative, Pépieux, 11700 Capendu, Aude, tel.(68) 91.41.04. SW of Minerve. Cave 4km E of Pépieux on D52, nearer Olonzac. 8–12 hrs; 14–18 hrs. Produces one of the best well-known reds called 'Les Cathares'. Also a fruity white.

Cave Co-operative 'Costos Trousos', 11160 Trausse-Minervois, Aude, tel.(68) 78.31.15. D620 NE from Carcassonne. Right at Caunes on D115. 8–12 hrs; 14–18 hrs. No English spoken. Good red aged in wood. Look for '82, '83.

LIMOUX

Société des Vignerons de Blanquette de Limoux

Blanquette de Limoux, 'the oldest sparkling wine in the world', is regarded by many as equal to any outside Champagne and you can get the best of it here. You can also buy some other local wines, but not the best in Languedoc.

ave du Mauzac, 11300 Limoux, Aude, tel. (68) 31.14.59. 24km S of Carcassonne on D118. 8–12 hrs; 14–18 hrs. Phone.

CORBIÈRES

Caves Saury-Serres

Don't miss it. Not growers, but they bottle and mature wines from Corbières, Minervois, Fitou and Limoux. In an old cave is a fascinating display of how wine used to be produced, with old implements, including a superb nineteenth-century stone press, pumps, tractors, displays of how wine growers used to live and dress, a cooperage, forge and saddle-room. A buffet of local dishes, including salted meats from the black mountains, smoked fish, local goat cheese, honey cakes and *cassoulet*, is served at noon, with wines, and is a bargain. It is worth coming a long way to see. Some nice older wines, too.

11200 Lézignan-Corbières, Aude, tel.(68) 27.07.57. 100m from Lézignan railway station, just off N113 Narbonne–Carcassonne and A61 motorway. 9–12 hrs; 14–19 hrs every day. Cellars free; wine museum 8F (30 mins). Mme Saury-Serres would like you to mention this book when you visit.

Château de Caraguilhes (Lionel Faivre)

Some of the best Corbières wines, produced by traditional methods in a vineyard already known in 1532. The careful and serious producer uses no chemical weedkillers, insecticides or additives. 'Château de Caraguilhes' red is kept two years in bottle before being sold, and will keep much longer. Medium weight, subtle, full bodied. Excellent with meat, cheese and charcuterie. You will be surprised at such quality from Corbières. We saw it on sale at Harrods. The 1982 is good. Blanc de Blancs, a little 'green',

St-Laurent de la Cabrerisse, 11220 Lagrasse, Aude, tel.(68) 43.62.05. W of Lagrasse 10km on D3 where it meets D613. Monday–Friday 8–18 hrs; phoning preferred. Weekends, phone. Some English spoken.

is a refreshing aperitif. Red *Vin de Pays* is fruity, light on alcohol, and good for hot weather drinking.

Caves des Côtes d'Alaric

Good cheap 'green' (young) wines. Peyres Nobles red is very good. Kept in wood to mature, it has an unusual bouquet, a powerful taste, is full in the mouth and quite smooth.

11200 Camplong, Lézignan, Aude, tel.(68) 43.60.86. D114, off D212 Lézignan–Lagrasse road. 8–12 hrs; 14–18 hrs.

Château les Ollieux

A red wine worth taking home to keep a year or two. Decant it and see if very knowledgeable friends can name even the area! It is very carefully produced in centuries-old modernised caves under the personal supervision of Françoise Surbézy-Cartier, whose family have owned the château since 1855. 'Château les Ollieux' label red is carefully selected after eighteen months. It has won three Mâcon gold medals in nine years.

Montserat, 11200 Lézignan, Aude, tel.(68) 43.32.61. Just off D613, 20km SW of Narbonne, marked as 'les Ollieux' on Michelin yellow. 8–12 hrs; 14–18 hrs. Some English spoken.

Other Corbières caves to visit:
Co-opérative Agricole, Ferrals-lès-Corbières, 11200 Lézignan, Aude, tel.(68) 43.62.47. 7km S Lézignan on D611. Monday–Friday 8–12 hrs; 14–18 hrs. Saturdays 9–12 hrs in July, August. Outstanding value red 'Chevalier de Béranger' won Mâcon gold medal 1984. Three hundred and twenty growers in Co-op.
Cave Co-opérative de Lagrasse, 11220 Lagrasse, Aude, tel.(68) 43.10.62. 8–12 hrs; 14–18 hrs. English spoken. Good value red and white.
Cave Co-opérative, Thézan, 11200 Lézignan, Aude, tel.(68) 43.32.13. D611, 17km S of Lézignan. Visits working hours; tastings.
Château Beauregard (Simone Mirouze), Bizanet, 11200 Lézignan, tel.(68) 45.12.13. N113 W from Narbonne 5km, left on D613, first left after Abbaye de Fontfroide. Visits and tastings in working hours. English spoken. The vineyards have been in same family for 150 years and have been completely replanted. High quality red, good colour, keeps well; unusual, subtle rosé *perlant* (very slightly sparkling).

Caves des Côtes d'Alaric

Le Mont Alaric (Cave Co-opérative), Monze, 11800 Trèbes, tel.(68) 78.68.01. Near Carcassonne. E on N113, right on D3. Monday–Friday 8–12 hrs; 14–18 hrs. Saturdays 8–12 hrs. Wines sold in 12-bottle cartons or 22-litre *cubitainers*. Red 'Selection' is good value.

Société Co-opérative, Fraissé-des-Corbières, 11360 Durban, 8km SW Durban by D27, D206. 9–12 hrs; 15–18 hrs. Quality red at low price.

Union des Co-opératives des Corbières Maritimes, 11480 Portel-des-Corbières, Aude, tel.(68) 48.28.05. D3 NW from Sigean. Monday–Friday 8–12 hrs; 14–18 hrs. Some English spoken. Three important villages (Portel, Peyriac, Sigean) produce quality strong 'Maritime' wine under the name of Le Rocbère.

Other places in Narbonne to vist:

Les Vignerons du Val d'Orbieu, route de Moussan, 11100 Narbonne, tel.(68) 42.38.77. 8–12 hrs; 14–18 hrs. English spoken. Group of local producers. Val d'Orbieu wine is some of the best in the Midi. Deep-coloured, fruity red.

Paul Herpe, quai de Lorraine, 11100 Narbonne, tel.(68) 32.03.25. Monday–Friday 9–12 hrs. Very useful. Family *négociants* since 1919. Wines of Languedoc – sparkling Limoux, Corbières, Fitou, Minervois, La Clape (area between Narbonne and the sea). Bargains in 33-litre containers for bottling yourself; or take it to your gîte or caravan for daily drinking.

FITOU

Cave Co-opérative

Very useful cave for holidaymakers on this coast. Among the good wines of Corbières and Rivesaltes (a natural sweet wine) is a superb Fitou 'Vieille Réserve' which will keep well. Do try it.

11510 Fitou, Aude, tel.(68) 45.71.41. 8–12 hrs; 14–19 hrs. English spoken.

Les Vignerons du Cap Leucate

Another Co-op useful for holidaymakers, with Corbières, Rivesaltes and choice of three grades of Fitou.

11370 Leucate, tel.(68) 40.01.31. In old Leucate village. Business hours.

Other Fitou caves to visit:
Cave Pilote, Villeneuve-les-Corbières, 11360 Aude, tel.(68) 45.91.59. 8.15–12 hrs; 14–18 hrs. English spoken and an English cassette played for cave visits. High quality Fitou wines, aged in wood and capable of longer keeping. Also Corbières wines.
Cave Co-opérative, 11350 Paziols, Aude, tel.(68) 45.40.56. D611 3km S Tuchan. 8–12 hrs; 14–18 hrs. English spoken. Fitou and Rivesaltes wines but best known for good Corbières.

SABLES DU GOLFE DU LION

Domaine de Jarras-Listel

Huge vineyards in the sands of the Mediterranean coast. One of six Domaines belonging to Les Salins du Midi, originally a sea-salt producing company, but now the biggest vineyard owners in France. Barley is planted between the vines to stabilise the sand. The most modern technology is used but the wine remains *Vin de Pays* because AOC status is given on an area basis, not individual properties. The cellars are nineteenth-century and the red is kept a

30220 Aigues-Mortes, Gard, tel.(66) 38.32.32. A579 from Aigues-Mortes (SE Montpellier) towards Grau-du-Roi; signboard on left 3km. Every day in summer; Monday–Friday in winter: 9–12 hrs; 14–17 hrs.

year in oak. They have experimented over the years with different grapes and now have an enormous acreage of Cabernet Sauvignon. Though known best for Blanc de Blancs dry whites and sparkling rosé, especially the *sur lie* wines, they produce good Cabernet reds. The best, Domaine du Bosquet, is matured a year in oak in caves near Sète built by the Nazis as munition stores. At Aigues-Mortes are sixty-four giant tanks.

Corbières

Further Information

Conseil Interprofessionel des Vins de Fitou, Corbières et Minervois, RN113, Lézignan-Corbières, 11200 Aude.

Food

A variety of dishes has been created in Languedoc to suit the different climates and seasons, from winter in the mountains to summer on the Mediterranean coast. Olive oil, tomatoes and aubergines are the main coastal ingredients, with fish both from the sea and the shallow lagoons (*étangs*). In the mountains, goose and pork, with their fat, and duck and dried beans are basics, along with beef, which is sometimes tough, so it is stewed slowly in *daubes* and *estouffades*, and lamb which is better.

Cassoulet is the great dish to fight winter in the mountains, and I like it well enough to eat any time except midsummer. I have mentioned the Toulouse version in Area 4. The Carcassonne version usually has lamb instead of goose confit, with the same haricot beans, pork, sausage, herbs and garlic. An old Minervois or Fitou red wine is superb with that. For lighter appetites, try *oeufs à la Languedocienne* (fried eggs on slices of fried aubergines with a garlic and tomato sauce). *Pot au feu Languedocienne* is the usual pot au feu of beef and vegetables with salt pork added.

Sète is the fishing port of this area and apart from the usual Mediterranean fish (including sardines and tuna – though smaller than the Atlantic fish), plenty of shellfish comes in. *Langouste à la Sétoise* is lobster in a spicy sauce with tomatoes, cognac and garlic (not unlike *sauce Armoricaine*) and *riz à la Sétoise* is mussels dressed in vinaigrette served with a rice salad made with tuna fish and tomatoes. Rice has been encouraged as a crop near the coast to replace vines.

Thau lagoon now produces excellent mussels and oysters. Strangely, local people, even on the coast, still eat a lot of *morue à la Languedocienne* (salt cod, potatoes and garlic in a creamy blend) – a hangover from days of real poverty, when mosquitoes ruled and the *vignerons* scratched a living from run-down vineyards making wine for café plonk. I get a nasty taste in my mouth remembering some of that wine!

They *did* have snails from their vineyards. Pesticides, however, have destroyed most of them. Holidaymakers pay fortunes for the few remaining, and most are imported from afar. But they are still prepared the same way – *escargots à la Languedocienne* (snails in spicy sauce with ham, anchovies, tomatoes and chopped walnuts) and *escargots à la Narbonnaise* (in mayonnaise with ground almonds).

You can still get *poularde à la Languedocienne*, too – a farmyard chicken, part poached, then roasted, surrounded by aubergines and tomatoes, stuffed with cèpes or mushrooms and served with a young red wine very slightly chilled.

Hotels

Lézignan

Tassigny, place Lattre de Tassigny, Lézignan-Corbières, 11200 Aude, tel.(68) 27.11.51.

Two star. Meals and rooms C. Shut Sunday evenings; restaurant also Mondays, part of September.

Le Bon Coin, 46 ave Georges Clémenceau, 11200 Lézignan, tel.(68) 27.01.18.

Simple family hotel liked by locals for good cooking and value. Meals C–M; rooms C. Shut Friday night, Saturday lunch, mid October–mid November.

Minerve

Relais Chantovant, Minerve, 34210 Olonzac, Hérault, tel.(69) 91.22.96.

Recommended by wine growers for food value. Meals C; rooms VC. Shut 15–30 October, Mondays in July, August.

Ornaisons

Relais du Val d'Orbieu, Ornaisons, 11200 Lézignan, tel.(68) 27.10.27. On D24, 15km W Narbonne.

Old mill, comfortable, quiet; gardens, pool. Meals M–E; rooms M. Open 15 March–1 November.

Sigean

Château de Villefalse, Sigean, 11130 Aude, tel.(68) 48.21.53.

A 'Château Hotel Indépendent'. 7km from sea; just off A9, between Narbonne and Perpignan. Regional style house and cooking. Meals M; rooms C–M. Shut Tuesdays, Wednesday lunch; January, February.

Leucate

Hotel Jouve, Leucate, 11370 Aude, tel.(68) 40.02.77.

On the beach. Open mid March to mid October. Meals C–M; rooms C. Restaurant shut Monday except in July, August.

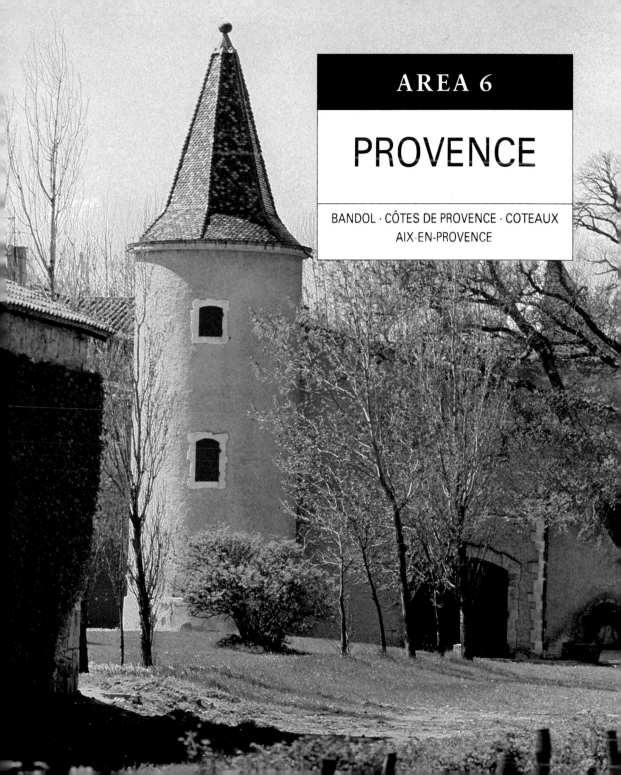

PROVENCE

BANDOL · CÔTES DE PROVENCE · COTEAUX
AIX-EN-PROVENCE

For a long time most Provence wine was made to be drunk locally, particularly by holiday-makers who knocked back a bottle of ice-cold, but potent, rosé over lunch and slept under umbrellas until evening. Even the red was made to be drunk cold and young.

Most wines are still like that. But some very serious wine makers, aiming at gaps left in the French national markets by increased prices of the old favourite wines, make longer-lasting red wines kept a year in cask and intended to be drunk when five to six years old at room temperature.

Many of the newer growers have come from other wine areas, buying vineyards in the hills which were almost abandoned. They

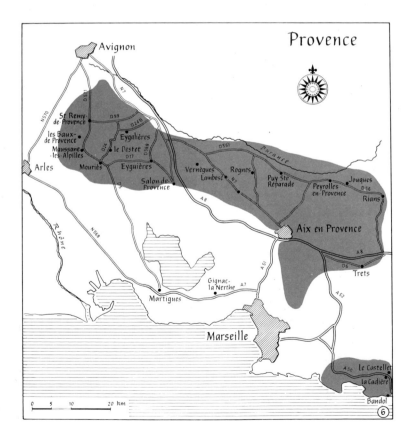

have introduced different grapes, especially Cabernet Sauvignon, to improve ageing quality and Syrah to keep the fruit in older wines. Some of these reds are excellent value, especially if you can buy them when about two years old to keep. The old grape varieties for red were Carignan, with a coarse taste; Grenache, used much in the Rhône valley, giving colour, filling the mouth and leaving a strong taste; Cinsault, with a light, fruity, acidic taste, almost essential in rosé wines; and Mourvèdre, for late-maturing, deep-coloured wines such as Bandol.

The main appellations in Provence are Bandol AOC, Cassis AOC (producing the best white wines of the area, dry, with little acid, a yellowy colour and expensive), Côtes de Provence (recently given an AOC and best known for rosé, although it also has reds, which are usually drunk chilled when young, and some older château-named wines, most of which are now good), Coteaux d'Aix en Provence (the château-named wines which are very often better, in my view, than Côtes de Provence), and Coteaux des Baux-en-Provence (nearly all red and rosé; often excellent value in reds because they are little known).

Palette AOC wines from a small area south of Aix are rare and dear. Reds are full-bodied and good, rosés are light red, not pink, and whites, which are very rare, are not unlike Graves.

Bandol red wines are different and the best reds in Provence. Made with a minimum of fifty per cent Mourvèdre grapes and often sixty per cent, they are kept two years in cask, plus another year in bottle before being sold, and get better up to ten years. The best can last twenty years. They rival the fine wines of Côtes du Rhône, and being robust, they put up with travel buffetings.

Some fairly good wines are produced in the hills behind St-Tropez towards Gassin. They were renowned long before the arrival of Bardot. But if the vineyards here offered tastings to passing travellers, they would find themselves swamped by campers and day visitors! If you see a board offering tastings, grab your chance.

Tastings

BANDOL

Moulin des Costes et Mas de la Rouvière (Paul et Pierre Bunan)

The best red wine I know in Provence. It can last ten to twenty years. Wines of two vineyards are made into separate wines – 'Moulin des Costes' from grapes grown on terraces on this steep Fontanie hill, with views to the mediaeval village of Le Castellet, below which grapes grow to make 'Mas de la Rouvière'. They are made of sixty-five per cent Mourvèdre grapes whose wine shoots 'reach the sky'. The dark red grapes give the wine finesse and enough tannin to make it a wine for ageing. Wines stay in vats ten days to extract tannin, complete fermentation in barrels, are not bottled for at least two years, and are not sold until they've been at least six months in bottle. They should be kept five to six years, and are even better after ten. The tannin softens, they become full bodied, strong, long lasting on the palate and are rugged enough to stand transporting. Oddly, the rest of France (including even the Gault-Millau magazine) only recently seems to have discovered that these Bandol wines can be laid down and kept. The reds rather overshadow a pleasant dry white.

BP 17, 83740 La Cadière d'Azur, Var, tel.(94) 98.72.76. Take D559 up the mountain from Bandol, then the little road left to La Cadière. Lane on the left is marked to Moulin des Costes and others. Follow signs. Or leave Motorway A50 at La Ciotat, drive through La Cadière. 8–12 hrs; 14–18 hrs. English spoken – ask for Laurent Bunan.

Domaine Tempier (Lucien Peyraud)

The oldest estate in the area, a fine natural wine aged in oak for twenty-eight months or more. Distinct blackberry aroma when young, richer later. The Peyraud family did much to build the deserved reputation of Bandol wine.

Le Plan de Castellet, 83330 Var, tel.(94) 98.70.21. Over A50 from La Cadière (*see above*). Monday–Friday 9–12 hrs; 14–18 hrs. Phone.

Domaines Ott, Château Romassan

The Ott family has made wine in Provence for 100 years. They have three estates, Clos Mireille at La Londe les Maures (tel.(94) 66.80.26), which produces a very good and expensive white wine, Château de Selle at Taradeau (tel.(93) 68.86.86), and this one. You can visit them all. Ott use the most modern methods and

Le Castellet, 83330 Var, tel.(94) 98.71.79. Visits and tasting in working hours. English spoken.

machinery and make very good red wine but are best known to holiday-makers for outstanding rosé.

CÔTES DE PROVENCE

Château Grand'Boise (Nicole Gruey)

Wine has been made at this fortified mansion since 1612. Award-winning red AOC wine Cuvée 'Mazarine'. Also white and rosé.

Vineyards surrounding La Cadière, looking across to the semi-deserted ancient village of Le Castellet

13530 Trets, Bouches-du-Rhône, tel.(42) 29.33.12. Local road CVO 11 from Trets, which is 27km E of Aix by N96, then D6. 9–12 hrs; 14–17.30 hrs. Phone.

Les Baux de Provence (NE of Arles) Mas Sainte-Berthe

A new cave built on to a sixteenth-century manor farm. Mme Hélène David makes a good light example of little-known and underestimated red recently made AOC. Visitors very welcome.

13520 Les Baux de Provence, tel.(90) 97.34.01. At foot of Rocher de Baux. 9–12 hrs; 14–18 hrs all week.

Mas de Gougonier (Nicolas Cartier)

Natural culture without chemicals (*culture biologique*); olives and almonds, too. Nice red kept a year in wood, forty per cent Cabernet – fruity, well made, cherry colour. On very pretty road in attractive area below Alpilles mountains.

Le Destet, 13890 Mouriès, tel.(90) 47.50.45. 19km NE Arles on D17 is Maussane; take D78 E 6km towards Destet. Mas is on left. Every day 8–12 hrs; 14–18 hrs.

Domaine de la Vallongue

'All amateurs of good wine welcome,' says Philippe-Paul Cavalier, whose vineyards in gorgeous scenery produce red wines aged in oak, with a taste lasting long in the mouth. Best kept up to eight years. Also a rosé; both have 12 degrees alcohol, so are potent.

13810 Eygalières, tel.(90) 95.91.70. Among Les Alpilles hills, 5km E and S from Eygalières on D24. 9.30–12 hrs; 14.30–18 hrs.

Terres Blanches (Noel Michelin)

Outstanding AOC wine, eighteen months in wood, flowery aroma, fruity and spicy taste, round and elegant. No chemical fertilizers, weedkillers or insecticides used. Filtered once through wood shavings. Quite well known in Britain.

13210 St-Rémy-de-Provence, tel.(90) 95.91.66. 6km E of St-Rémy on N99, small road right. Monday–Saturday 8–12 hrs; 14–18 hrs.

Other Baux de Provence caves to visit:

Domaine Lauziers, 13890 Mouriès, Bouches-du-Rhône, tel.(42) 04.70.39. (Post – 24 rue du Clos, Auriol, 13390.) D17 E from Maussane, left at Destet. Monday–Saturday 8–12 hrs; 13.30–18.30 hrs. The Boyer family bought this abandoned vineyard in 1959. Now make good wine aged in wood.

Caves de Sarragan, Val d'Enfer, 13520 Les Baux de Provence, tel.(90) 97.33.58. W edge of city. Every day 9–12 hrs; 15–19 hrs. Cathedral-like caves with outside views over city and to Alpilles hills. Very welcoming. AOC red and rosé.

The eighteenth-century fountain by sculptor Aixois Chastel at Château Beaupré

COTEAUX AIX-EN-PROVENCE

Château Beaupré (Baron Christian Double)

The château was built in 1793 but was partly destroyed in 1909 by an earth tremor, after which it was rebuilt. The eighteenth-century fountain is by the sculptor Aixois Chastel who designed several fountains still seen in Aix-en-Provence. Old vines, grapes hand-picked, red aged in 100-year-old barrels, to be drunk at room temperature. Good value. Also rosé and dry white natural wines. Rooms in the château are let as Gîtes Ruraux for holidays.

Les Plantads, 13760 St-Cannat, tel.(42) 28.23.83. On N7 NW of Aix just before St-Cannat. Open every day 9–12 hrs; 14–18 hrs.

Château Barbebelle (Brice Herbeau)

Fine old house; one of the oldest vineyards in Provence. In 1961 a first-century family mausoleum was found of local lords who were also Roman citizens. Wine-making equipment and caves improved in 1974 to produce an AOC red wine which has won gold medals at Mâcon. Traditional Aix wines (red and rosé) are called 'Château Barbebelle', to be drunk young. 'Cuvée Jas Amour' follows the new fashion in Provence using Cabernet Sauvignon with Syrah and Grenache grapes. An excellent wine.

13840 Rognes, Bouches-du-Rhône, tel.(45) 50.22.12. 7km N on N7 from Aix, right on D543. Château on left 2km before Rognes. Visits every day 9–12.15 hrs; 13.45–18 hrs (19 hrs in summer).

Château Bas (Georges de Blanquet)

Superb, typically Provençal, property, with an ancient tower and even the ruins of a Roman temple to Diana just outside its park. The wine is made naturally, with no chemical weedkillers or sprays, and matured in 200-year-old oak casks. Wild herbs and flowers grow in the vineyards. A friend swears you can taste not only the grape but thyme, rosemary and pine.

1311 Vernègues, Bouches-du-Rhône, tel.(90) 59.13.16. 25km NW of Aix. Leave N7 at Cazan, just after Lambesc; left 4km on D22. 8–12 hrs; 13.30–17.30 hrs.

Château du Seuil

Seventeenth-century Lord of the Manor's house. Outstanding AOC red wine, well made, enough tannin for it to keep and improve for seven to eight years. Also rosé and white.

13540 Aix-en-Provence-Puyrichard, tel.(42) 92.15.99. 9km NE of Aix on N7, turn right on D543; right again after 3km to Puyrichard. Open every day 9–12 hrs; 14–18 hrs.

Château Pigoudet

'Come and drink the glass of friendship,' says Gilbert Chapuis. Fine Provençal house built on the remains of a Roman villa, with a restored old wayside shrine and a Roman chapel. Superb country-side and views. Very good red AOC Cuvée Spéciale 'Descartes' (try 1981 – quite expensive but well worth it), rosé, sparkling rosé (made by Champagne method), and cheap red or rosé *Vin de Pays* 'Les Fourances'.

Route de Jouques, 83560 Rians, Var, tel.(94) 80.31.78. NE of Aix, take N96 to Peyrolles (21km), then right on D561. Caves between Jouques and Rians. Open office hours.

Château Vignerolles (Charles Sardou)

Bought by the Sardou family over 100 years ago from the Hospice d'Arles, so the vineyard and one wine are called 'Mas de l'Hôpital'. It's in the sunniest region of France and the vines get 2750 hours of sun a year. Ten years ago, Charles Sardou added Syrah from Tain-Hermitage and Cabernet Sauvignon from Médoc to the usual vines of Provence (Cinsault, Grenache, Carignan). The wines are aged in five 100-year-old Hungarian oak hogsheads, each with a capacity of 30,000 bottles (just the thing for a party). The red is full bodied and attractive, the rosé fruity, and the white quite delicate.

13700 Gignac la Nerthe, Bouches-du-Rhône, tel.(42) 88.55.15. Between Arles and Aix, on N368 SE of huge Etang de Berre, near Marignane. Open Tuesday–Saturday 14–19 hrs; Saturday also 8–12 hrs.

Château La Coste (R. et J. Bordonado)

Beautiful house designed in 1682 by the great Italian architect Palladio, founder of a style even copied for the Washington White House. The cellars are seventeenth-century, too. Abandoned for years, it has now been totally restored. To the usual Provence grapes, the family added 100 hectares of Grande Syrah and Cabernet Sauvignon for red wines, Mourvèdre for rosés, and Sauvignon Blanc for whites. Red wine 'Cuvée Lisa' is aged a year in wood, and should be kept until it is five to six years old when it is robust and *franc* (natural and sound). Also a red *Vin de Table*.

Puy Ste Réparade, 13610 Bouches-du-Rhône, tel.(42) 61.89.98. Little D14 N from Aix or D96 N, left on D596, left on D561 to Puy Ste Réparade, D14 S for cave. Open Monday, Wednesday, Saturday 8–12 hrs; 14–18 hrs. Ask for tasting. Not automatic.

Further Information

Comité Interprofessionel des Côtes de Provence, 3 ave Jean-Jaurès, 83460 Les Arcs sur Argens, Var.
Syndicat des Coteaux d'Aix-en-Provence, Maison des Agriculteurs, ave Henri-Pontier, 13626 Aix-en-Provence.

Food

With so many holiday-makers and residents from other spots, Provence regional cooking has been almost smothered by international, nouvelle and modern classical cooking, not to mention fads and genuine diets. And this was always a trading coast, with fruit and vegetables pouring in from North Africa. But some things remain – olives, herbs, peaches, fishes of the Med which have no equivalent in Britain. And *bouillabaisse*. This fish stew with saffron and oil can be made of almost any fish, but should include *congre* (conger eel), *rascasse* (scorpion fish) and *galinette* (gurnard), and must be marinaded in olive oil, fennel, onion and other herbs. Some cooks put in mussels, others regard this as a tourist gimmick, and no Provençal would dream of wasting expensive shellfish like lobster in a long-cooked stew of many flavours. Nor would a Provençal accompany it with *rouille* (strong garlic and chilli mayonnaise beloved especially in North Africa). That is served with *bourride*, a stew of white-fleshed fish, which I prefer. If I never had another *bouillabaisse*, I would not worry. There are so many individual fishes to taste – fresh sardines, red mullet (*rouget* – the small ones are best), monkfish (*lotte* – expensive), sea bass (*loup de mer*, cooked with fennel), *thon* (small tunny). I like the habit of taking *aïoli* (garlic mayonnaise) with fish but not with the traditional salt cod.

Olives are still served with everything. *Alouettes sans têtes* are not beheaded skylarks but beef olives, with slices of meat wrapped round stuffing and braised. You can buy olives marinaded in oil and flavoured with different herbs. And olive oil comes in different types. First it has to be virgin (*vierge*), meaning just pressed, nothing added. There's *vierge semi-fine* with high acidity, *vierge fine* with half the acidity and *vierge extra*, the best, with very little acid. *Huile rafinée* means it has been refined to get rid of acidity – or a bad taste; *huile pure* is a mixture of virgin and

refined. It seems that virgins can't be refined in the olive business.

Etuvée is an *estouffade* – pot roast meat with herbs and aromatic vegetables cooked in a sealed container. *Pissaladière* is like a pizza with a topping of onion puréed in olive oil, with anchovies and olives – no tomatoes. *Ratatouille* is a stew of *any* summer vegetables in oil – courgettes, red and green peppers, aubergines, onions, tomatoes, garlic or anything you like. Do try tiny raw broad beans dipped in grated cheese with your white wine aperitif. *Brousse*, the small round cheeses of sheep's or sometimes cow's or goat's milk, such as *banon*, are eaten locally with rosé wine. They are too 'sour-milky' for a mature red, which they would spoil. *Caviar Niçois* has nothing to do with sturgeon – it is a paste of anchovy, olives, thyme, mustard and garlic. *Artichaut à la barrigoule* is artichoke stuffed with pork, sausage meat and mustard.

When we were young in Provence and too busy having fun and broke to eat in a restaurant, however humble, we lived on *pan bagna* – a long roll cut lengthwise, soaked in olive oil and filled with tomatoes, boiled eggs, anchovies, onions, olives, sometimes lettuce, and left to marinade.

Hotels

La Cadière

Hostellerie Bérard, La Cadière, 83740 Var, tel.(94) 29.31.43. 9km above Bandol.

Charming hotel away from coastal crowds. Beautifully and sympathetically run. Heated pool. Wonderful meals by patron-chef René Bérard. Meals C–E; rooms C–M. Shut mid October–end November.

Aix-en-Provence

Mas d'Entremont, 13090 Aix-en-Provence, tel.(42) 23.45.32. 3km from Aix on N7 to Celony.

Old Provençal farmhouse in a small park, cleverly converted. Taste the wine of nearby Château La Coste – Château Lisa red. Meals and rooms M. Restaurant shut Sunday evening, Monday lunch. Open 15 March–1 November.

Le Pigonnet, 5 rue Pigonnet, Aix-en-Provence, 13000 Bouches-du-Rhône, tel.(42) 59.02.90.

In an old Provençal bastide, with flower garden and pool. Meals and rooms M. Restaurant shut Sunday evening in winter.

Mas de la Bertrande, Beaurecueil, 13100 Aix-en-Provence, tel.(42) 28.90.09. 7km E of Aix on N7.

Pretty Provençal house. Friendly service and welcome. Meals and rooms M. Pool. Shut Sunday evening, Monday; 10–25 February.

Les Baux-de-Provence

Oustau de Baumanière, Val d'Enfer, Baux-de-Provence, 13520 Maussane-les-Alpilles, Bouches-du-Rhône, tel.(90) 54.33.07. In valley W of Baux.

A beautiful house with splendid views of the Alpilles hills and some rooms in an old farmhouse among the olives. Relais et Châteaux Hotel, 3 Michelin stars for cooking, so expensive. Meals E–VE; rooms VE. Shut Thursday noon, Wednesday from 1 November–31 March, also mid January–1 March.

Mas d'Aigret, Baux-de-Provence, 13520 Maussane-les-Alpilles, tel.(90) 97.33.54. On D27A E from Baux.

Old farmhouse in lovely position. Good straightforward cooking; simple rooms (2 are in cellars). Meals and rooms C–M. Shut 3 January–15 March.

Rians

L'Esplanade, Rians, 83560 Var, tel.(94) 80.31.12.

Simple Logis de France. Meals and rooms C.

Salon-de-Provence

Abbaye de Sainte-Croix, Salon-de-Provence, 13300 Bouches-du-Rhône, tel.(90) 56.24.55. 5km NE by D16.

Another pricey Relais et Châteaux, converted from old abbey. Meals and rooms E–VE. Shut 1 November–1 February. Restaurant Monday lunch.

St Rémy

Auberge La Graio, 12 bd. Mirabeau, St-Rémy-de-Provence, 13210 Bouches-du-Rhône, tel.(90) 92.15.33.

Town centre; flower garden; pleasant rooms. Good value meals. Meals and rooms C–M.

SOUTHERN RHÔNE

CHÂTEAUNEUF-DU-PAPE · TAVEL
LIRAC · GIGONDAS

Gigondas wine has been awarded its *Appellation d'Origine Controlée*. We had drunk little of it in Britain, but a French wine expert told us that it was the most underrated red in France, sold in the bad old days as Châteauneuf-du-Pape. One of Britain's biggest buyers said that it had a bouquet of manure. So on our way south to the Côte d'Azur, we decided to drop in for an afternoon.

We tasted extensively and agreed with the Frenchman. We had

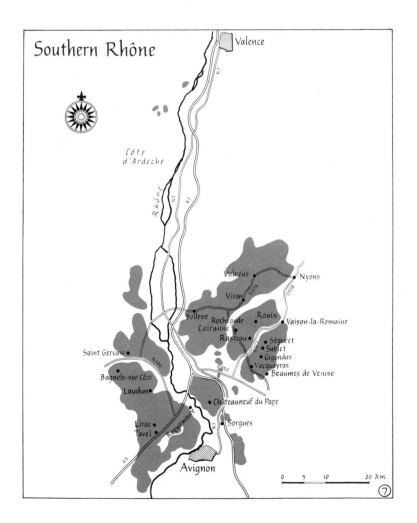

found a bargain. But Sablet, the next village, was en fête. Stalls piled high with sweets, sausages and sandwiches filled the streets of the sleepy hillside wine village. Music from the village band and a group called 'Les Teddy Boys' echoed through the hillside vineyards. We danced, ate and drank wine from barrels in the village square as we joined a huge open-air lunch at trestle tables.

That was in 1972 and our bargain in the strong dark-coloured wine of Gigondas with its rich, fruity taste lasted until about 1980 when the fashion for Rhône wines hit France. Even now, it is very good value because the world thinks first of Châteauneuf-du-Pape when buying Rhône wines, especially Southern Rhône. So much inferior wine was labelled 'Châteauneuf du Pape' that it became a joke until Baron de Roy de Boiseaumarié led the campaign to stop fake labelling.

You must know your maker still. Some wines are magnificent, some mediocre, for it is not an easy wine to produce. Thirteen varieties of grape are allowed in the appellation, and most makers use nine, including some white grapes for red wine. As with all wines, the soil is the first key. Flattish smooth stones (*galets*) radiate heat even at night, so grapes mature round the clock, giving them ripeness and thick skins, the wine dark colour and great tannin. Grenache grapes give good alcohol, Cinsault and Syrah give fruit and mellowness, white grapes give bouquet. But the wine should be at least five years old to soften the tannin and is best up to ten or even fifteen. The modern attempts to make lighter, younger wines to fit fashion and keep money flowing could be the curse of the Rhône.

Though Gigondas has been 'discovered' there are several good lesser-known wines worth seeking out – Tricastin red, Roaix red (for younger wine, two to four years old), Sablet red (smooth, fruity, easy to drink), Chusclan rosé (nearly as good as Tavel, but can be drunk when two years old), Séguret red (good fruit, robust for travelling, best when three to four years old), Valréas red (underrated, velvety, best when four to five years old) and rosé (dry, refreshing, drunk young), Vacqueyras red (almost as good as Gigondas; spicy; needs to be kept at least three years, improves up to ten; very good value, so try the pricier wines), Lirac (do try the red and rosé – before they get 'discovered'; the reds are smoother and more elegant than other Rhône Villages, with lighter feeling; the rosé is nearest to Tavel), Lubéron (from far east of Avignon, is only rated VDQS and is very cheap; reds are best young – under three years old – and served cold when they leave a ripe fruit taste in the mouth; whites are light and attractive).

Of the well-known wines, Beaumes de Venise's full-bodied red is overshadowed by the sweet, deservedly popular Muscat vin doux, which is made by adding wine alcohol to strong sweet wine to bring it up to 21.5 degrees. Paris is suddenly drinking it young. I prefer the traditional matured wine. Roll it round your tongue for ages and savour it! Rasteau is made the same way, as a fortified wine, and is kept in cask to mature for several years. There is a 'white' (deep gold) and 'red' (tawny, made by leaving the skins to ferment with the must). Of Rasteau unfortified wines, red is much better than white or rosé.

To catch the market for young, light wines, some Tavel rosé producers are keeping wines in tanks and bottling them young, producing a pale pink wine. This seems to put it among the Provence rosés for quaffing as a refresher. Tavel was always different – made from different grapes, aged in wood, served cold but not iced and could be drunk throughout the meal. Happily, you can still get this orange-coloured mature wine.

Most AOC wines of this area are called Côtes-du-Rhône or Côtes-du-Rhône-Villages (which means that they are allowed to add the name of the village or commune). They must all come from seventeen named communes in the Vaucluse, Gard and Drôme départements but may be red, white or rosé. Reds are potent (at least 12.5 degrees alcohol), whites must have 12 degrees. Grape types are controlled, with red allowed up to sixty-five per cent Grenache grape, making them 'fleshy' (or

Vineyards in Beaumes de Venise

mouth filling) and highly coloured. Villages wines are usually *rude* (rough) when young and develop and improve with time. Most rosés should be drunk young.

Until recently, Villages wines were regarded in the trade as the best value in France. Alas, because of rising Burgundy and Bordeaux prices, they have become much sought after, and prices have risen accordingly. But they are still very good value.

Tastings CHÂTEAUNEUF-DU-PAPE AREA

Domaine de Beaurenard (Paul Coulon)

One of the best Châteauneuf wines – mauvish colour, floral bouquet, long-lasting taste, long keeping. The Domaine has won medals consistently since 1927. Also a wine museum with tastings at Rasteau (*see* page 114).

10 route d'Avignon, 84230 Châteauneuf-du-Pape, Vaucluse, tel.(90) 83.71.79. 8–12 hrs; 14–17 hrs.

Domaine Chante-Cigale

Superb, long-lasting wine, made traditionally at vineyards which have been in the same family since the time of the Avignon Popes (fourteenth century). The grapes are hand picked, the wine has three weeks fermentation, and spends at least eighteen months maturing in oak barrels.

Route d'Avignon, 84230 Châteauneuf-du-Pape, tel.(90) 83.70.57. 8–12 hrs; 14–18 hrs.

Roger Sabon

Family vineyards, run by Roger Sabon and his three sons, keeping scrupulously to traditional methods. Old vines, with the best grapes made into red Châteauneuf which is kept in oak for fifteen to twenty-four months. The rest is made into a wine called *Râpe* ('drunk by employees', rough on the throat).

ave Impériale, 84320 Châteauneuf-du-Pape, tel.(90) 83.71.72. Monday–Saturday 8–12 hrs; 14–18 hrs.

Père Anselme

The Brotte family, *négociants* who bottle and mature wine from all over the Rhône valley, were largely responsible for the growing fame of Rhône wines from 1930. They pick the wines extremely carefully and have a huge stock from Châteauneuf-du-Pape to Tavel, Gigondas, Séguret, St-Joseph and Hermitage, so it is an excellent place to visit. Very interesting wine museum of old barrels, presses and implements.

BP No 1, 84230 Châteauneuf-du-Pape, tel.(90) 83.70.07. Every day 8–12 hrs; 14–18 hrs, including wine museum.

Clos des Papes (Paul Avril)

The family has made wine here for more than 300 years. The red is mellow, with enough tannin to give it flavour, and fleshy. A good white wine, too.

13 route de Sorgues, 84230 Châteauneuf-du-Pape, tel.(90) 83.70.13. 8–12 hrs; 14–18 hrs.

Château de Beaucastel (Perrin family)

A fine red wine, carefully made and kept eighteen months in wood. No chemicals or synthetic pesticides used. A good white, too.

84350 Courthezon, tel.(90) 70.70.60. NE of Châteauneuf over motorway, on N7. Monday–Friday 9–12 hrs; 14–17 hrs.

Other Châteauneuf-du-Pape caves to visit:

Domaine de Mont-Redon (Jean Abeille), 84230 Châteauneuf-du-Pape, tel.(90) 83.72.75. D68 N of Châteauneuf; lane on left. Visits (phone) 8–12 hrs; 14–18 hrs. The tasting and buying cave is also open all day from 8–20 hrs, including weekends. The wines of 'Mour Redon' were known in 1334 and it is now the largest estate here. Some vintages the red wine is kept in wood for three years. Always fruity and superb. The 1982 is splendid. So is the '83 white.

Los Mont-Olivet (Le Fils de Joseph Sabon), 13 ave Saint-Joseph, 84230 Châteauneuf-du-Pape, tel.(90) 83.72.46. Tastings at Cave 'Reflets', Chemin du Bois la Vitte, Châteauneuf-du-Pape, Monday–Friday 8–12 hrs; 14–18 hrs; Sat 8–12 hrs. Beautifully smooth wine which is kept two to five years in oak casks before bottling.

Domaine du Vieux Lazaret (Jérome Quiot), ave Baron le Roy, 84230 Châteauneuf-du-Pape, tel.(90) 39.73.55. Must phone. The family have been at Hers Château, 6km from Châteauneuf, since 1792, and have three Domaines making Châteauneuf-du-Pape, Côtes de Provence and Côtes du Ventoux, all of which are excellent AOC wines with fine bouquet.

TAVEL AND LIRAC

Château d'Aquéria

Do try the famous rosé, top of Tavel, dry, full bodied and potent, not just a refresher but a wine to drink with good food. It should not be iced, just cold (about 12°C, 54°F). This cave also makes a good value, deep coloured red, with fruit, charm and body. Beautiful old house; vineyard started in 1595.

30176 Tavel, Gard, tel.(66) 50.04.56. E of Tavel on D177 under A9 motorway. Monday–Friday 8–12 hrs; 14–18 hrs.

Les Vignerons de Tavel

A superb Tavel rosé. Described as 'one of the most conscientiously run co-operatives in France'.

BP No 3, route de la Commanderie, 30126 Tavel, tel.(66) 50.03.57. Every day 8–12 hrs; 14–18 hrs.

Domaines de Garrigues (Jean-Claude Assemat)

Two separate Domaines which produce a mellow, well-rounded wine, which is fresh but has little acidity. Very good value. Also a white.

Roquemaure, 30150 Gard, tel.(66) 50.15.52. Little port on Rhône river and D980 between Avignon and Orange. 8–12 hrs; 14–18 hrs.

Other Lirac-Tavel caves to visit:
Domaine Castel-Oualou (Marie Pons-Mure), 30150 Roquemaure (*see* Domaines de Garrigues above), tel.(66) 50.12.64. Monday–Saturday 9–12 hrs; 14–18 hrs. Red wines renowned in France. Also rosé and white.
Château de la Fontaine, 30126 Lirac, Gard, tel.(86) 52.20.34. 9–19.30 hrs. Handles wine of three owners – Philippe Testut of Lirac (well known for Chablis, too), Comte de Régis of Château Segries, Lirac, and Domaine de Lanzac, Tavel, all producing red, rosé and white. The Testut red is fine value.
Domaine du Devoy (Lombardo Frères), St-Laurent-des-Arbres, 30126 Gard, tel.(66) 50.01.23. Vineyard on N580 NE of Lirac. 8–12 hrs;

14–18 hrs. The Lombardo family produced wine near Carthage until Tunisian independence in 1964, when they bought this abandoned vineyard then completely overgrown with woods, where they produce a modern, light, easy to swallow, fruity red, and a floral, fruity rosé.

Château Saint Roch (Antoine Verda), 30150 Roquemaure, Gard, tel.(66) 50.12.59. On small road GR42A W from Roquemaure towards D580. The family owns other vineyards in the Châteauneuf area. This red Lirac is a traditional, carefully aged wine which has won many medals and is internationally known.

GIGONDAS AREA

Domaine St-Gayan (Roger Meffre)

84190 Gigondas, Vaucluse, tel.(90) 65.86.33. 9–11.45 hrs; 14–18.30 hrs.

The leading AOC Gigondas red wine, kept twelve months in wood, at its best between six to ten years and even twenty with some vintages. A superb wine from very old vines, with a strong flowery aroma, and a lovely mellow taste. The 1981 won a Mâcon gold medal; the excellent '82, fruity and round, won a gold medal in Paris. Also a strong, well constituted Côtes-du-Rhône-Villages and Côtes-du-Rhône red, to be drunk young, and a rosé and white. All worth buying.

Other Gigondas caves to visit:

Cave de Vignerons, 84190 Gigondas, tel.(90) 65.86.27. 8–12 hrs (including Sunday); 14–18 hrs. Co-op making two types of red – one by modern methods which is very fruity and ready in three to five years, the other made traditionally, best drunk between five to ten years and not sold until it has been aged eighteen months in wood, and a further eighteen months in bottle; a very good wine. Both can be served with aromatic fish (turbot, red mullet, etc.), any meat and cheese. Serve lightly *chambré* (18°C, 64°F).

Domaine Raspail-Ay (François Ay), 84190 Gigondas, tel.(90) 65.83.01. Monday–Friday 8–12 hrs; 14–18 hrs. Much respected locally.

Domaine les Gallières (Roux family), 84190 Gigondas, tel.(90) 65.85.07. 8–12 hrs; 14–18 hrs. In the same family over 200 years. One of the best Gigondas wines.

Pierre Amadieu, 84190 Gigondas, tel.(90) 65.84.08. Every day 9–12 hrs; 14–18 hrs. Apart from caves at Gigondas, the family mature wines in a disused railway tunnel at Pierrelongue on D5 near Vaison-la-Romaine. Always regarded as one of the best Gigondas, though some think it 'woody', with a little too much tannin from the oak casks. I like it.

Château de Montmirail (Maurice Archimbaud), 84190 Vacqueyras, Vaucluse, tel.(90) 65.86.72. Open every day (except Sunday) in office hours. A big estate which produces AOC Gigondas and AOC Côtes-du-Rhône Vacqueyras wines. The Cuvée de Beauchamp Gigondas is unusual. Vines are only twenty-five years old, but the family have been *vignerons* for centuries. It is said that the wine can be drunk young, but I have not tried it. It goes on ageing and improving for ten years, so why drink it young? A flowery bouquet, spicy, raspberry taste, low tannin and acid and very pleasant. Also very good value.

Cave des Vignerons, BP No 1, Vacqueyras, 84190 Vaucluse, tel.(90) 65.84.54. Monday–Saturday 8–12 hrs; 14–18 hrs. It is said that mediaeval troubadours got inspiration from Vacqueyras wine, so they call these Les Vins du Troubadour. The alcoholic content of the Côtes-du-Rhône-Villages must have made him sing. Smooth and easy to drink, too. Best at five to six years. Also a mouth-filling Gigondas which needs to be kept eight to ten years.

Vieux Clocher (Maison Arnoux), 84190 Vacqueyras, tel.(90) 65.85.18. 8–12 hrs; 14–18 hrs. English spoken. The family have been vineyard owners since 1717 and vinify not only their own grapes but those from other estates, making Vacqueyras, Gigondas and Châteauneuf-du-Pape, as well as Côtes-du-Rhône. The wines are made excellently, with strict selection of grapes. Very highly regarded in France.

Domaine de Verquière (Chamfort Frères), 84110 Sablet, Vaucluse, tel.(90) 46.90.11. Sablet is 4km N of Gigondas. 8–12 hrs; 14–19 hrs. Charming little village of wine makers. This Domaine has made wine for centuries from vineyards well tended over generations. Less weight than Gigondas wines, less spicy, fruitier and almost too easy to drink! This is possibly the best of Sablet, well balanced, with a good body – like an athlete.

BEAUMES-DE-VENISE AREA

Cave des Vignerons

Home of the superb Beaumes-de-Venise sweet white wine which is in vogue from Paris to London and New York for elevenses, as an aperitif, but especially with desserts. Its heady rich taste of Muscat grapes with a flavour of ripe peaches is too much for food. It starts with 15 degrees alcohol, is boosted to 21 degrees with pure wine alcohol (like sherry) and should be kept a few years. It is aged two years before it is sold but is still young and what the French call *rude*, meaning rough or harsh. Expensive and rates like sherry to the Customs man. Red Côtes de Ventoux also made.

84190 Beaumes-de-Venise, Vaucluse, tel.(90) 62.94.45. Between Carpentras and Gigondas. 8.30–12 hrs; 14–18 hrs.

Union des Caves de Ventoux

Mont Ventoux is a rugged peak which dominates this area. In my youth they held car hill-climbs up it. It is usually snow capped, but vineyards abound in the stony ground of its foothills and the wines, mostly red, have an AOC. This cave is a union of five Vaucluse wine co-operatives representing 3,000 growers, and has very modern equipment. Too much like a factory (California style) for me, but the wines are fine.

Route de Pernes, 84200 Carpentras, tel.(90) 60.24.66. 9–12 hrs; 14–18 hrs.

Domaine de St-Sauveur (Guy Rey)

Historic estate with a twelfth-century chapel. For long a convent, it has been a vineyard for 150 years and produces a delightful Beaumes-de-Venise and an honest, good value red wine.

Rue Joseph Vernet, Aubignan, 84810 Vaucluse, tel.(90) 62.63.31. 3km S of Beaumes, 6km N of Carpentras. 9–12 hrs; 14–18 hrs.

Other Côtes-du-Rhône and Villages caves to visit:
Domaine de Chanabas, 84420 Piolenc, Vaucluse, tel.(90) 70.43.59. N7, 7km N Orange, right under railway from village. Every day 8–20 hrs. Robert Champ produces very quaffable cheap red, rosé and white.

Domaine Haut-Castel (Arène), D980 route de Barjac, 30200 Bagnols-sur-Cèze, Gard, tel.(66) 89.67.19. 4km N by N86, left on D980. 11km S of Pont St-Esprit. 9–12 hrs; 14–19 hrs. Reliable Côtes-du-Rhône red; also rosé, white and cheap table red in 32-litre *cubitainers*.

Le Serre de Bernon (Vignerons des Quatre Chemins), Laudun, 30290 Gard, tel.(66) 82.00.22. Near N86 S of Bagnols-sur-Cèze. Monday–Friday 8–12 hrs; 14–18 hrs (also Sunday 1 June–30 August). Old Benedictine vineyard area. Known for good cheap white wine. Also red, rosé.

Cave des Vignerons, Rasteau, 84110 Vaison-la-Romaine, tel.(90) 46.10.43. 10km W of Vaison. 8–12 hrs; 14–18 hrs. Good chance to try Rasteau sweet white, fortified with wine alcohol to 21.5 degrees. Aged in cask for several years. Excellent and rare. Also Côtes-du-Rhône-Villages red, plus white and rosé. Very modern plant with experimental vine plantings.

Paul Coulon (Beaurenard), Rasteau, 84110 Vaison-la-Romaine, tel.(90) 46.11.75. 8–12 hrs; 14–17 hrs. Other half of Domaine de Beaurenard at Châteauneuf-du-Pape. Very good value Côtes-du-Rhône red. Also rosé. Interesting wine museum with implements from earlier days.

Florimond Lambert, 84110 Roaix, Vaucluse, tel.(90) 46.11.33. 6km W of Vaison on D975. Tastings any reasonable time. 'Our' village, where we have stayed in the Cuer family farmhouse gîte under the Templars' castle surrounded by vines, drinking the wine and contemplating in the sunshine the snows of Mont Ventoux. Opposite the post office is a tasting and selling cave belonging to 'Uncle' Cuer, with a bargain in nice red wine. Up the lane alongside, to the old village and chapel, is the Lambert property where you taste good Côtes-du-Rhône-Villages wine under vines; very good value. On the little road to Ségurat, a superb hilltop mediaeval village, is the Ségurat–Roaix wine co-op, producing good red.

La Vigneronne (Cave Co-operative), 84110 Villedieu, Vaucluse, tel.(90) 35.23.11. N of Vaison by D51, D94. 8–12 hrs; 14–18 hrs. 'Drunk as a Templar' they said around here for centuries after the Knights

Templars' Order was disbanded for debauchery and even murder, and one of the easy-to-drink wines here, mellow and full bodied, is called 'Cuvée des Templiers'.

Cave des Vignerons, 26790 Rochegude, Drôme, tel.(75) 04.81.84. 8km SE of Bollène by D8. 9–12 hrs; 14–18 hrs. When Thomas Jefferson was US Ambassador to Paris in 1784–9 this was the wine he gave to George Washington (he himself also liked Château Lafite). You can taste nine separate cuvées, all inexpensive, including a remarkably cheap table wine. Most red is drunk one to three years old, though it can be kept longer.

Domaine du Petit Barbaras (Raymond Feschet), Bouchet, 26790 Drôme, tel.(75) 04.80.02. Just N of D94; 13km E of Bollène. 9–12 hrs; 15–19 hrs. Little Barbara is best in red. Lively and spicy, yet soft and fruity. Coteau du Tricastin wine came from 'nothing' to AOC status recently. Little known and still excellent value.

Caves les Coteaux, Visan, 84820 Vaucluse, tel.(90) 41.91.12. N of D94 Bollène–Nyons road. 8–12 hrs; 14–18 hrs. Visan AOC has full colour, flavour and is full of alcohol. Try 'Confrérie-Saint-Vincent', which is aged in oak, and the above-average Visan white. Good choice here.

Domaine de la Taurelle (Mme Roux), Mirabel-aux-Baronnies, 26110 Nyons, Drôme, tel.(75) 27.12.32. D538 Mirabel to Nyons, turn right half way. Every day 9–19 hrs. Lovely countryside. Hillside vineyard in same family since 1872. Wine includes a good keeping Côtes-du-Rhône La Taurelle and cheap *Vin de Pays* red. Also Blanc de Blancs.

Co-opérative Agricole Nyonsais, 26110 Nyons, Drôme, tel.(75) 26.03.44. 8.30–12 hrs; 14–18 hrs. Get your Côtes-du-Rhône-Villages wine, black olives and olive oil here – all AOC, the only place in France with this honour for all three. The red wine is good value. So is *Vin de Pays* du Grignan.

Romain Bouchard, Au Val des Rois, 84600 Valréas, Vaucluse, tel.(90) 36.04.35. 14km W of Nyons on D941. Visits any time. Phoning not necessary but makes certain. Romain Bouchard comes from a

The old still at the entrance to Châteauneuf-du-Pape

famous Beaune family of vignerons (since 1681) and has been here twenty-one years. Cardinal Maury, writer and Archbishop of Paris in the eighteenth century, said: 'To see the sunny side of life look at it through a glass of Valréas.' The vineyard was part of the personal Domaine of the Popes of Avignon. Superb Côtes-du-Rhône is hard to beat (over 12.5 degrees of alcohol). Also strong white and rosé. Reasonable prices.

Cellier de l'Enclave des Papes, BP 51, 84600 Valréas, Vaucluse, tel.(90) 41.91.42. 4km S of Valréas. 8–12 hrs; 14–18 hrs. Phoning preferred. English spoken. Co-op. Very high quality, strong wines (13 degrees plus) – Valréas can be kept up to ten years to mature.

Other caves near Avignon to visit:

Cave Co-opérative, 84310 Morières-lès-Avignon, tel.(90) 22.45.45. 8km E Avignon on N100. 8–12 hrs; 14.30–18.30 hrs. Côtes-du-Rhône red, white, rosé; tasting cave.

Château de Bourdines (Gérard Baroux), route d'Entraigues, 84700 Sorgues, tel.(90) 39.36.77. Sorgues is 8km NE Avignon on D225, then go right under motorway, right again. Monday–Saturday 16–19 hrs. Well-made and fruity red Côtes-du-Rhône; good cheap *Vin de Pays* in 22-litre *cubitainers*.

Caveau du Château de Domazan, Domazan, 30390 Gard, tel.(66) 57.02.45. 14km W Avignon on N100. Visits 14.30–18 hrs. Five respected vignerons, who make their own wine, set up this cave for tastings and selling. All produce AOC wines. Good choice of reds.

Further Information

Comité Interprofessionel des Vins des Côtes-du-Rhône, 41 cours Jean-Jaurès, 84000 Avignon.

Hotels

Food *see* Area 6 (Provence) and Area 8 (Rhône Valley (above Valence)))

Montélimar

Les Hospitaliers, Vieux Village, Le Poët Laval, 26160 La Bégude-de-Mazenc, Drôme, tel.(75) 46.22.32. From N7 at Montélimar, E on D540, 19km; left up hill before village inn.

Favourite of my *French Selection* readers. Inspired conversion of mediaeval fort and village. Splendid views. Excellent cooking. Yvon Morin is an expert on Châteauneuf-du-Pape wines; fine cellar. Meals M–E; rooms M. Shut 15 November–1 March; restaurant shut Tuesday in low season.

Nyons

Auberge du Vieux Village, Aubres, 16110 Nyons, Drôme, tel.(75) 26.12.89. 4km E Nyons.

Pretty views of Alpine foothills. Good country cooking. Meals and rooms C–M. Shut Wednesday lunch.

Colombet, 53 place Libération, 16110 Nyons, tel.(75) 26.03.66.

Very good cheap menus. Meals C–M; rooms C. Shut early November–early January.

Suze-la-Rousse

Relais du Château, Suze-la-Rousse, 26130 Drôme, tel.(75) 04.87.07. 7km E Bollène on D94.

Peaceful country. Recommended by *vignerons*. Meals C–M; rooms C. Shut mid December–mid January.

Rochegude

Château de Rochegude, 26790 Rochegude, Drôme, tel.(75) 04.81.88. 14km N of Orange.

Relais et Châteaux hotel; historic château with thirteenth-century tower. Fine grounds, splendid view. Meals M–E; rooms M–VE. Open 15 March–end October; restaurant closed Monday lunch.

Vaison-la-Romaine

Le Beffroi, Haute Ville, Vaison-la-Romaine, 84110 Vaucluse, tel.(90) 36.04.71.

Up hill in mediaeval part of charming market town with Roman remains. Meals and rooms C–M. Open 15 March–12 November, 12 December–5 January; restaurant shut Monday, Tuesday lunch.

Gigondas

Montmirail, Gigondas, 84190 Beaumes-de-Venise, tel.(90) 65.84.01. 2km E of Vacqueyras.

Well-run quiet modern hotel in huge park below mountains. Provençal dishes. Good local wines. Meals and rooms C–M. Open 1 March–1 December. Restaurant shut Monday.

Les Florets, Gigondas, tel.(90) 65.85.01. 1½km by VO lane.

Our old favourite converted farmhouse has grown a little, especially in fame. Still charming. Quiet; simple rooms. Regional dishes. Wines from own Vacqueyras vineyards. Meals and rooms C–M. Shut Wednesday; January, February.

Carpentras

Safari, ave J.-H. Fabre, Carpentras 84200 Vaucluse, tel.(90) 63.35.35.

Much praised by my *Travellers' France* readers. Modern with pool. Superbly run. Meals and rooms C–M. Restaurant shut Sunday evening, Mondays in winter.

Roquemaure

Château de Cubières, Roquemaure, 30150 Gard, tel.(66) 50.14.28. N of Avignon on Rhône.

Recommended by so many *vignerons* for value that I offer it though unseen. Eigh-teenth-century house in a garden. Meals M; rooms C. Restaurant shut Tuesdays.

Tavel

Auberge de Tavel, Tavel, 30126 Gard, tel.(66) 50.03.41.

Michelin star well deserved. Bargain cheap menu. Seventeen Tavel wines in cellar. You can taste a glass each of five of the best; you pay, but it is a good way to taste. Meals and rooms C–M.

Châteauneuf-du-Pape

Logis d'Arneval, Châteauneuf-du-Pape, 84230 Vaucluse, tel.(90) 83.73.22. 3km on D17.

Very much favourite of the *vignerons*. Meals C–M; rooms C.

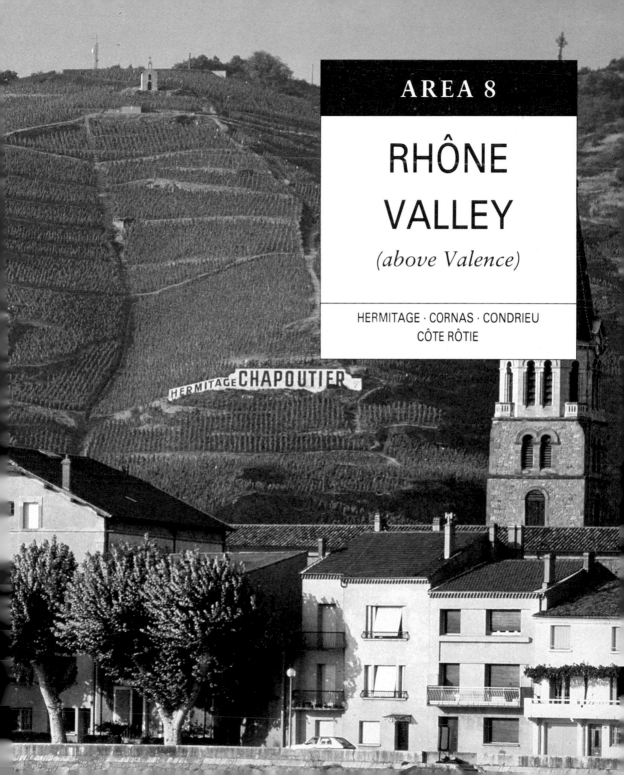

AREA 8

RHÔNE VALLEY

(above Valence)

HERMITAGE · CORNAS · CONDRIEU
CÔTE RÔTIE

By modern standards, the steep slopes where Syrah grapes for Hermitage wine are grown are 'unworkable'. They would surely be abandoned if they did not produce such a gorgeous wine. They are often terraced with dry stone walls, like the old fields of our West Country and everything has to be done by hand. Heavy rainstorms can wash the shallow top soil down towards the river and it must be replaced – though not so often as in Condrieu a little further north.

With the top wines of Bordeaux and the *grand cru* wines of Burgundy's Côte de Nuits, Hermitage wines are the longest-lasting reds in France. Usually they do not reach their peak for ten years. The 1979 wine will not be drunk until into the 1990s. So, with capital tied up and the high cost of labour, wines are inevitably dear. The white wine costs even more, although it is ready in three to five years. There is only a quarter as much white as red. White Hermitage is an experience not to be missed. It is full flavoured without being heavy, dry, but mellow, not acidic, and fruity at two to three years, smoother later.

Even books on wine call Crozes-Hermitage a 'minor' Hermitage. Perfectly excusable, for they come from the next village to Tain-Hermitage and are made from the same Syrah grape. But most vineyards are lower, with more clay in the soil and are worked by machines, which is cheaper. They are lighter wines and mature in three to five years. They go well with chicken, game, red meat and cheese but are not in the class of Hermitage, nor the price range. Production is expanding, as an alternative to pricey Burgundies. White wine is not so good. I prefer the white St-Joseph from over the river. Why is it called Crozes-*Hermitage*? Because the wise *vignerons* of Crozes decided that it would do their product no harm if their neighbour's illustrious name were tacked on to it. They were right.

St-Joseph has just been re-discovered by the French. I say 're' because it was the wine of French kings a few centuries back, and much beloved by our Victorian ancestors. They called it 'Mauves',

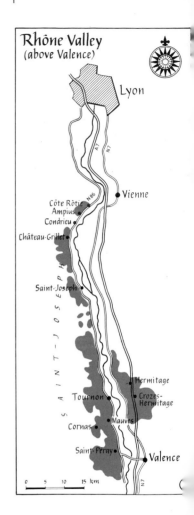

after the village where much is produced, and I have seen stone wine jars marked 'Mauves' in old London inns – but not recently. White wines smell of apricots, are rich and full and almost as good as white Hermitage, but hard to find, so buy some while you are in Mauves. Red wines are deep coloured, earthier than Crozes-Hermitage when young, excellent value when three to five years old and excellent wines when eight years old. I have been a secret St-Joseph drinker for over ten years. The vineyards are interesting, as the vines are trained up one stake.

Cornas red is the ultimate in a Syrah wine – so dark that you can hardly see through it when young and with such a strong aroma of blackcurrants that it seems like a dry, rough Ribena, but it softens beautifully with the years and is a charming wine, rich and heady. Alas, rare and fairly pricey.

Condrieu white wines come from the rare Viognier grape and are uncommon because of the steep slopes and the washing away of soil by rain, so that understandably some vineyards have been abandoned. A most unusual wine. Still rarer is Château Grillet, also made from the Viognier grape. There is only one owner, M. Neyrat-Gachet, who rescued some abandoned vineyards. Buy a bottle if you can find it. It is expensive but an interesting experience and a fine weapon for silencing the guest who knows it all.

Wines of Côte Rôtie (just below Vienne) are grown on two facing hills so steep that workers use cable and winch, which have replaced the mules. The hills are called Côte Brune and Côte Blonde. Soil scientists say that this is because Côte Brune is of darkish clay while Côte Blonde is of lighter silico-calcareous soil. I prefer the local story that a Seigneur of Ampuis gave his blonde and his brunette daughters a vineyard each as a dowry. A mere scientist would say these slopes were not worth working, anyway. Nowadays the wines are usually blended to make a subtle red wine to drink with light meats and poultry.

Tastings

Jean-François Chaboud

For five generations the family have made St-Péray sparkling wine by the Champagne method. For a long time it was the most famous sparkling wine outside Champagne and it is still one of the best.

21 rue Ferdinand Malet, 07130 St-Péray, Ardèche, tel.(75) 40.31.63. Opposite Valence on the Rhône on N86. 9–12 hrs; 14–19.30 hrs.

Pierre Darona

Makes a good still white wine, with delightful bouquet, as well as sparkling wine.

Les Faures, 07130 St-Péray, tel.(75) 40.34.11. 8–12 hrs; 13–21 hrs.

Marcel Juge

Cornas wines are so full of tannin that it is essential to keep them. Marcel Juge's wines age fairly quickly – in about five years – and are delightfully and persistently fruity with a flavour of soft, red fruits. Matured in oak casks. A good buy, but not cheap.

07130 Cornas, tel.(75) 40.36.68. Every day 8–20 hrs.

Pierre Coursodon

Deservedly high reputation for red and white St-Joseph wines, well worth trying. The white is exceptional – an apricot taste, like white Hermitage, but can be drunk younger. Red needs at least three years to develop – he suggests eight years. Alcoholic, with a strong perfume. Very good value. Vineyard is *en challets* – little terraces held up by dry stone walls. White wine is dearer than red.

Place du Marché, Mauves, 07300 Tournon, tel.(75) 08.29.27. S of Tournon on W side of Rhône by N86. 9–12 hrs; 14–19 hrs.

Bernard Gripa

St-Joseph wines are made, but the cave is known especially for St-Péray sparkling wine.

Mauves, 07300 Tournon, tel.(75) 08.14.96. On N86. Monday–Saturday 8–12 hrs; 14–19 hrs. Phoning preferred but not essential.

Délas Frères

For serious lovers of Rhône wines, the phone call is worth making, for here are many of the best, including Hermitage, Crozes-Hermitage, St-Joseph, Châteauneuf-du-Pape and Cornas. The Délas family ran the firm for 150 years until it amalgamated with Champagne Deutz in 1977. Huge exporting business.

St-Jean-de-Muzols, 07300 Tournon, tel.(75) 08.60.30. 2km N of Tournon by N86. Visits and tastings only by phoning. Ask for M. Chapelle. English spoken.

Cave Co-opérative des Vins Fins

Very good place for tasting and buying. Superb strong and fruity white Hermitage, good red, lighter Crozes-Hermitage which still needs to be five years old, and an outstanding 1981 'blackcurranty' St-Joseph red. Very fair prices.

22 route de Larnage, 26600 Tain-l'Hermitage, Drôme, tel.(75) 08.20.87. 9–12 hrs; 14–18 hrs.

Maison Chapoutier

You can hardly miss the massive sign on a vine-covered hillside. Max Chapoutier owns several domaines and is the best-known producer of Hermitage. His white wine Chante-Alouette has been called 'sublime' and could even make a pop-star sing like a lark. There are also other excellent wines from Côtes-du-Rhône, including a Châteauneuf-du-Pape 'La Bernadine', red and white St-Joseph 'Deschants' wines which are outstanding value, and good Côte Rôtie from his own properties up there near Vienne.

BP 38, Tain-l'Hermitage, 26600 Drôme, tel.(75) 08.28.65. Monday–Friday working hours; Saturday morning.

Georges Vernay

Original fruity Condrieu red, favourite at the nearby Hostellerie Beau Rivage, with two Michelin stars (*see* Hotels). If you have never tried the white wine of Condrieu, this is your chance. It can almost rival Hermitage. Subtle, satisfying. Perfume of violets when young. Ages well. Viognier is the name of the rare grape, as well as of this cave. The whole area is only seventeen acres and they are on steep slopes with a soft top soil which is sometimes washed down the hill by rain and has to be laboriously replaced.

Caveau de Viognier, RN 86, 69420 Condrieu, Rhône, tel.(74) 59.52.22. On N86, 11km SE of Vienne. 9–12 hrs; 14.40–17 hrs.

E. Guigal

You cannot miss the vineyards. The sign stands clear on a hillside. The biggest producers in Côte Rôtie, growing and buying-in grapes. Like most producers, they blend Côte Blonde and Côte Brune grapes to make a fine red wine, spicy and with an aroma of raspberries. They also make a very nice wine from Côte Brune grapes only.

RN 86, Ampuis, 69420 Condrieu, tel.(74) 56.10.22. 8–12 hrs; 14–18 hrs.

J. Vidal-Fleury

Leading wine maker in Ampuis, producing Côte Rôtie wines described as 'sappy', soft and highly flavoured. They also produce a good Condrieu and a lovely Muscat de Beaumes-de-Venise tasting of peaches and honey.

BP No 12, Ampuis, 69420 Condrieu, tel.(74) 56.10.18. Monday–Friday 8–12 hrs; 14–17 hrs.

Further Information

Comité Interprofessionel des Vins des Côtes-du-Rhône, 41 cours Jean-Jaurès, 84000 Avignon.

Picking grapes on the steep hills in Hermitage

Food

Modern cooking was virtually invented by Fernand Point at the Pyramide in the old Roman city of Vienne, at the very top of this wine road, and Lyon, still for my generation the capital of French gastronomy, is only 30km further north.

They say that the Northern Rhône Valley is covered in vines, fruit trees and Roman ruins, but it is a culinary bridge between the Lyonnaise and Provence and the influence of both are obvious in the dishes of the South and North Côtes-du-Rhône. And the game of Forres is not far away.

You are liable to be offered all the traditional Lyonnaise dishes, even such splendid old-fashioned delights as *gratinée lyonnaise* (beef consommé with port and eggs stirred in, topped with toasted bread and cheese), *gras-double* (ox tripe fried with onion, wine vinegar and parsley), *omelette à la lyonnaise* (omelette filled with onions and parsley), *jambon au foin* (smoked ham simmered in water with herbs – originally with hay!), *rosette* (pork sausage not unlike salami), and, of course, *saucisses de Lyon*. There are, alas, two types of Lyon sausage, and you have to watch when ordering. I was brought up on a long, dried sausage, but the fresh garlic sausage for boiling is the one most people mean by Lyon sausage these days, partly because it is used in the great regional dish of *saucisses en brioche*, served with hot potato salad. These are not the dishes you would get in the Michelin-starred or Gault-Millau-toqued gastronomic temples which built Lyon's reputation but in restaurants where the workers of this big industrial city eat and in the small towns and villages a long way down the Rhône. And the strong red wines of the Côtes-du-Rhône go splendidly with them, as they do with the charcuterie and cheeses.

Hotels

Condrieu

Hostellerie Beau Rivage, 2 rue Beau Rivage, Condrieu, 69420 Rhône, tel.(74) 59.52.24.

Old house covered in vines, with terrace and dining room views of the Rhône. It has two Michelin stars but is equally known for Rhône wines chosen by the owner Mme Paulette Castaing. Meals M–E; rooms C–M. Shut 5 January–mid February.

Bellevue, Les Roches de Condrieu, 38370 Isère, tel.(74) 56.41.42. 1km S of Condrieu.

Restaurant overlooks the Rhône. Deservedly well-known for its cooking, but odd closures. Meals C–E; rooms C. Shut 4–14 August; mid February–mid March; Sunday evening October–April; Tuesday lunch April–October; and Mondays.

Tain-l'Hermitage

Commerce, 1 ave République, Tain-l'Hermitage, 26600 Drôme, tel.(75) 08.65.00.

Used by visiting wine buyers. Comfortable – all rooms have toilet. Meals C–E; rooms C. Shut mid November–mid December.

Tournon

Château de Tournon, 12 quai M-Seguin, Tournon, 07300 Ardèche, tel.(75) 08.60.22.

A vignerons' inn; 3-star Logis de France with casserole for good regional dishes. Meals C–E; rooms C–M. Shut 1–15 November; Sunday in winter; Saturday lunch in summer.

Hotel de la Gare, 6 ave de la Gare, Tournon, 07300 Ardèche, tel.(75) 08.05.23.

Much praised locally for excellent traditional cooking at bargain prices. Bargain wines, too. Simple rooms. Meals and rooms C. Shut Saturday lunch, Sunday; mid December–mid January.

St-Péray

Les Bains, 14 ave 11 Novembre, St-Péray, 07130 Ardèche, tel.(75) 40.30.13.

Quiet, big garden. Pleasant provincial cooking. Meals and rooms C. Shut 20 December–31 January.

Pont de l'Isère

Chabran, Pont de l'Isère, 26600 Tain-l'Hermitage, Drôme, tel.(75) 84.60.09. On N7 9km N of Valence, 9km S of Tain-l'Hermitage.

Great chef with two Michelin stars, three red toques from Gault-Millau, he is not entirely devoted to 'modern' dishes and serves excellent roast dishes in regional style with honest fresh vegetables, honestly cooked, without being made into mousses or cooked with Pernod. Super choice of Rhône wines at fair prices. 'Contemporary' look of hotel rather startling. Meals M–E; rooms C–M. Shut Monday, plus Sunday evening in winter, Tuesday lunch in summer.

AREA 9

JURA,
SAVOIE AND
BUGEY

ARBOIS · CÔTES DE JURA

It is strange that so few travellers explore the tranquil, beautiful Franche-Comté country of fast mountain streams, rich in fish, waterfalls, peaks and green valleys – a land of natural food and refreshing, fruity wines.

Jura wines were served to Roman Emperors from the first century AD and to Kings and Emperors of France. Arbois is very

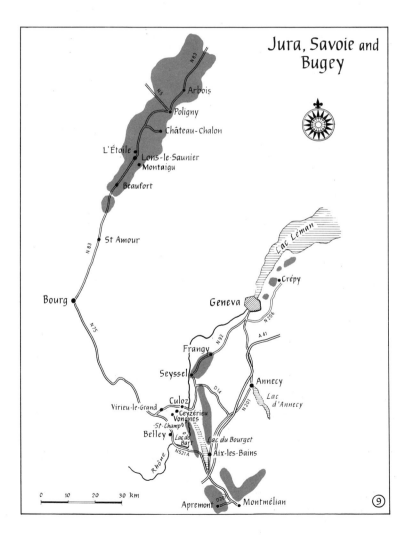

Jura, Savoie and Bugey

much the wine capital. Those delicious white wines are made of Chardonnay or Pinot Blanc grapes, with a touch of Savagnin, to give them that slight taste of sherry, a full yellow colour and rather nutty smell. Pleasant and fruity, they become very aromatic after a few years. Those made entirely of Chardonnay need ageing three years or so.

Reds made from Pinot Noir are rather like a very light Beaune, while Trousseau grapes make a deep-coloured full-bodied wine kept three years in oak and capable of being kept in bottle much longer. Few outsiders know these older reds, which are rather like a delicate Burgundy. Rosé d'Arbois is pale red, tastes like light red and varies enormously. Sometimes it is delicate and fruity, other times acid and thin.

Côtes de Jura wines are much like Arbois. L'Etoile makes the best white wines of Jura. They are lovely with fish, but are hard to find.

Jura makes two very rare wines. Vin de Paille is a dessert wine made from bunches of red and white grapes dried for two months, traditionally on straw, now often in a draughty attic. This dries the juice and intensifies sugar concentration. It produces a rich amber-coloured liquid, almost like a liqueur, sold in half bottles because it is rare and pricey.

The famous Vin Jaune of Jura is made from Savagnin grapes only, picked so late that the snow has sometimes started, and fermented slowly over months. Then it is left to age in oak barrels for at least six years with no topping-up. The result is a deep yellow wine with a very heady bouquet and a taste of dry honey, not unlike a fino sherry. Best known is Château-Chalon Vin Jaune. You can buy the wine usually at about eight years old, but it is much better if kept for another ten years or so, better still kept for 100! They say that the wine was invented by mistake when a cask of Savagnin was forgotten for years. Certainly fifty years ago at Henri Mair's Château Monfort at Arbois they found a barrel bricked up for about 200 years. Half of it had evaporated,

but the rest was nectar, so they say that the wine is indestructible.

Savoie wines are refreshing after a day's skiing or walking, but there are dangers in judging them this way. In years when ripening conditions are difficult in the hills, reds can be thin and whites like battery acid, especially those made with the Jacquère grape. But Roussette dry white wines made with the Altesse grape have fruit and just enough acidity and are excellent as an aperitif or with charcuterie, hors d'oeuvres, fish and fowl. Though most Savoie wine is crisp dry white, they also produce good reds, fair rosés, richer whites and sparkling wine. Seyssel dry white wines are made entirely of Roussette (Altesse) grapes and are light with a flowery bouquet and refreshing flavour. Seyssel Mousseux sparkling (made by the Champagne method) is very light and pleasant. Not much is made, alas.

Red Savoie AOC wines from Pinot Noir and Gamay grapes are light in colour, attractively fruity and are drunk young and cold. Surprisingly good reds are made from Mondreuse grapes, fruity, smooth and easy to drink, with an aroma of strawberries and violets. They can be kept several years to improve and are served *chambré*. They are little known in Britain.

Bugey produces light, very quaffable wines with VDQS appellation. The reds are light, fruity, not very alcoholic, tasting like a light Beaujolais – drunk cold and young. The whites, more like Savoie, are also light.

Freely translated, the motto of Savoie vignerons is: 'The more you drink, the straighter you think.' Well . . .

Arbois

Tastings

JURA

Château Monfort (Henri Maire)

They say in France that Arbois is known for Louis Pasteur who studied fermentation here and Henri Maire. In his tasting 'Tonneaux' Henri shows a film *The Glory of Pasteur* as well as a film of his own five Domaines, his caves and wine making at Château Monfort. Here is stored the world's biggest reserve of *vin jaune* (yellow wine) maturing over decades. And here the original cask is said to have been found (*see* introduction to this section). He makes red, rosé, white, yellow and Vin Fou, the wine you must have seen advertised on hoardings as you drive through France. It is a sparkling wine, made originally by the family for home drinking. 'Bottles were opened only at Christmas, except for those which had exploded,' says Henri.

39600 Arbois, Jura, tel.(84) 66.12.34. Tasting rooms in Arbois open every day, including holidays, 9–18 hrs at Aux Tonneaux Henri Maire, place de la Liberté, rue de l'Hôtel-de-Ville, tel.(84) 66.15.27. Vineyard and cave visits are arranged here but it pays to phone first. English spoken.

Château l'Etoile (J. Vandell)

Etoile was an important wine district until most of its sons were killed in the 1914–18 war. Now it produces only 180,000 bottles of AOC white wine. They are considered to be the best of Jura, so they are not easy to find. They should be opened two hours before you drink them and served chilled but not too cold. This château also makes an AOC L'Etoile sparkling wine by the Champagne method (*brut*, *sec* and *demi-sec*), Vin Jaune, Vin de Paille white, and Côtes-de-Jura red and rosé, plus a wine aperitif called Macvin (could it be wine and whisky? – no, it is grape juice with *marc*, the wine spirit). The ancient château is a ruin.

L'Etoile, 39570 Lons-le-Saunier, Jura, tel.(84) 47.33.07. SW of Arbois on N83; 5km W of Etoile. Monday–Saturday working hours.

SAVOIE AND BUGEY

Jean Perrier

Important producer of Savoie wines. Family has owned the vineyards for five generations. They have won many gold medals. Wine *négociants* as well as growers, offering a good range of Savoie wines. 'Tourists and buyers warmly invited to taste our wines.'

St-André-les-Marches, 73800 Montmélian, Savoie, tel.(79) 28.11.45. 14km SW of Chambéry, just before Montmélian. Visits and tastings 14–18 hrs. 'A little English spoken.'

Jean-Claude Perret

No times given to me but you can taste the wines, of which a rosé from Gamay grapes is praised. Also a small Savoyard museum.

Caveau du Lac, St-André-les-Marches, 73800 Montmélian, tel.(79) 28.13.32.

La Cave de la Ferme (François et Bruno Lupin)

For several generations, the Lupin family have produced La Roussette de Frangy, the fruity, flavoursome dry white wine from Altesse grapes. They run this little farm auberge for travellers to taste their wine and their home-made regional dishes.

74270 Frangy, Savoie, tel.(50) 77.01.15. Every day except Wednesday. Payment.

BUGEY

Eugène Monin

Generations of the family kept the flag of Bugey flying when the appellation was threatened with extinction. His two sons and their wives work with him and they produce 150,000 bottles a year, winning many gold medals, including at the great Mâcon Fair; 70,000 bottles are of their excellent Blanc de Blancs sparkling made by the Champagne method. Also red wines are made with Pinot and Gamay, and two Bugey whites with Roussette or Chardonnay grapes. All wines are light and attractive.

Vongnes, 01350 Culoz, Ain, tel.(79) 82.92.33. 8–12 hrs; 13.30–20 hrs. On small roads NE Belley 8km. Tasting caveau in middle of the village with board 'Maison Monin'.

Further Information

Syndicat Régional des Vins de Savoie, 3 rue du Château, 73000 Chambéry, Savoie.
Société de Viticulture du Jura, ave du 44 R.I. BP No 396, 39016 Lons-le-Saunier, Jura.

Food

Wine is used a lot for cooking in both Jura and Savoie, and the *vigneron* Henri Maire even offers recipes to his customers, including a family recipe for *coq Château Montfort*. You poach a jointed chicken gently in butter and Arbois Jaune wine, with spices, garlic and a bouquet garni, reduce the sauce, mix it with a roux of flour and butter, then add a cup of cream. Half the sauce is put in an oven dish, topped with grated Jura cheese, the chicken pieces added, then topped with the rest of the sauce and more cheese and put in a low oven until brown on top. Delicious – but the wine is pricey!

The splendid fresh mountain trout are fried in butter and a glass of wine poured into the dish to make the sauce.

From Savoie come most of France's raspberries and her best strawberries. Pears are superb and apples, cherries and plums grow liberally, and off tourist tracks you find wild strawberries. Freshwater fish, too, abound in the lakes and rivers – the usual trout, perch, pike and char, with less usual delicacies such as the *lavaret*, salmon-like, but white fleshed, and *lotte des lacs* (burbot – not like sea lotte). Trout weighing over 30lb have been landed from Lake Léman (Lake Geneva), and *soupe aux poissons* here is of freshwater fish.

Crayfish (*écrevisses*) from mountain streams are used for lovely dishes and their shells are boiled to make a stock for sauces. Sauce Nantua, named after the lake in Bugey once full of crayfish, is a rich cream sauce with puréed crayfish and butter (and truffles if you can afford them). It is superb with free-range chicken from Bresse, fed for nine weeks on nothing but cereal and skim milk. Their AOC regulations are so tight that even the feathers must not vary in colour! An area, too, for *quenelles de brochet* (pike in fluffy light mousse).

Hill lamb of Savoie is delicious, but it is really a dairy and cheese area.

The Franche-Comté, which includes Jura and which we often *call* Jura, has many dishes similar to its Swiss neighbour, including cheese fondu and *brési*, the delicious thinly sliced, air-dried beef.

Cheeses are legion and nearly all delicious. Most famous are gruyère and cancoillotte. Gruyère includes in most French people's minds emmental, gruyère, Comté and Beaufort, these last two seen rarely outside France. More emmental is produced in Haute-Savoie. The main ingredient of cancoillotte is mettons (whey solidified by heating).

Gougères, in various sizes and served hot or cold, are made of choux pastry dotted with rough cut lumps of gruyère (not grated). Delicious with red or white wine.

Similar dishes, from heavy winter stews to lighter fish and chicken, taste very different when cooked with Jura and Savoie wines rather than with Burgundy.

Alas, my winter-sporting days are over. I helped long ago to form the Non-Ski Club for people wanting to sit in the sun sipping wine, enjoying the ballet of skiers in their colourful pants falling around in the snow, and conserving our energy for what the skiers call 'Après-Ski' but do not have enough energy left to enjoy. But any winter-sporter must have met the comforting Alpine gratins – dishes with a brown topping of cheese or breadcrumbs, with a wide choice of meat, fish and vegetables underneath, from crayfish, smoked mountain ham or sliced sausages, to leeks, Swiss chard, macaroni, mushrooms or potatoes. *Gratin savoyard* is of thinly sliced potatoes baked in stock, topped with cheese. For *gratin dauphinois*, says the local Tourist Board which has tired of inferior versions of its great dish, the sliced potatoes must be simmered in milk with garlic until the milk totally disappears, then covered in cream and knobs of butter, sprinkled with nutmeg and baked in a dish rubbed generously with garlic. That way it is superb.

Hotels

Arbois

Le Paris, 8 rue de l'Hôtel-de-Ville, Arbois, 39600 Jura, tel.(84) 66.05.67.

André Jeunet, master of classical cooking and a favourite of my *Travellers' France* readers, has handed over the cooker to son Jean-Paul, formerly with Troisgros, the 'Modern' temple at Roanne. A few dishes are more inventive and ornate, but he still offers excellent old timers like fillet steak in shallot sauce. Also chicken in Jura Vin Jaune. Meals C–E; rooms C–M. Open 15 March–15 November. Restaurant shut Monday evening, Tuesday except July, August.

Poligny

Hostellerie des Monts-de-Vaux, 39800 Poligny, Jura, tel.(84) 37.12.50. Poligny is 10km SW of Arbois; 6km E on D472.

On the edge of a lovely forest, it is a relais de poste converted into a Relais et Châteaux hotel. Nicely furnished. Good service. Meals M; rooms E. Shut 1 November–end December; hotel Tuesday, Wednesday morning low season; restaurant Tuesday and Wednesday lunch low season.

Artemare

Hostellerie du Valromey, Artemare, 01510 Virieu-le-Grand, Ain, tel.(79) 87.30.10. D904, 14km W of Ruffieux, just above N tip of Lac du Bourget.

Nice country inn recommended by vignerons. Meals C–M; rooms C. Shut 2 December–2 January; restaurant Monday 1 September–30 June.

Ambérieu-en-Bugey

Savoie, 2km on Route Bourg, Ambérieu, 01500 Ain, tel.(74) 38.06.90. 45km NW of Belley; 30km SE of Bourg-en-Bresse.

Meals C–M; rooms C.

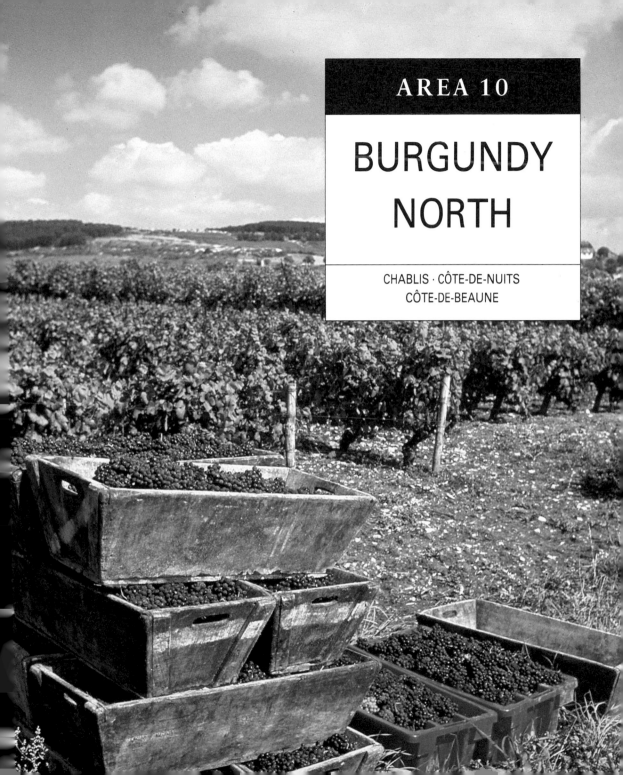

AREA 10

BURGUNDY NORTH

CHABLIS · CÔTE-DE-NUITS
CÔTE-DE-BEAUNE

The correct toast as you raise your glass in Burgundy is: *'Grande Soif!'* – 'Great Thirst!' But now you must add to it: 'And Bulging Wallet.'

Even a teetotaller must know that for various reasons, such as bad weather and heavy buying with the Almighty Dollar and the Unyielding Yen, the price of *premiers crus* Burgundy has been pushed up. But to travel the great wine road N74 and its appendages through what is so aptly called Côte d'Or is a saddening experience for those who adore great Burgundy wines and used to

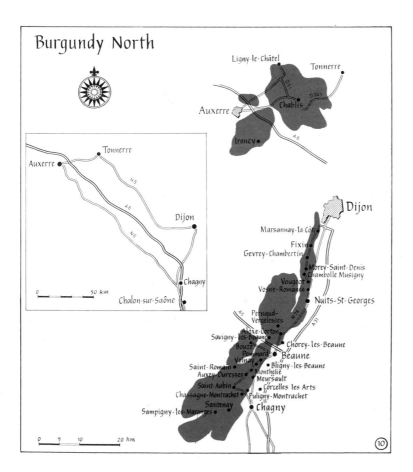

treat themselves to the odd bottle. At my age I am pretty sure that I shall never be able to afford to taste another aged Richebourg, Chambertin, or La Tâche Vosne-Romanée before I die, and the price of all wines but the fairly humble comes as a shock. Ah, well – at least I *have* tasted them – though not, alas, the 'Queen of Wines' Romanée-Conti.

We used to say that the road from Dijon to Santenay read like a restaurant wine-list. It would have to be a pretty posh restaurant to have all those great wines in its cellar.

I write only in sadness. If you study only superficially the care put into growing, handpicking, choosing the grapes, making the wine, caring for it, bottling and maturing it for up to ten years, and consider the capital lying virtually idle for so long, the price of *grands crus* is not so surprising. What surprises me is that anyone can afford them.

You are unlikely to be invited to taste these great wines unless you are a big buyer or related to the vigneron. But, as with Bordeaux, there are very pleasant wines indeed which you can taste and which are more likely to be within your price range.

I have the greatest admiration for people who can write books on Burgundy wine. To the layman it is all such a jumble. Vineyards are often only the size of an allotment. One man may own several but all in different communes. The communes are only a few kilometres apart yet produce different wines. How they manage to make Pommard, Beaune, Volnay and Monthélie in the same tiny cellar beats me. I would probably get them all mixed up. Then there are slightly bigger vineyards where six or more *vignerons* or *négociants* may own a part each. So a well-known wine name could have several owners. Or two wines can have the same name. And when you go to taste a wine in Monthélie you may be offered also wines from Volnay, Savigny and Meursault.

There are none of those huge single-owner vineyards which you find in Bordeaux. The nearest to this is Château Pommard with twenty hectares (fifty acres). The great Clos de Vougeot, once the vineyard of Cistercian monks, enclosed in a wall for protection from robber bands, now has around eighty owners, surrounding the château where the modern *Chevaliers du Tastevin* hold their lively tastings and dinners (*see* Area 11 – Burgundy Côte Chalonnaise).

Even Chambertin and Chambertin Clos-de-Bèze have a dozen owners, so wines must vary. But I refuse to believe that there is a bad Chambertin. Hilaire Belloc, reporting a dream that he was dead and confessing to St Peter, gave it its rightful place. 'I am sorry St Peter – it was a long time ago. I cannot remember the name of the French village nor of the girl. I cannot even remember what we ate for dinner. But, my God, the wine was Chambertin!'

Gevrey-Chambertin is not the same thing. Gevrey tacked the name of its famous vineyard on to the name of the village for publicity reasons. There are good *premier cru* wines in Gevrey, and the village wine AOC is very pleasant. So is the AOC Pommard if you like wines full of alcohol, sturdy, firm and rich. With game, goulash and Cheddar cheese, I do.

A number of 'lesser' wines of the Côte d'Or may not be quite so good as their better-known neighbours but are pleasant and much cheaper. Most of these you can taste and may well decide that they are worth buying. You don't find them too easily in Britain. Fixin, for instance, is very like Gevrey-Chambertin – not quite so fine but it is robust, and does not mind the bumping around of travelling. It is best five to ten years old. Then there is the Marsannay rosé, made from Pinot Noir grapes, fruity, with a delicate bouquet and not unlike Tavel. Drink it young (one to three years old), or keep it until it is full bodied and drink it right through the meal. The red Marsannay, if you can find it, has very good Pinot flavour, is fruity, and can be drunk from three to five years. Good value.

Definitely look for wines of Bourgogne Haute-Côte-de-Nuits, the area west of Nuits-St-Georges where vineyards were neglected or abandoned for years. More and more are coming back into production under good *vignerons* who are proud of their wines.

View of the town, church and vineyards of Chablis

The reds, though slower to mature than most Haute-Côte-de-Beaune wines, are very good value with prices so high. Whites are very good and rare. Others worth trying for value are St-Aubin, especially the flowery white, St-Romain, with whites which last well, reds with a real Pinot smell and pleasant earthiness, and Chorey-lès-Beaune. Monthélie wines are not well known even in France. They are much underrated and the best, like Château de Monthélie, as just as good as Volnay or Pommard, the names under which they used to sell. These mature more quickly and are cheaper. Auxey-Duresses whites are charming when young. For bargains try Santenay, especially La Maladière – it is fruity, with a nutty bouquet, and can be drunk quite young (three to five years).

Chablis, a wine to which I am addicted, has also shot up in price, although the excellent 1985 year may redress the balance when the wine is open and ready by about 1990. *Grand cru* and *premier cru* wines, which are far superior to the average AOC Chablis, are much dearer but worth the extra money. They must be kept to mature as the *vignerons* tell you, not drunk young as too many French people do. How long depends on the year and the maker. But my Simonnet-Fèbvre *premier cru* Tonnerre '84 should be ready in 1988, while the '83 *grand cru* 'Les Preuses' will not be ready until 1990. Be sure to taste AOC Chablis before buying. Some of those in our supermarkets taste of virtually nothing. And as for the alleged 'Chablis' in the US – it is enough to make the French village change its name. California has some good wines, but Chablis isn't one of them. When President Nixon was going round the Simonnet cellars he said: 'We have a great Chablis in California. Have you tried it?' And a forthright Burgundian said: 'Only when I made a bet to give up wine for a week.'

Chablis and Meursault have such fine white wines that we can forget that many of the great Côte d'Or communes produce white, too. The full-blooded red Aloxe-Corton can be fit for an Emperor. Back in 775 the Emperor Charlemagne was addicted. His wife complained that it stained his white beard, so he ordered that part of the vineyard be planted to produce a white wine. Voltaire lapped up red Volnay while pouring his guests a cheap Beaujolais!

The multitude of small growers in Burgundy used to send their wines to a *négociant*, who would buy them, mature them, and sell them under a label such as Côte-de-Beaune-Villages, Côte-de-Beaune or even a brand name. Many growers have realised that they can make a better living by cutting out the shipper and selling direct – in cask or bottles. That is why, along the N74 wine road in particular, you may see handwritten notices saying *Vente Directe* or *Dégustations* – tastings. You may find yourself in a scruffy cellar the size of your dining room and a man will offer you a wine almost certainly young and needing to be kept a year or two. He will be happy if you buy two or three bottles. It is cash-in-hand and all his.

The big boys in the wine trade sneer mightily at these 'tastings'. They would, wouldn't they? It is *their* middleman's profit being cut out. Obviously some of this wine is mediocre. But some is good. The only test is: 'Do you like it and is it value for money?' But do ask how long it should be kept.

More doubtful than 'Direct Sell' producers are labels (often used by the bigger companies). *Mis en bouteille dans Nos Caves* (bottled in our cellars) means nothing. All Burgundy is bottled in cellars. *Mis en Bouteille au Château* could mean anything. The château could be in Paris – or Leamington Spa. Some *négociants* or shippers keep offices in a château and bottle there wine bought from all over the place. Look particularly for *Mis en Bouteille par le Propriétaire* (bottled by the grower) or for the grower's name followed by *Propriétaire, Propriétaire-Récoltant, Viticulteur*, or *Vigneron*. But *Propriétaire à Nuits-St-Georges* does not mean that the wine comes from his vineyards.

A word of advice from Jean-Louis Laplanche, the owner of Château de Pommard: 'We bottle only the best cuvées from each harvest, carefully selected by repeated tasting. This allows for the great vintages as well as for the lesser ones to offer a wine of great distinction. One may have more body and warmth, another has more balance and subtle aromas. Therefore do not be swayed by preconceived notions of the "vintage of the century" or by little annotated cards. Each bottle is a separate achievement.'

Do spend some time in Beaune. It may be crowded and noisy but it is a superb old town – the essence of Burgundy and its wine. And visit the Musée du Vin de Bourgogne, Logis du Roi, just north of the Hospices. In an old palace of the Dukes of Burgundy, it is a fascinating museum of wine from earliest days and there are guided tours every day 9–11.30 hrs; 14–17.30 hrs.

Tastings CHABLIS AND AUXERROIS

Simonnet-Fèbvre

Our 'supplier' since we were introduced to the wines by ex RAF pilot Paul Rémaux d'Equainville who owns the Moulin des Pommerats hostelry at Venizy. I have memories of some rich but delicate Fourchaumes, and we still have some 1983 to be drunk around 1990. The fruity '84 will be ready before it. But to taste Chablis fit for the local patron St Martin try Simonnet *grand cru* 'Les Preuses'. It has an incredible depth of taste. Superb. They produce, too, a Crémant de Bourgogne white sparkling wine and Irancy 'Palotte', sometimes called 'Red Chablis', and known since the twelfth century. It has concentrated acidic fruitiness that softens later.

La Maladière, 9 ave d'Oberwessel, 89800 Chablis, Yonne, tel.(86) 42.11.73. Office hours. If possible ring the owner Jean-Pierre Simonnet, who speaks perfect English and will explain his wine-making.

Domaine Laroche

Excellent Chablis which has won many awards. *Premiers crus* Fourchaumes and Vaillons matured in oak are outstanding, *grands crus* 'Les Clos' and 'Blanchots' are magnificent and should be kept ten years if possible. Some of the wines are at 'L'Obédiencerie' in the cellars of the monks who fled here from Tours in the ninth century and started it all. There is a thirteenth-century wine press, too.

10 rue Auxerroise, 89800 Chablis, tel.(86) 42.14.30. 9–12.30 hrs; 14–18.30 hrs.

La Chablisienne (Cave Co-opérative)

Formed in 1923, it has played an important part in seeing Chablis through bad years when frost and hail have destroyed grapes and vines. It now produces one of the best wines, 'Grenouilles'.

9 boulevard Pasteur, 89800 Chablis, tel.(86) 42.11.24. Monday–Saturday 8–12 hrs; 14–18 hrs.

Other Chablis caves to visit
Guy Robin, 13 rue Marcelin-Berthelot, 89800 Chablis, tel.(86) 42.12.63. Visits 'all day, every day'. Much respected locally, friendly to visitors. Three generations of *vignerons*.

Christian Mignard, 40 rue Auxerroise, 89800 Chablis, tel.(86) 42.12.27. This is their tasting caveau, open April–September, but they still prefer a phone call. Superb *premier cru* 'Montée de Tonnerre'.

Frederic Prain, Côte de Léchet, 89800 Milly-Chablis, tel.(86) 42.40.82. Visits from Wednesday 12 hrs–Friday 18 hrs, phone first; English spoken. The cave is among the vineyards and you can see the grapes – very rare here.

Auxerrois

Caves de Bailly, quai de l'Yonne, 89530 St-Bris-le-Vineux, Yonne, tel.(86) 53.34.00. 9km SE of Auxerre by N6, D956. Saturday, Sunday 14.30–17.30 hrs. Or phone. Cave visits and tastings 7F. Co-operative producing one of the best sparkling Crémant de Bourgogne by the Champagne method. Also pleasant Blanc de Blancs.

CÔTE DE NUITS

(S of Dijon to Corgoloin, S of Nuits-St-Georges)

Domaine Pierre Gelin

Fixin has no *grands crus* AOC wines but the Clos du Chapitre *premier cru* from here is as good as much Gevrey-Chambertin and cheaper. Worth the phone call. Best at five to ten years. At nearly three times the price, you can buy a Chambertin Clos-de-Bèze, or a 'Réservée' red Burgundy for half the price. Wines kept in wood for eighteen months and excellently made.

62 route des Grands Crus, Fixin, 21220 Gevrey-Chambertin, Côte d'Or, tel.(80) 52.45.24. 9–12 hrs; 14–17 hrs. Phone.

Domaine Berthaut

Vincent and Denis Berthaut produce the other great *premiers crus* Fixin 'Les Arvelets'. The 1982 was splendid. Also a *premier cru* Gevrey-Chambertin and very good Fixin AOC 'Les Crais'.

9 rue Noisot, Fixin, 21200 Gevrey-Chambertin, tel.(80) 52.45.88. Working hours.

MARSANNAY

(3km N of Fixin on D122)

Regis Bouvier

A vineyard known in the Middle Ages and kept by Dukes of Burgundy and Kings of France, which produces a good value red AOC Burgundy 'Clos du Roi' from Pinot Noir grapes which is fruity and can be drunk at three to five years. A true Burgundian village.

52 rue de Mazy, 21160 Marsannay-la-Côte, tel.(80) 52.21.37.

Laurent Goillot-Bernollin

Not many producers in Gevrey-Chambertin are interested in travellers or amateurs. They get too many trade callers. From their seventeenth-century house, this family have produced good wine for around 100 years, making only AOC Gevrey-Chambertin. Worth buying. Friendly, likeable wine with a lovely smell.

29 route de Dijon, 21220 Gevrey-Chambertin, tel.(80) 34.36.12. 9–12 hrs; 14–19 hrs. Phone preferred, but not necessary.

Jean Taudenot

A very respected family, *vignerons* through many generations, they offer a good range, including Charmes Chambertin, a Gevrey, local Morey-Saint-Denis red (good value) and Chambolle-Musigny (a fine wine with a touch of iron). Lovely old house and *clos*.

21220 Morey-St-Denis, Côte d'Or, tel.(80) 34.35.24. 8–12 hrs; 13.30–19 hrs. Tastings only 'for buyers' but a very useful address for keen amateurs or travellers wanting to buy a few bottles.

La Grande Cave (F. Chauvenet)

Very important place as it offers a big choice of wines from the Côte d'Or. Vougeot itself is complicated because the renowned wall-enclosed Clos Vougeot has eighty owners, not one, and variations in wine quality are enormous. The château itself is the headquarters of *Les Chevaliers du Tastevin*, a brotherhood which has done wonders to publicise Burgundy. This *confrérie* awards its labels to wines submitted and found by blind-tasting to be truly good. That helps the wine world wide, though they do say in the village inns that some wines have lasted suspiciously long. You

21640 Vougeot, Nuits-St-Georges, Côte d'Or, tel.(80) 61.11.23. 9–12 hrs; 14–19 hrs.

can visit the château – which is spectacularly lit up on weekends –
in July and August.

Domaine Bertagna

Top wines of the commune of Vougeot outside the Clos walls.
You will see the sign clearly. Known especially for *premier cru*
'Les Petits Vougeot' and 'Clos de la Perrière'. They also have
vineyards at Morey-St-Denis, Chambolle-Musigny, Vosne-
Romanée and Nuits-St-Georges.

Rue du Vieux Château,
21640 Vougeot, Côte d'Or,
tel.(80) 62.86.04. Visits and
tastings 8–19 hrs every day,
including Sundays and
holidays. Ask for Madame
Saint-Martin.

Jean Grivot

You have to be mighty lucky and well connected to be given a
tasting of Romanée-Conti, 'Queen of Wines', or the gorgeously
velvety *grand cru* Richebourg, but it is worth a phone call to try
Jean Grivot's *premier cru* commune Vosne-Romanée with its
heady perfume. It will cost you a bit to buy and you will have to
keep it a few years but, believe me, it will keep up with inflation,
and give you immense pleasure when you drink it.

Vosne-Romanée, 21700
Nuits-St-Georges, tel.(80)
61.05.95. You must phone.

Dufouleur Père et Fils (Xavier Dufouleur)

One of the most respected families in Nuits. They have been
vignerons here since the sixteenth century, have marketed their
own wines since 1848, and produce traditional wine, using oak
casks for maturing. Wines reach their best in ten to twenty years.

17 rue Thurot, 21700
Nuits-St-Georges. Tasting
cave open 8.30–12 hrs;
14–18 hrs. No need to
phone.

Henri Remoriquet

Henri's grandparents were vineyard workers who saved up to buy
a few parcels of vines in 1892. Since 1950, when Henri took over,
the vineyards have grown progressively and now produce wines
respected in the French wine trade, for true taste and flavour.
Premier cru 'Les Saint-Georges' and 'Rue de Chaux', AOC Nuits-
St-Georges 'Les Allots', are both well made, fruity and tannic
enough to age well. He and his son have also started a vineyard in

25 rue de Charmoise, 21700
Nuits-St-Georges, tel.(80)
61.08.17. Monday–Friday
8–19 hrs.

Hautes-Côtes-de-Nuits and produce a wine from there. This area from the south hills of Nuits had virtually collapsed, but has now revived and is producing wine well worth trying. Wines have to pass a tasting test to use the name. Reds are slower to mature than Hautes-Côtes-de-Beaune and are best when four to eight years old, served *chambré*.

VILLERS-LA-FAYE

Domaine Fribourg

Another Bourgogne Hautes-Côtes-de-Nuits, run by father and son, producing a good red and the rare white, which is good value.

Villers-La-Faye, 21700 Nuits-St-Georges, tel.(80) 62.91.74. Village on D8 SW of Nuits. In working hours, but phone if possible to make sure someone is around.

CÔTES DE BEAUNE

Château de Corton-André (Pierre André)

One of the great houses of Burgundy. A visit to the old château is an experience. The tasting room is in the old cellars. Pierre André founded the company in 1923, bought the château in 1927 and added his name. The company has a huge estate of 174 acres in Burgundy, and another in Côtes-du-Rhône. It also buys selected grapes and has agreements with other growers to help them produce better wines and market them. These include wines of Chablis, Burgundy, Mâcon, Beaujolais, Côtes-du-Rhône and Provence. Among the wines produced in their own Burgundy estates are Clos de Vougeot, and four *grand cru* Corton – 'Clos du

BP 10, Aloxe-Corton, 21420 Savigny-lès-Beaune, tel.(80) 26.44.25. Every day 10–18 hrs. No need to phone. Just ask for Madame Courbin.

Roi', 'Corton Pougets', 'Combes' and 'Corton le Château' (certain *grand cru* vineyards can use the name 'Corton' without the prefix 'Aloxe', which is pronounced Alose, like 'dead loss'). They produce *premier cru* Aloxe-Corton, Pommard, Savigny-lès-Beaune and a Bourgogne Rouge, and also that magnificent white Burgundy Corton-Charlemagne, which I have not tasted often enough (*see* introduction to this section).

Domaine Goud de Beaupuis, Château des Mulots

A family Domaine since 1787, with an old stone pressoir still in use and wines matured in oak in eighteenth-century caves for twenty-two months. Plenty of alcohol. Beaune, Savigny, Chorey, Pommard, Aloxe-Corton.

21200 Chorey-lès-Beaune, tel.(80) 22.20.63. 3km N of Beaune. 8–20 hrs every day, all year. English spoken. Phoning not essential but helps.

J. Calvet et Cie

This great international wine company (wine makers, bottlers, maturers, wholesalers, founded 1818 and exporters to Britain for more than 150 years) has superb cellars in the mediaeval fortifications of Beaune. You taste wine in a fifteenth-century tower. Everyone is helpful.

6 boulevard Perpreuil, 21200 Beaune, tel.(80) 22.05.32. Visits and tastings every day except Monday 8–11.30 hrs; 14–17 hrs.

Cave des Batistines

Négociants and wine merchants selling Burgundy wines; visits to old cellars and museum of wine-growing implements.

20 rue Fg Madeleine, 21200 Beaune, tel.(80) 22.09.05. 9–19.30 hrs. Tastings every day, including Sundays and holidays.

Château de la Creusotte (Albert Morot)

Respected small producer with caves beside the vineyard, making Beaune in oak and ageing it in oak casks. Most wine is sold direct.

21200 Beaune, tel.(80) 22.35.39. 10–18 hrs. Phone if you can.

Bouchard Aîné

Superb cellars, most interesting visit. The idea is to tell people more about Burgundy wine. Tastings are only for trade callers, but you get a Kir (one part Crème de Cassis – alcoholic blackcurrant liqueur to four parts dry white Aligoté wine). You can buy *premier cru* Beaune, Fixin Mazières, Mercurey or white Mâcon.

36 rue Ste-Marguerite, 21200 Beaune, tel.(80) 22.07.67. 9–12 hrs; 14–16.30 hrs. So many people wanted to visit these famous family-owned cellars that they have been forced to ask you to phone. Ask for Terry Price. English spoken.

Tasting prior to an auction in Beaune

Patriarche Père et Fils

The biggest cellars in Burgundy, in what was formerly the convent of the Nuns of the Visitation, founded by the grandmother of the Marquise de Sevigné, and bought by Jean-Baptiste Patriarche in 1796 when his cellars at Savigny-lès-Beaune became too small. The nuns' cellars have been joined to other underground passages, including the fourteenth-century cellars of the monks of Chartreuse, to make a labyrinth. Patriarche are *négociants*, but they also own vineyards and château of Château Meursault. A tasting of really good wines, the proper way, with the little silver flat Burgundian cup called a *tastevin*, which is as well, for you can taste twenty-one wines, and twenty-one glasses of wine in about thirty minutes might take effect! They give you a comment card. It says: 'Taste sensibly'.

Couvent des Visitandines, 21204 Beaune, tel.(80) 22.23.30. Visits with tastings, 9.30–11.30 hrs; 14–17.30 hrs, takes 40 minutes, cost 25F (adults), 15F (students); children under 18 free. The fee is given to charities in Beaune (appropriate for a former convent). Closed 15 December–1 March.

Maison Joseph Drouhin

The *négociants* are run by one of the great Burgundy wine experts, Robert J. Drouhin. They are also vineyard owners in Chablis and Chambolle-Musigny and make some delicious and well-known wines such as 'Marquis de Laguiche' Montrachet and Puligny-Montrachet 'Clos du Cailleret'. You may buy the wines at Denis Perret (*see* below).

7 rue d'Enfer, 21200 Beaune, tel.(80) 24.68.88. Visits and tastings must be arranged by phone. The caves are in cellars which used to belong to the Kings of France and Dukes of Burgundy from the thirteenth to seventeenth centuries.

Denis Perret

Caves selling good Burgundy of five *négociants-vignerons* (Drouhin, Bouchard Père et Fils, Louis Jardot, Louis Latour and Chanson) from 30F to 400F a bottle.

49 rue Carnot, 21200 Beaune, tel.(80) 22.35.47.

Cave Exposition de la Reine Pedauque

Ancient caves with hundreds of thousands of bottles and barrels, including the greatest *crus* of Burgundy and some of the oldest wines. Set up by vineyard owners of Clos des Langres near Nuits-St-Georges and in Mâcon and Beaujolais. Good cross-section of Burgundy wines to taste with information and explanation.

Porte St-Nicolas, 21200 Beaune, tel.(80) 22.23.11. Visits with tastings in business hours. English spoken.

Château de Pommard

Château Pommard used to have a huge notice outside offering 'Free Tastings Every Day' (next to one saying 'Safe Driving Demands Sobriety') but so many tourists poured in that they now charge a nominal 20F to help cover the cost of wine tasted and staff time. Founded in 1726, it is the largest remaining undivided estate (fifty acres) of the great growths of Burgundy. The owner, Jean-Louis Laplanche, personally oversees everything from pruning the vines to choosing only the best *cuvées* from each vintage for putting under the Château de Pommard label. He says that the wines cannot be appreciated before a minimum of four to ten

21630 Pommard, Côte d'Or, tel.(80) 22.07.99. Visits with tastings Easter–3rd Sunday in November. 8.30–18.30 hrs every day, price 20F.

years according to the vintage. When I was last there in 1986, the 1980 wine, with a strong bouquet of violets and softness, was ready for drinking. The '79, which is going to be great, and the powerful '81, needed keeping for a few more years. The '79 fits exactly Serena Sutcliffe's description of Château Pommard – 'big, tannic and beefy' – which is how I have thought of Pommard since my first glass. They are not like that every year. Be warned – prices in 1986 were 120–150F a bottle and you would have to pay a lot more than that in restaurants. Superb bottles, pretty labels.

Domaine Parent

This vineyard has been in the Parent family since 1740. They still use traditional methods to make some beautiful wines, described as the 'perfect example of Pommard' (just as they supplied it to Thomas Jefferson when he was US Ambassador to France). Le Clos Micault, aged for at least ten years, is a lovely full-bodied Pommard of the type I love. 'Les Epenots' is strong wine but can charm you into thinking it a softy!

Place de l'Eglise, 21630 Pommard, tel.(80) 22.15.08 (Jacques Parent) or (80) 22.61.85 (François Parent). Phoning essential.

Château de Monthélie (Robert de Suremain)

Delightful village. For long Monthélie wines were sold as Volnay or Pommard. They were given an AOC in 1935; red is made from Pinot Noir grapes, white from Chardonnay, and in most other ways the wines resemble nearby Burgundies, but reds mature faster than Pommard or Volnay and are usually cheaper. Whites do not always keep well. I would skip them. These from the château and those produced by Parent (above) are the best and are very good value. De Suremain also produce a good white Rully *premier cru*.

Monthélie, 21190 Meursault, tel.(80) 21.23.32. 5km SW of Pommard by D973. Phoning essential for appointment.

Other Monthélie caves to visit:
Denis Boussey, Monthélie, 21190 Meursault, tel.(80) 21.21.23. 9–12 hrs; 13.30–19 hrs. Must phone. You have to buy a minimum of six bottles. A journalist I know bought this wine for the Boussey name on the

label! He got a good wine – Champ Fulliot. The fourth generation of Bousseys produce also Meursault, Volnay, Pommard and Savigny-lès-Beaune, all matured in oak. You taste in 300-year-old vaulted caves.

Paul Garaudet, Monthélie, Meursault, tel.(80) 21.28.78. Visits Saturdays or phone. Old-established, well-known Côte-de-Beaune family with vineyards also in Meursault, Volnay and Pommard; nearly all old vines. All wines matured in wood.

Château de Meursault, 21190 Meursault, tel.(80) 21.22.98. Visits every day including Sundays and holidays 9.30–11.30 hrs; 14.30–17.30 hrs. Probably the most rewarding visit in Burgundy. The sixteenth-century château which, until recently, belonged to le Comte de Moucheron, is superb. The cellars, holding half a million bottles and 1,000 oak maturing casks, were partly dug by the monks of Cîteaux Abbey in the thirteenth century. The Meursault white wines produced here are gorgeous – in another world from some produced by small growers. A park replanted with vines in 1975 produces an AOC Bourgogne from Chardonnay grapes called 'Clos du Château'. They also mature wines from other vineyards which they own or part-own, including Pommard, Beaune-Grèves and Volnay 'Clos des Chênes'.

Marc Colin, Gamay St-Aubin, 21190 Meursault, tel.(80) 21.30.43. St-Aubin is alongside Chassagne-Montrachet on N6, 1km W of where it meets N74. Phone if possible. St-Aubin wines are little known and usually much cheaper than other Côte d'Or wines which are no better. Most reds are drunk young (aged two to four years) and are light, fruity and stylish. Whites are drunk at the same age and have a lovely flowery taste, rather like the smell of roses. Do try Colin's *premier cru* white 'La Chatenière' – well worth the trouble of phoning. Also red and the delicious white Chassagne-Montrachet (inevitably pricey these days – reds are less known and better value). St-Aubin is an old village of *vignerons'* houses classed as an historic monument.

Domaine Prieuré-Brunet

Where Côte-de-Beaune begins (or ends) is a spa where 'wine and water meet'. Spend your money on wine before you lose it at the casino. Red wines are earthy and fruity when young and are not often kept long. Good value. White is rare. Since 1804 the Prieuré family have built up an international reputation for reliability. Try 'La Maladière'. This Domaine, with fifteenth-century caves, is well worth visiting because the family own vineyards in Chassagne-Montrachet, Meursault, Volnay, Pommard and Beaune (Clos du Roy) and you can get any of the wines here, including white Bâtard-Montrachet – the great white of Burgundy. They do welcome visitors.

21590 Santenay, tel.(80) 20.60.56. On D974, 4km W of Chagny or D113A, 4km S of Chassagne-Montrachet. No need to phone. 10–12 hrs; 15–19 hrs.

Further Information

Comité Interprofessionel des Vins de Bourgogne et Mâcon, Maison de Tourism, ave du Maréchal-de-Lattre-de-Tassigny, 71000 Mâcon, Saône-et-Loire.
Comité Interprofessionel de la Côte d'Or et de l'Yonne pour Vins AOC de Bourgogne, rue Henri Dunant, 21200 Beaune.

Food

Dijon has a Gastronomic Fair in November for which you need a great thirst, a great appetite and at least the *spirit* of youth. Apart from flowing wine and groaning tables, they offer you little hammers (once wood – now of plastic). If you see someone you fancy you simply tap them on the head. If they walk away, that's 'No'. If they hit you back, that's 'Maybe'. If they grab your hammer, that's 'Yes'.

As a young man I remember setting off after a splendid Burgundian dinner to find more good red wine and armed with a

hammer. I next remember breakfasting in a square, where the fountain gushed real red wine, off sausages with Dijon mustard from a nearby stall, and wine from the fountain, with a girl I did not recall having seen before but who seemed to be a close friend. Now I am content to eat and drink to satisfaction.

The Burgundians believe in flavoursome solid dishes to go with their flavoursome, strong wine. Here in the ordinary cafés and restaurants traditional regional cooking is alive and well, unmoved by the delicate lightweight dishes fashionable in the starred restaurants. *Coq au vin*, made with honest Burgundy, not plonk, or with Gevrey-Chambertin and called *Coq au Chambertin* in the posher places; true *boeuf Bourguignon*; cold *boeuf à la mode* (beef stewed in red wine with vegetables and herbs, served cold in its own jelly); *saupiquet* (ham in a piquant sauce of cream, wine vinegar and juniper berries); *jambon persillé* (cold ham layered with parsley in a jelly); *oeufs pochés en meurette* (eggs poached in red wine sauce – a great dish in the vineyards); Dijon's *râble de lièvre* (saddle of hare marinaded in *marc* – the wine spirit – and roasted with grapes and shallots, with a pepper cream sauce). Blessedly these dishes are not dying out under the bombardment of 'health food' advice. In season the game of the Morvan is still served, too, including *marcassin farci* (young wild boar stuffed with sausage), although I prefer the autumn older boar (*sanglier*) which is quite different from pork, and delicious smoked.

These dishes and the freshwater fish stews popular around Chablis are made for the Côte d'Or wines of Burgundy, most of which simply cannot be drunk young and are certainly not light. Can you imagine drinking an old Aloxe-Corton with Nouvelle Cuisine's almost-raw duck's breast in raspberry vinegar? Or Chablis with a featherlight vegetable mousse?

Hotels

Chablis

Ilostellcrio doc Clos, 89800 Chablis, Yonne, tel.(86) 42.19.63.

Opened summer 1986 and given a Michelin star *beforehand* because of its chef's reputation! Meals C–E; rooms C–M. Shut January; Tuesday lunch, Wednesdays except 1 June–30 September.

Dijon

Chapeau Rouge, 5 rue Michelet, Dijon, 21000 Côte d'Or, tel.(80) 30.28.10.

Excellent traditional Burgundian cooking with a touch of mousse vegetables. Wines chosen by expert. Meals M; rooms M–E.

Gevrey-Chambertin

Aux Vendanges de Bourgogne, 47 route de Beaune, 21220 Gevrey-Chambertin, tel.(80) 34.20.24.

Clean modern hotel among vineyards with regional dishes much appreciated by my *Traveller's France* readers. Meals and rooms C. Shut 27 January–10 March; Sunday evening, Monday.

Fixin

Chez Jeanette, Fixin, 21220 Gevrey-Chambertin, tel.(80) 52.45.49.

Simple Logis with true Burgundian cooking which I like (real coq au vin, *oeufs meurettes*, snails, *jambon persillé*, etc.). You are unlikely to find country cooking much better. Terrace and garden for eating in summer. Meals C–M; rooms C. Shut Thursday and 25 December–20 January.

Morey-St-Denis

Auberge Castel de Très Girard, rue Girard, Morey-St-Denis, 21220 Gevrey-Chambertin, tel.(80) 34.33.09.

Logis de France with a 'casserole' for regional dishes; among vineyards and favoured by *vignerons*. Meals C–E; rooms C–M.

Nuits-St-Georges

Des Cultivateurs, 12 rue Gén.-de-Gaulle, 21700 Nuits-St-Georges, tel.(80) 61.10.41.

Relais Routiers with bar-restaurant used by locals in charming, busy little town. Simple but comfortable sound-proofed bedrooms, but front noisy in summer. Traditional dishes. Good value. Cheap wines. Old France atmosphere. Meals and rooms C.

La Côte d'Or, 1 rue Thurot, Nuits-St-Georges, 21700, tel.(80) 61.06.10.

Two-star Michelin. Precise, careful cooking by Jean Crotet, known to be a perfectionist; food beautifully presented. Meals E; rooms M. Shut 1–23 July; 2–20 January; Sunday evening; Wednesday.

Bouilland

Hostellerie du Vieux Moulin, Bouilland, 21420
Savigny-lès-Beaune, Côte d'Or. Right off N74 to
Savigny-lès-Beaune, then D2 N.

Attractive position beside a little river; lovely
views; big garden. Young patron-chef Jean-
Pierre Silva seeks fresh local ingredients and
cooks excellently, tied neither to tradition nor
modern fashions. Fresh farmyard chicken in
honey and wine vinegar; real farm cheeses.
Wines from 50F to 1500F! Splendid choice of
Burgundies. Meals M–E; rooms C. Shut
Tuesday lunch, Wednesdays; 15 December–
22 January.

Beaune

Central, 12 rue V. Millot, 21200 Beaune, tel.(80)
24.77.24.

In the noisy centre but after M. Cluny's splen-
did dinners and a bottle of Beaune, who
would notice? His meals are praised by my
Travellers' France readers. Meals and rooms
C–M. Open 21 March–17 November. Shut
Wednesdays out of season.

Meursault

Soleil Levant, route Beaune, Meursault, 21190 Côte
d'Or, tel.(80) 21.23.47.

Vignerons' recommendation. Motel style but
known for Burgundian dishes. Meals and
rooms C.

St-Gervais-en-Vallière (15km SE of Beaune by D970, left on D94 to Chaublanc)

Moulin d'Hauterive, St-Gervais-en-Vallière, 71350
Verdun-sur-le-Doubs, Saône-et-Loire, tel.(85)
81.55.56.

Delightful hideaway in beautifully furnished
old mill. The only sound is the little river
washing the walls. Fishing. Garden and park.
Thoughtful and imaginative cooking. Fine
wines. Much praise from my *French Selection*
readers. Meals and rooms M. Shut 30
November–1 March; Sunday evening,
Monday except 1 June–1 September.

Chagny

Hostellerie Château de Bellecroix, Chagny, 71150
Saône-et-Loire, tel.(85) 87.13.86. 2km S of Chagny
on N6, then VO. Marked on yellow Michelin 70.

Fairy-tale château with pointed towers. Commanderie of Knights of St John from 1199;
combines twelfth- and eighteenth-century
architecture. Park. Talented young chef combines some fine old dishes with a flair for
modern décor on the plate. Another hotel
which my *French Selection* readers have
praised. Very good wine list from Rully to
veritable Chambertin, Côte-de-Beaune and
Côte Chalonnaise. Meals C–M; rooms M.
Shut 21 December–1 February; Wednesdays.

BURGUNDY

Côte Chalonnaise

MERCUREY · RULLY · MONTAGNY

The Côte Chalonnaise is west of Chalon-sur-Saône between Chagny and Mâcon and it does not seem like wine country. You pass through woods and past meadows and to find the vineyards you must usually take to lanes often wide enough for only one car and with grass growing up to your window in summer.

Mercurey is on the D978 and is quite a busy little one-street village. Givry, on D981, has more than 3000 inhabitants. But to find Bouzeron, Rully and Montagny you must take tiny winding roads off to the right coming from Chagny on D981.

Rully is a charming little place dominated by a big hilltop church and so sleepy that on my last visit I thought that everyone must have emigrated. Not a person nor a car did I see as I drove round by the sportsfield, parked by the church and walked around for about twenty minutes. A dog noisily defending the courtyard of Domaine du Prieuré brought Armand Monassier's director

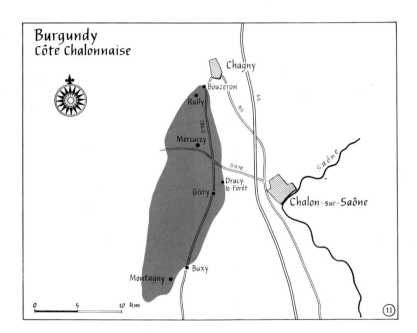

from the cellars. That was where everyone was, it seemed – in cellars or in vineyards.

This isolation from the world may be the prime reason why until very recently so few people, even in France, knew much about these red and white Burgundy wines. For years they were superb bargains, especially the still white wines of Rully, to which Barbara, my wife, is much addicted. Only the Mercurey red wines were known very far from here and they were rather looked down upon as a poor man's substitute for Beaune, Volnay and Pommard.

Then the trade buyers came, looking for alternatives to the Côte d'Or reds, Chablis and Pouilly-Fuissé because of inflated prices. As there is not much Mercurey red and less Rully red or white, prices have risen. But the wines are still excellent value.

Rully white is delicious when drunk two to three years old. A little bottle age helps. After three years, the wines start to lose fruit and become a bit tougher. They become different wines. Mercurey whites are not so attractive but make you drunk more quickly. Perhaps it is lucky that they are rare.

Rully red wines can be drunk quite young (two or three years old). But I believe that Mercurey red wines have suffered by being drunk far too young – because of fashion in France and ignorance in Britain and the US. They are made with the same grapes (Pinot Noir) as the wines of the Côte d'Or and have far too much tannin and iron until they are three–four years old. They are even better kept five or six – longer in a good year. The bad ones are dry and rough.

There is no love lost between Mercurey and Rully, and in the 1920s Mercurey had the influence and Rully was only allowed to make its red wines into red sparkling Burgundy, which sold well in the US, despite prohibition. Most of the white was made into sparkling Burgundy, too, by the Champagne method. That had been brought to Rully by François Brazile Hubert, a cellarman from the Champagne, in 1831, not so long after it was taken to

Saumur in the Loire – the first place to use it outside Champagne.

Much less of these Vins Mousseux and Crémant de Bourgogne sparkling wines is made now, although some are excellent. More than seventy per cent of white Rully is now still wine. High tax on sparkling wine in Britain and the US is blamed, making the differential between sparkling Burgundy and Champagne small, so people drink Champagne. Anyway, if you can sell wine for a reasonable price after two years, why go to all the fuss of the Champagne method to make it sparkle?

Montagny, near Buxy, makes the next best white wine, but it is more like a white Mâcon. Bouzeron (near Chagny) has just got the AOC for its wines from the Aligoté grape, which are bottled and drunk in the spring after the harvest. They are good by Aligoté standards, but I find them too acidic unless mixed with crème de cassis to make a Kir. Just mix one part of crème de cassis (blackcurrant liqueur) with four parts of wine and ice thoroughly – a splendid summer aperitif.

Opposite: *Rully*

Tastings

Apart from the main streets of Mercurey and Givry, the wine folk around here are not much used to travellers and many vineyards are owned by shippers who bottle elsewhere. So there are few places to taste. Especially in Rully, the most rewarding wine village, you will be asked to phone ahead – from the village inn, Du Commerce, perhaps, over a glass of Rully! Otherwise there may be no one at home.

Domaine du Prieuré (Armand Monassier)

M. Monassier, for long a successful Paris restaurant owner (Chez les Anges), has owned vineyards here since 1960 and produces our favourite white Rully – delicate, fresh with a definite grape-and-

Rully, 71150 Chagny, tel.(85) 87.13.57. Almost opposite the church. Business hours. Better to telephone.

apple taste. Well worth taking home. His red has an aroma of strawberries and keeps well. He is a great enthusiast. His red Mercurey 'Clos de la Vigne De Devant' is very fruity.

Caves Delorme-Neulien (Domaine de la Renarde)

Rully, 71150 Chagny, tel.(85) 87.10.12. 8.30–12 hrs; 13.30–18 hrs. Preferable to phone ahead for tastings. Not necessary for buyers. Ask for M. Lafond, who speaks English.

The most important Domaine in this area, owning all of the 45-acre Varot vineyard; it is most unusual in Burgundy to find one vineyard in such a big single *parcel* (plot). Altogether Jean-François Delorme has 148 acres in Rully, Mercurey, Givry and Bouzeron, so it is worth making the effort to arrange a tasting. You can find not only excellent Rully and Mercurey red and white wines but also the red Givry 'Clos du Cellier aux Moines' which Serena Sutcliffe has described as having the smell of 'all the herbs of Provence'. Bouzeron white wine is made from Aligoté grapes, is fresh and fruity, bottled earlier than the other whites around here made with Chardonnay, and drunk with fish or mixed with crème de cassis (blackcurrant liqueur) to make Kir. His white Rully is pungent, his red like velvet and violets. But the Delorme family, here since 1900, have always been known for their sparkling wine made by the Champagne method – the white 'André Delorme' and Crémant de Bourgogne, and a sparkling red.

Domaine de la Croix Jacquelet

71640 Mercurey, Givry, tel.(85) 47.14.72. No need to phone but tastings 'free for buyers'.

This company's vineyards total 148 acres, producing Rully red, Mercurey red and the rare white, and Bourgogne Rouge.

Antonin Rodet

71640 Mercurey, Givry, tel.(85) 45.22.22. Phone if possible; ask for Dominique Pernot (or Jean-Michel Ricard or Marc Vachet). English spoken.

Antonin Rodet, the established family business which matures, bottles and ships wines from all over Burgundy, is now owned by the great Antonin Rodet's son-in-law the Marquis de Jouennes d'Herville. His seventeenth-century Château de Chamiry and its vineyard here at Mercurey are classed as national monuments. The lively young director Bertrand Devillard is keen to produce

Barrels stacked in the middle cave of Domaine de la Croix Jacquelet

red wines of lightness and elegance rather than heavy and alcoholic, which is the way much Mercurey turns out. Most of his red wine is ready in four to five years. The 1982 red won a bronze medal at the International Wine and Spirit Contest in London in 1985. But his 1982 white won a gold in London and in Bordeaux. It is a delightful aromatic wine, the best white Mercurey I have tasted.

François Protheau

I was impressed by the Mercurey red wines when I tasted them at the London Wine Fair in 1986 but I have not tasted the Rully wines. The family have been *vignerons* since 1720. 'Clos l'Évêque' and 'Clos des Corvées' are both well above average wines but have that rustic touch of Mercurey with some iron – which I like and my wife Barbara doesn't.

Château d'Étroyes, 71640 Mercurey, Givry, tel.(85) 45.25.00. 14–17 hrs. Phone to ask for tastings.

Pinot Noir grapes

Hotels

Food *see* Area 10 (Burgundy North)

Chagny

see Area 10 (Burgundy North).

Rully

Hotel du Commerce, place Sainte-Marie, Rully, 71150 Chagny, Saône-et-Loire, tel.(85) 87.20.09.

Simple clean inn; 16 bedrooms (4 with toilet). Good value regional meals. Meals and rooms C.

Hotel Rully, RN6, Rully, 71150 Saône-et-Loire, tel.(85) 87.09.69.

On N6, 5km S Chagny, 4km E of Rully. *Vignerons* say that it specialises in Burgundian cooking. I do not know it. Garden and grounds. Pool. Meals C; rooms C–M.

Mercurey

Val d'Or, Mercurey, 71640 Saône-et-Loire, tel.(85) 47.13.70. On D978.

Meals very popular, so book. Cheaper menus are outstanding value, dearer meals very good. Jean-Claude Coyny's rather modern version of Burgundian cooking. Excellent

jambon persillé. Good desserts. Not only Mercurey wines but Rully from his brother-in-law Jean Coulon. Meals C–E; rooms C. Shut Tuesday lunch 15 March–15 November; Sunday evenings 15 November–15 March; early December–early January; few days early September.

Dracy-le-Forêt

Le Dracy, Dracy-le-Forêt, 71640 Givry, tel.(85) 41.55.88. 3km W of Chalon-sur-Saône on D978 – 3km N of Givry on D981.

Modern, pleasant, among lawns; comfortable rooms; a little faceless. Good value meals in restaurant alongside. Meals and rooms C–M.

Givry

Halle, place Halle, 71640 Givry, Saône-et-Loire, tel.(85) 44.32.45.

Good straightforward Burgundian family cooking; simple comfort. Meals C–M; rooms C. Shut November; Sunday evenings, Mondays.

AREA 12

MÂCON AND BEAUJOLAIS

BROUILLY · CHÉNAS · FLEURIE
POUILLY-FUISSÉ

Georges Duboeuf, who is variously called the King or the Pope of Beaujolais, is known personally to almost every great chef and wine trader in the world and would certainly not remember me. But I owe him a small 'thank you' if only for my stomach's sake.

One nasty November night a few years back, I arrived dutifully with friends at his cave to taste and take away the Beaujolais Nouveau. After a smell, a swirl and a swallow I admitted that I didn't want to drink any more because it always gave me hiccups and an acidic stomach.

Without so much as a snort he disappeared into the cellar and brought back for me a bottle of Fleurie which was about two years old, flowery, soft, delicious and as seductive as a cuddly blonde under the influence of Champagne.

Nouveau Beaujolais has improved since those days, largely through the efforts of M. Duboeuf who sends lots of his carefully chosen wines to be independently tasted and analysed to make sure which ones are suitable for drinking young. But I still prefer a two- or three-year-old Fleurie or a five- or six-year-old Moulin à Vent.

Many of my friends in the wine trade are saddened that the fashion for 'Primeur' (Nouveau) Beaujolais has resulted in good wine which would have been delicious in three or four years being rocked and rolled around French roads, then swilled before it has had time to stop swirling. The earthy growers of Burgundy would drop their *tastevins* laughing if they could see the snobs of Paris and London solemnly going through a tasting ritual, then pronouncing wise words on the merits of the year's vintage of Primeur when the stuff has not had time to stop revolving round the bottle. Every bottle drunk like that puts up the price of Beaujolais later.

On Beaujolais I agree with the man who writes best about wine for amateur consumers, like me – Alexis Lichine, wine producer in Bordeaux, *négociant* almost everywhere. In his *Guide to the Wines and Vineyards of France* (Papermac and Knopf) he says:

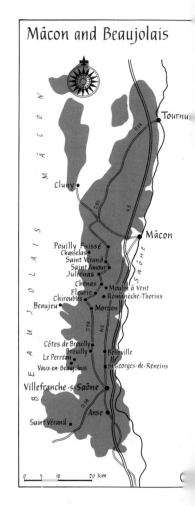

'Forget the delicate sniffs and sips, the ruminatory gargles, the suspenseful silences with which we approach the great Burgundies and Bordeaux. The wines of Beaujolais are meant to be swallowed and gulped and unabashedly enjoyed.'

But do allow yourself a sniff long enough to enjoy that lovely fruitiness of the Gamay grape at its best.

Even I can remember when much Beaujolais never reached a bottle. It went in barrels, mostly to Lyon and Paris, where it was lapped up in bars and none-too-pricey restaurants from carafes, or straight into the glass. The local joke was that three rivers flow into Lyon – the Saône, the Rhône and the Beaujolais.

But as it became more respectable and was put into bottles, producers set out to make wine which kept well, some of which, like Morgon, needed to be kept. Now the fashion is for lighter wines with lighter food, and some wine makers are aiming to make wines which can be drunk younger – even Morgon.

So it is useful to know something about each of the different Beaujolais, which can have quite different characteristics even though they may be made with the same Gamay grape grown only a few kilometres apart. The answer, of course, is not just in the making but in the soil.

I am told that it is the granite-based soil of the Beaujolais which makes the Gamay grape produce such a gorgeously fruity wine from that mauve juice. Only the Touraine Gamays can compare. Certainly the best wines, the *crus* (such as Fleurie) and the best Beaujolais Villages AOC come from the north of Beaujolais. Those from the south are mostly lighter and good for making Nouveau. Some Chardonnay grapes are grown in the north near the Mâcon area and are used for making white wine, very similar to Mâcon Blanc.

Of the *crus*, Brouilly is the largest, producing a charmingly soft wine with a lovely Gamay smell that is best drunk young. It's a café-bistro wine. Côte de Brouilly, a better wine, does not open up for about three years.

Moulin-à-Vent is deep in colour, smooth and rich, and is best drunk after three or four years. Good vintages improve for ten years, and I agree with experts that it often seems more like a Côte d'Or Burgundy than a Beaujolais.

Chénas is not quite so good as Moulin but should be kept. It has a lovely flowery smell and super fruitiness in the back of the throat, which stays quite a long time. St-Amour is lighter in colour, livelier than its neighbours but delicate. It can be drunk young, but is better kept three years. The white of this commune is sold as St-Véran.

Morgon wines have quite a different bouquet and for me a different taste from the others. Most of them are dead when drunk young but have a rich flavour and are quite substantial after two or three years, and some are really rich after five or six years. If you go to the Duboeuf cellars, try to buy some Domaine Lieven, which he bottles. It is grown in the vineyards of Princesse de Lieven, who is Mrs Charles Piat (a name you may well have noticed on Beaujolais bottles!). Morgon was for long the favourite Beaujolais of Paris, but with the light food fashion the in-wine is now Chiroubles, which is light, fragrant, tasty and willing, and ready before the others (just the sort of companion to take to a party). Alas, the fashionable French are drinking it by February and you are lucky to find any by summer, when it would go well with salad snacks.

Luckily there is enough Fleurie to go round. A seductive wine, charming, very fruity, 'easy to say and easy to drink', as locals put it. The French maintain that you should drink it within eighteen months of the vintage but that depends on the vines, and locals often keep it three years.

Juliénas is said to be the epitome of Beaujolais. Deep purple in colour, gorgeously fruity at six months to a year, spicy as well at two to four years. Considering the steep slopes and problems of growing the vines, it is very good value.

Perhaps because it is so difficult to pronounce well, the white

Mâcon Pouilly-Fuissé is the favourite of connoisseurs and would-be connoisseurs, particularly in the US, and its price has risen steadily beyond the range of most of us, which has upset my younger daughter Louise considerably. I know no producer or *négociant* who falls over himself to give free tastings! It is rightly the pride of Mâcon, but I do not know why it is so much more popular than Chablis, providing you get the right Chablis. If there is any inferior Pouilly-Fuissé, I have not met it lately – although in the bad old days you could not trust the label outside Burgundy. They are mostly fruitier and softer than Chablis, and they usually have more body, especially the wines of Solutré. I suppose it is no longer necessary to warn people not to muddle Pouilly-Fouissé with Pouilly-Fumé, the completely different wine from Pouilly on the Loire. Pouilly-Loches and Pouilly-Vinzelles are not so good as Fuissé but are the same style and cheaper. A good cheaper alternative to Pouilly-Fuissé is St-Véran. Lovely when three to five years old.

White wines, made mainly with the Chardonnay grape plus a little Pinot Blanc, now make up sixty per cent of Mâcon production. They are taken much more seriously now than ten years ago – possibly because they are often good value. Mâcon Blanc AOC is fresh, fruity, slightly acidic and is drunk within two years. Mâcon Blanc Supérieur is more alcoholic, fruitier and has greater body. It is now usually called Mâcon Villages.

Mâcon red is probably better known to most Britons. Though quite like Beaujolais, the wines are normally a bit rough and acidic for me. They should be kept until they are three to four years old.

I am sorry that I have given so few places where you can taste wine in the Mâconnais, but I did not get much response there to the idea of individual travellers tasting and buying wine direct. Most of the wine is made by co-operatives and whilst they were friendly, they wanted a lot of notice for callers. But the Maison de Tourisme in Mâcon is helpful and gives tastings (*see* Further Information).

Tastings

Cave Co-opérative

A good white Mâcon, round, fresh and fruity. Has a mural showing Viré's twinning (*jumellage*) with Montmartre in Paris. Why didn't my Kent village think of that?

Viré, 71260 Lugny, Saône-et-Loire, tel.(85) 33.11.64. Just W of N6 about 19km N of Mâcon. Business hours. Pay by the glass.

André Degueurse

To a lover of Burgundy, the village is almost a shrine. From here, in 1660, Claude Brosse the local grower took his wines to Paris in an ox-cart and got an order from Louis XIV. Like him, André Degueurse is just a small local grower, but you should try his white Mâcon Chasselas, and his red Mâcon and Beaujolais, too. Chasselas is at the very meeting place of Mâcon and Beaujolais, and the village has the right to produce both AOC wines. Chasselas table grapes are still grown, too – as at Versailles.

Chasselas, 71570 La Chapelle de Guinchay, Saône-et-Loire, tel.(85) 35.11.99. SW of Mâcon neighbouring Fuissé. Friday, Saturday, Sunday 10–12 hrs; 15–17 hrs. Otherwise phone to make sure someone is there.

Le Cellier de la Vieille Eglise

Tasting cave set up by the producers' association (*Association des Producteurs du Cru Juliénas*) in an old deconsecrated (*désaffectée*) church with coloured frescos devoted to Bacchus and his worshippers. Three good wines – Juliénas (one of the best of Beaujolais), Beaujolais Villages and St-Amour (the neighbouring commune whose name has helped the wine's popularity). Amour is certainly a sprightly wine, though one critic suggested unromantically that it has a slight taste of bananas. It takes about three years to ripen, so obviously it is no instant aphrodisiac. It is said that the name came to the village because the Canons of Mâcon Cathedral, who owned it, did not allow their vows to stand in the way of full enjoyment of their *droits de seigneur*. Apart from St Valentine's Day, the day to drink it with a suitable

Juliénas, 69840 Rhône. 10–12 hrs; 14.30–18.30 hrs, every day in June, July, August; shut Tuesdays rest of the year. No need to phone.

companion is 20 August – St Amour's Day. It must be a sign of old age, but I prefer the sturdy Juliénas wines, which have a marvellous fruitiness when drunk in the first six months to a year, turning to spice and richness when over two years old. They are called 'real Beaujolais', and are not for lovers of lightweight wines.

Pouilly Fuissé

Château du Bois de la Salle (Cave Co-opérative des Grands Vins)

Where the producers make and keep wine. Tasting and buying but best to phone if you want to be shown round. You pay for tastings. Groups must give eight days written notice. Same three wines as at the tasting cave Vieille Eglise.

69840 Juliénas, tel.(74) 04.42.61. 9–12 hrs; 14–17 hrs.

Cave du Château de Chénas

This co-operative, in a Louis XIV château, is one of the very best places to visit in Beaujolais, for not only are its wines outstanding but you have a chance to compare Moulin-à-Vent with the cheaper Chénas. Moulin-à-Vent is named after the vaneless old windmill which stands high on a hill on the Chénas to Romanèche-Thorins road overlooking a sea of vines producing Fleurie, Chénas and Moulin-à-Vent. Some of its wines come from the commune of Chénas, the rest from Romanèche-Thorins. Moulin-à-Vent wine is the King of Beaujolais – big, strong, dark and tough, described sometimes as more like a red Burgundy in need of ageing than a Beaujolais. It is fruity when young and tannic. It does become more elegant with age, but is never like the flowery, light wines so popular now. Chénas is very similar to Moulin, but lighter and a little more velvety. A splendid place to taste the wines (at a price) is on the terrace of Daniel Robin's restaurant-among-the-vines, 'Robin-Relais des Crus' at Les Descamps, down the road from Château de Chénas. Robin is also a wine grower (Domaine des Bruneaux). The vaulted cave of the Château de Chénas is the biggest in Beaujolais, and some 250 growers belong to the co-operative.

Chénas, 69840 Juliénas, Rhône, tel.(74) 04.11.91. Visits Monday–Saturday midday 8–12 hrs; 14–18 hrs, also Saturday afternoon 1 April–30 October. No need to phone. Tastings free except for groups.

Georges Duboeuf

Georges Duboeuf is Pope of Beaujolais, *négociant* par excellence, and, according to many, the man with the best nose and palate in Burgundy. He travels each year through the Beaujolais and Mâconnais tasting wines (8,000 in a year, I am told), taking back more than 3,000 for exhaustive laboratory analysis. From these he finally takes only those fine wines which are 'balanced, fruity, stylish and have individuality'. The wines justify his enthusiasm. He supplies many of the leading restaurants of France and of cities from the US to Hong Kong. It was he who made Beaujolais Nouveau a considered wine, not just any old cheap Beaujolais to be rushed to Paris as a stunt. He has a fine turn of phrase, too. He

Romanèche-Thorins, 71570 La Chapelle de Guinchay, Saône-et-Loire, tel.(85) 35.51.13. Office hours. Make an appointment for tasting, either by phone or by calling.

Moulin à Vent

calls Morgon 'truculent'. And of his best choices for 1984 he said: 'They represent the quintessence of Beaujolais, brilliant ruby with violet hue, a strong floral note in which raspberries, blackcurrants and bananas dominate, wines that are well balanced, elegant, aristocratic, subtle, and finish with the delightful taste of fresh grapes.' So, you see wine tastings here are serious and for the true lover of Beaujolais.

Caveau de Dégustations des Viticulteurs

A cave where, for a nominal amount, you can taste the best Fleurie wines, chosen by a tasting jury. Pleasant bar with tables and vaulted cellars where wines mature.

Fleurie, 69820 Rhône, 10–12 hrs; 14.30–18.30 hrs. No need to phone. Wines 3F 50 a glass.

Cave Co-opérative des Grands Vins

Do you remember, on the BBC TV programme *Year of the French*, seeing a magnificent lady called 'Queen of the Beaujolais'? That was Mademoiselle Marguerite Chabert, who has run this big co-operative cave for years and was still doing so when I last heard though surely touching eighty. And one of the best two wines is rightly named after her, 'Cuvée Président Marguerite', for it is a

Fleurie, 69820, tel.(74) 04.11.70. Open every day 9–12 hrs; 14–19 hrs. No need to phone to taste or buy; phone to be shown round cellars. Tastings 4F a glass.

typical Fleurie, elegant, with a lovely bouquet, and called locally 'feminine'. I have certainly met girls a lot harder than this wine, not to say less charming. But I love Fleurie. It has such an attractive soft taste and is a wine which can genuinely be at its best after only eighteen months, although some, like the 'Cardinal Bienfaiteur' of this cave, are more powerful and need to be kept longer. These are usually made from older vines. The cave also produces good AOC Beaujolais Villages for drinking young.

Caveau de Morgon

Not a wine to drink in November after the harvest. It improves for years and when older is superb with Burgundian dishes. The attractive caveau is in the Louis XVII Château de Foncrenne in the middle of a big, pretty public park. There is a display of old wine-making tools and a miniature zoo.

Le Bourg, 69910 **Villié-Morgon**, Rhône, tel.(74) 04.20.99. Every day 9–12 hrs; 14–19 hrs. Small charge for tasting. If you phone for appointment you can see a seventeen-minute film on Morgon wines in English and taste the wine of the year.

Château de Corcelles

Restored fifteenth-century fortress with Renaissance galleries in its courtyard, fine woodcarvings in the chapel and a seventeenth-century Grand Cuvier eighty metres long, with wine maturing in huge casks. Visits to the château, with tastings and buying. Light, pleasant wines – Beaujolais Villages AOC.

Corcelles-en-Beaujolais, 69220 Belleville-sur-Saône, Rhône, tel.(74) 66.00.24. Check opening times.

Maison de Beaujolais

A sort of restaurant set up by *Belleville Syndicat d'Initiative* for tasting wines and local specialities (paying), and giving information on wines.

St-Jean-d'Ardières, 69220 **Belleville-sur-Saône**, Rhône, tel.(74) 66.16.46. On N6, 1½km N of Belleville. Shut Thursday, January. Check opening times.

La Cave Beaujolaise

A co-operative. Modern wine-making equipment in modern building, but you taste wines in fine old caves of an eighteenth-century château. Beaujolais Villages AOC is fruity and light. Château Les Loges wine is full bodied and matures excellently.

Château des Loges, **Le Pérreon**, 69830 St-Georges-de-Reneins, tel.(74) 03.22.83. From St-Georges-de-Reneins on N6 go W on D20 and D49. 9–12 hrs; 14.30–19 hrs. You pay for tastings.

Cave Co-opérative Beaujolaise

The little town stands on a hillock, with this modern co-op, which has 140 growers belonging to it, at the bottom. The tasting bar alongside is open Saturdays 8–11.30 hrs; 14–17 hrs. Other days, phone.

69620 **St-Vérand**, Rhône, tel.(74) 71.73.19. 8–12 hrs; 14–18 hrs. 20km SW of Villefranche-sur-Saône.

Cave de Clochemerle

Gabriel Chevallier, author of *Clochemerle* about a village urinal placed in view of a church, opened this cave in 1956. In doing so, he settled an argument by saying that Vaux *was* Clochemerle. It was opened as a tasting cave and officially it still is. But in the tourist season it would be impossible to accommodate everyone, so you may have to buy or drink a bottle in the Auberge de Clochemerle, the simple village restaurant where they serve local dishes (tel.(74) 65.91.11). The wine is a typical Beaujolais of the villages. And if you have not read the book, do. It's fun.

69460 **Vaux-en-Beaujolais**, tel.(74) 03.26.58. 15km W of St-Georges-de-Reneins, which is on N6. Every day 10–12 hrs; 14.30–19 hrs. Check if tastings are being given. Anyway, you can buy the wine and taste it.

In many wine villages of Beaujolais the wine makers have set up little taste-and-buy wine caveaux. Some are only open in the tourist season. Most are open daily from 8 or 9 hrs until about 17 hrs, with two to two and a half hours for lunch from noon. But they do vary and may be open all day. You may well have to pay a nominal amount per glass. Here are some to look for:

Beaujeu – Le Temple de Bacchus, tel.(74) 04.81.18.

Chasselas – La Cadole du Char à Boeufs, tel.(85) 35.11.99. Open Friday, Saturday, Sunday, Monday 10–12 hrs or phone.

Chiroubles – La Terrasse de Chiroubles, tel.(74) 04.20.79. Open 10–11.45 hrs; 14.30–18.30 hrs; Sunday afternoons; lovely views.

Romanèche – on N6: Le Caveau des Viticulteurs du Moulin-à-Vent, tel.(85) 35.51.03; also restaurant.

Leynes – Relais Beaujolais–Mâconnais, tel.(85) 35.11.29. Must phone.

St-Amour – Le Caveau du Cru St-Amour, tel.(85) 37.15.99. Also restaurant Chez Jean-Pierre – fifty yards. Shut Thursdays.

Saint-Lager – Le Cuvage des Brouilly, tel.(74) 66.18.34. Open 10–12 hrs; 15–20 hrs except Tuesday mornings.

Saint-Vérand (Rhône) – Caveau des Viticulteurs de Saint-Vérand, tel.(74) 71.73.19.

Further Information

Comité Interprofessionel des Vins de Bourgogne et Mâcon, Maison de Tourisme, avenue du Maréchal-de-Lattre-de-Tassigny, 71000 Mâcon.

Union Interprofessionel des Vins de Beaujolais, 210 boulevard Vermorel, 69400 Villefranche-sur-Saône.

Hotels

Food *see* Area 10 (Burgundy North) and Area 8 (Rhône Valley)

Solutré-Pouilly

Le Relais de Solutré, Solutré-Pouilly, 71960 Saône-et-Loire, tel.(85) 35.80.81. 3km from Fuissé; 9km W of Mâcon on D94.

Attractive restaurant centred round a wood-burning stove, which serves old Burgundian dishes (*oeufs meurettes, andouillette Pouilly-Fuissé*). Rooms in annexe, lovely views over hills of Beaujolais, Pouilly, Roche de Solutré. Meals C–M; rooms C.

Mâcon

Bellevue, 416 quai Lamartine, 71000 Mâcon, tel.(85) 38.05.07.

Pleasant, old-style hotel with soundproofed rooms. The restaurant has been taken over by the son of the house who has added some imaginative modern dishes to the traditional Burgundian menus. Meals and rooms C–M.

Fleurville

Château de Fleurville, 71260 Lugny, Saône-et-Loire, tel.(85) 33.12.17. N6, 16km N of Mâcon.

Sixteenth-century château in a park, where the Comtesse de Ségur wrote *The Misfortunes of Sophie*. Attractive. Good traditional cooking. Meals (shut Monday lunch) C–M; rooms C. Shut 15 November–15 December.

Igé

Château d'Igé, 71960 Pierreclos, Saône-et-Loire, tel.(85) 33.33.99. Turn off N6 at Fleurville on D15 through Viré; left at Azé on D85.

Thirteenth-century fortified château of Counts of Mâcon. Nice old village and vineyards. Relais et Châteaux hotel. Meals à la carte M–E; rooms M–E. Open 15 March–5 November; weekends 5 February–15 March.

Romanèche-Thorins

Les Maritonnes, Romanèche-Thorins, 71570 La Chapelle-de-Guinchay, Saône-et-Loire, tel.(85) 35.51.70.

Pleasing house among greenery. Superb traditional cooking well deserving Michelin star (*poulet de Bresse au Beaujolais*) and wonderful list of Mâcon and Beaujolais wines. Meals M–E; rooms C–M. All shut 2–10 June; 15 December–25 January; Mondays. Hotel shut Sunday night 1 October–30 June; restaurant Tuesday lunch 1 July–30 September.

Juliénas

Chez la Rose, Juliénas, 69840 Rhône, tel.(74) 04.41.20.

Logis with 'casserole' for good regional dishes. Recommended by *vignerons*. Meals and rooms C. Shut 8–16 January. Tuesdays.

Belleville

Au Beaujolais, 40 rue du Maréchal Foch, Belleville, 69220 Rhône, tel.(74) 66.05.31.

Simple, one-star rooms but a restaurant true to old Beaujolais (*andouillettes Beaujolais, coq au vin, écrevisses à la crème*) with a wide choice of Beaujolais wines. Meals C–M; rooms C. Shut mid December–mid January; Tuesday evening, Wednesday.

Thoissey

Au Chapon Fin (Restaurant Paul Blanc), rue du Champ-de-Foire, Thoissey, 01140 Ain, tel.(74) 04.04.74. 5km E of N6 over M6 and river Saône from 6km N of Belleville.

My old favourite has lost a star from Michelin since I was last there, but the Blanc family still run it and the choice of Beaujolais wines is superb. Knowledgeable wine buyers still use it. Meals M–E; rooms C–M (some in old house, some in modern extension). Shut early January–early February; Tuesday except evening 15 June–23 September. The other, pricier, 3-star Georges Blanc hotel-restaurant is 23km away at Vonnas.

St-Georges-de-Reneins

Hostellerie St-Georges, 27 ave Charles de Gaulle, 69830 St-Georges-de-Reneins, Rhône, tel.(74) 67.62.78. N6, 9km N of Villefranche.

Keep it to yourself – only five bedrooms. Excellent Burgundian and Lyonnais dishes – super value. Meals C–M; rooms C.

Villefranche-sur-Saône

Plaisance, 94 ave de la Libération, tel.(74) 65.33.52, and La Fontaine Bleue, 18 rue Jean Moulin, tel.(74) 68.10.37.

These work together. Restaurant is behind the hotel. Hotel fairly modern. Restaurant good value. Fish direct from Brittany. Meals C–E; rooms C. Hotel shut 25 December–2 January; restaurant December and Sundays.

Château de Chervinges, Chervinges-Gleizé, 69400 Villefranche-sur-Saône, tel.(74) 65.29.76. 3km SW of Villefranche by D38.

Peaceful manor house in own grounds. Pool. Pleasant cooking. Own wines (also sold direct). Meals (dinner à la carte) M; rooms M–E; apartments E. Shut 2 January–28 February. Restaurant shut Sunday evening, Mondays.

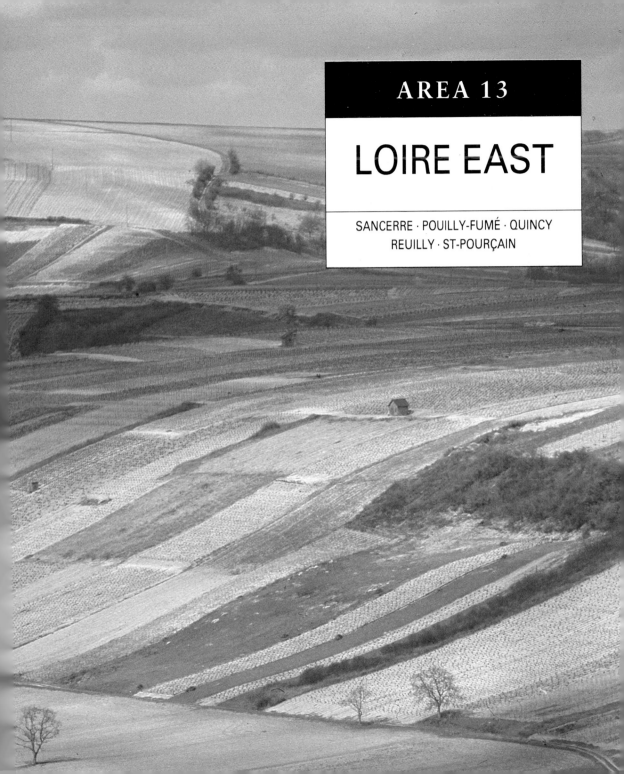

AREA 13

LOIRE EAST

SANCERRE · POUILLY-FUMÉ · QUINCY
REUILLY · ST-POURÇAIN

The best place to taste Pouilly-Fumé is in the 'Relais Fleuri' at Pouilly-sur-Loire, just off the N7. Here you can sit under the greenery on the terrace looking across the garden and a meadow to the river Loire. If you can lure Jean-Claude Astruc from his kitchen and get him talking about local wines, tell him that you want to try the odd glass and you may find yourself comparing the Guy Saget with the Blondelet and both with the Vieille Vigne wine of the co-operative. He always seems to be able to come up with something different. But do not drink too many glasses at one time, although M. Astruc's prices are very reasonable. You will not want to be too full of Fumé to enjoy his delicious cooking. The 'Relais Fleuri' is in a perfect position for a wine lover – the wine

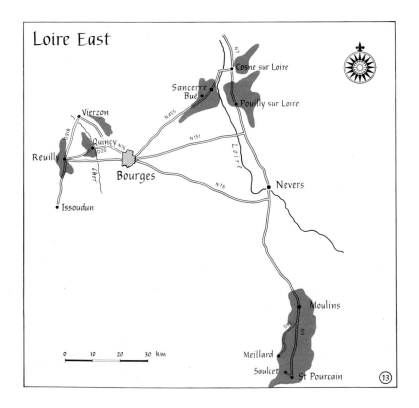

Loire East

Cosne sur Loire

Sancerre
Bué

Pouilly sur Loire

Vierzon

Quincy

Reuilly

Bourges

Nevers

Issoudun

0   10   20   30 km

Moulins

Meillard

Saulcet
St Pourcain

⑬

co-operative is opposite, Fernand Blondelet's cellars are 100 yards down the road (avenue de la Tuilerie) and another few hundred yards further on is the little town of Pouilly-sur-Loire with Guy Saget's caves among its shops and cafés.

Unlike the Mâcon Pouilly-Fuissé, made with the Chardonnay grape, this Pouilly-Fumé of the Loire is made from our old friend the Sauvignon grape. No one has ever given me a satisfactory explanation for its smoky, flinty taste. I found this taste very strong at one time but now I have to search for it a bit, so I am convinced that the wines are made differently now. But Barbara says that the smokiness is as strong as ever. Perhaps it is because I gave up smoking cigars. Anyway, the wines have a super, unusual taste and keep their freshness for at least four or five years whilst growing softer. I admire the growers – they put up with all sorts of problems like unpredictable late spring frosts and hail.

They make also a dry, light fruity wine from the Chasselas grape mixed with Sauvignon for lapping in litres – just called Pouilly-sur-Loire. Drink it very young.

Sancerre, across the river, makes twice as much wine as Pouilly and most of it is white. Sancerre and Pouilly are ardent rivals and will not admit that their wines are similar. In fact, I find Sancerre usually fruitier but not so interesting.

The hail storms seem to miss Sancerre. I am told locally that there are three types of soil, producing three different wines. Wines from around Bué are fruity and for drinking young. Chavignol's steep chalky slopes produce a distinguished wine to be kept three years or more. Ménétréol area wines are softer and less fruity.

Where Sauvignon grapes will not grow well in Sancerre, Pinot Noir has been grown to make rosé, and, in good years, red wine. In the unfathomable way of one-upmanship in Paris this rare red has suddenly become fashionable and they drink it young and cold. To me, it tastes raw. Pinot Noir does not make wines for drinking very young. Ask them in Beaune.

Quincy, west of Bourges, produces dry white wines from Sauvignon grapes with less individuality than Sancerre and Pouilly-Fumé. They are softer, but very aromatic and fruity and when drunk young make a good cheaper substitute. So does white Reuilly, which is not quite so smooth, but very aromatic. A spicy, light red Reuilly is made, too, but very little of it. Next fashion in Paris?

St-Pourçain-sur-Sioule is just off the N9 south of Moulins. Although in the *Allier département*, its wines are technically 'Loire', though are much like Burgundy. The light, refreshing and slightly cidery white wines are made from several grapes, including the local Tressalier. Red wines made from Gamay are more like a Beaujolais than Touraine and the Pinot Noir reds quite like Burgundy. Wines are good value.

Tastings

POUILLY-SUR-LOIRE

Caves de Pouilly-sur-Loire

The co-op is opposite the Relais Fleuri. Its 'Les Moulins à Vent' Fumé is dry and fruity, the 'Vieilles Vignes' has more body. They also make a light Pouilly-sur-Loire, and three little-known wines from around Gien and Cosne-sur-Loire (Coteaux du Giennois) – a fresh light Gamay red, a heavier Pinot Noir red and a rosé. Cheap and good value.

Le Moulin à Vent, BP No 9, ave de la Tuilerie, 58150 Pouilly-sur-Loire, Nièvre, tel.(86) 39.10.99. Avoid the N7 deviation around Pouilly – take the old road. Open Monday–Saturday 8–12 hrs; 14–18 hrs.

Domaine Fernand Blondelet et Domaine Tinel-Blondelet

One of the best Fumé wines. Fernand Blondelet is one of the most respected producers in the area. The younger generation runs the Tinel-Blondelet Domaine.

La Croix Canat, 58150 Pouilly-sur-Loire, tel.(86) 39.13.83. Notice on left, 250 metres past Relais Fleuri going towards Pouilly. 8–12.15 hrs; 13.30–19.30 hrs. Phone if possible. English spoken.

SANCERRE

Caves de la Mignonne

These caves were dug out in 1972, at great cost and trouble, to provide tasting cellars for Sancerre's two great gifts to gastronomy – wine and *crottin de chavignol*, a strong-smelling goat's cheese with a lovely flavour. (Don't be put off by the name – it only means 'goats' droppings!') Tastings, alas, are only given on special occasions, but it is a good place to buy the wines and cheese.

Route de Saint-Satur, 18300 Sancerre, Cher, tel.(48) 54.07.06. At N end of Sancerre village. Every day 15 March–15 November, 10–12 hrs; 14.30–18.30 hrs.

Domaine Henri Bourgeois

For me, the best property to visit in Sancerre, not only for quality wines but for choice. The Bourgeois family have been producing wine here for ten generations and also make, bottle and mature good wines from other properties. Quite one of the best white Sancerre wines is their 'Côtes de Mont Dâmnés' from south-facing slopes which have been known as far back as the eleventh century when lordly local landowners squabbled over them. Now they are in Bourgeois hands, and produce a delicious, strongly fragrant wine with a taste of its own which stays in the mouth for ages. 'Vigne Blanche' is a fresh, vital wine with a flowery smell. 'Duc Etienne de Laury', which needs to be kept in bottle for a year or more, is another very fragrant wine, produced from twenty-five-year-old vines. Red 'La Bourgeoise', from Pinot Noir vines planted fifty–sixty years ago, is the best red Sancerre I have tasted. Matured in oak barrels, it is full bodied and fruity and it would be criminal to drink it young. 'La Bourgeoise' white should be kept a while, too. It is powerful and easy to recognise after a few bottles. Chavignol is where the crottin cheese comes from. You need powerful wines with that.

Chavignol, 18300 Sancerre, tel.(48) 54.21.67. 2km W of Sancerre. Every day 8–11 hrs; 15–19 hrs. English spoken.

QUINCY

Raymond Pipet

Fifth generation *vignerons*, producing white AOC. Raymond Pipet offers tastings of his light, fine wines with a fresh bouquet 'in the tradition passed down by my *vignerons* ancestors'.

Quincy, 18120 Lury-sur-Arnon, Cher, tel.(48) 51.31.17. From N76 Bourges–Vierzon road turn W at Mehun on D20 for 4km. 9–12 hrs; 14–18 hrs.

Pouilly sur Loire

REUILLY

Gérard Cordier

Well known for Sauvignon white and Pinot Noir red. The Château de la Ferté, built 1636 by François Mansard, one of the greatest architects in history, is a delight, as fine as almost any in the Loire.

La Ferté, 36260 Reuilly, Indre, tel.(54) 49.28.98. Continue along D20 from Quincy (above) for 9km to Reuilly. La Ferté is 3km on D918 Issoudun road. Must phone.

Claude Lafond

An enthusiastic young grower makes a beautifully fruity and fresh Sauvignon white Reuilly for drinking young, an elegant and vital (*racé*) Pinot Noir which is said locally to be every bit as good as Sancerre red (keep it four years), and a wine which I believe is

Le Bois St Denis, 36260 Reuilly, Indre, tel.(54) 49.22.17. Every day 9–12 hrs; 14–19 hrs.

unique to Reuilly – a delicate rosé made from Pinot Gris grapes and recommended as an aperitif, with light summer salads or with dessert. Claude Lafond's father started growing vines in the 1960s, producing just 100 bottles in a year. When he was dying, eighteen-year-old Claude, studying to be an electronics engineer, promised Dad that *he* would continue with wine making. At thirty-five he has greatly increased the acreage, is one of the most respected growers in Reuilly and has won gold and silver medals at the Paris Concours for red and white wines.

ST-POURÇAIN-SUR-SIOULE

Jean et François Ray

Old-established family property producing a red largely from the Gamay grape, fruity and for drinking young, and a typical local dry white from the local Tressalier grape (also called Sacy) with Chardonnay and Sauvignon. These whites are worth trying – light and different from any I have tasted.

Saulcet, 03500 St-Pourçain-sur-Sioule, Allier. 2km along D46 W of St-Pourçain, right on D34. 8.30–12 hrs; 14–18.30 hrs.

Gérard et Jean-Louis Petillat

Leading local producer, making a refreshing, fragrant, dry white wine from Sauvignon and Chardonnay, and a sparkling Blanc de Blancs Chardonnay by the Champagne method. The rosé and one red wine are from Gamay grapes and are very easy to knock back. They also make a 'Grand Réserve' Pinot red, full bodied, well constituted and quite alcoholic to serve lightly *chambré* with meat and cheese. You might well get a bargain here. In the thirteenth century St-Pourçain wines were rated higher than both Beaune and the best whites of Burgundy, and cost more, too.

Domaine de Bellevue, Meillard, 03500 St-Pourçain-sur-Sioule, Allier, tel.(70) 42.05.56. From N9 N of St-Pourçain take D18 W over D34, then right on D217. Monday–Saturday 9–12 hrs; 14–18 hrs. English spoken. No need to phone.

Further Information

Sancerre – Union Viticole Sancerroise, 16bis avenue Nationale, 18300 Sancerre, tel.(48) 54.03.51.

Hotels   Food *see* Area 10 (Burgundy North) and Area 16 (Loire Valley)

Pouilly-sur-Loire

Relais Fleuri, ave de la Tuilerie, Pouilly-sur-Loire, 58150 Nièvre, tel.(86) 39.12.99.

Old-style inn with nice garden, Loire river views and excellent cooking; good value. Meals C–M; rooms C. Shut 15 January–15 February; Wednesday evening, Thursday from October–Easter.

L'Espérance, 17 rue René Couard, 58150 Pouilly-sur-Loire, tel.(86) 39.10.68.

Only four rooms. Deserved Michelin star for regional dishes, and good local wine list, but pricey. Meals M–E; rooms C. Shut 1–20 December; 6–31 January; Monday; Sunday evening except July, August.

Sancerre

Hotel Panoramic et Restaurant, La Tasse d'Argent, Rempart des Augustins, Sancerre, 18300 Cher, hotel tel.(48) 54.22.44; restaurant tel.(48) 54.01.44.

Recommended by vignerons; I do not know them. Said to have wonderful vineyard views. Meals and rooms C–M. Restaurant shut January; Wednesdays from November–March.

Les Remparts, Rempart des Dames, Sancerre, 18300 Cher, tel.(48) 54.10.18.

Changed hands since my *Encore Travellers' France* readers praised it highly, but still known locally for excellent value. Regional dishes, Sancerre wines. Very cheap weekday menu. Good views. Meals C–M; rooms C.

Auberge Alphonse Mellot, 16 place de la Halle, 18300 Sancerre, tel.(48) 54.20.53.

Tasting restaurant only. 'Auberge Dégustation', with 'La Châtellerie' wines from patron's own vineyard served with local terrines, *crottin* (goat's milk cheese), smoked ham. Cheap menu and card.

St-Thibault (5km NE of Sancerre)

L'Auberge, 37 rue Jacques Combes, St-Thibault, 18300 Sancerre, tel.(48) 54.13.79.

Built 1610. Delightful garden with charming veranda; excellent local dishes and wines. Camille Cornille has handed over to the maître d'hôtel Hervé Huguet. Still good value. Meals C–M; rooms C.

L'Etoile, 2 quai de Loire, St-Thibault, 18300 Sancerre, tel.(48) 54.12.15.

Lovely position overlooking Loire. Happy place with regional dishes and grills over a wood fire. Simple rooms. Meals C–M; rooms C. Shut 15 November–1 March; Wednesday except July, August.

St-Pourçain-sur-Sioule

Chêne Vert, 35 bd Ledru-Rollin, St-Pourçain-sur-Sioule, 03500 Allier, tel.(70) 45.40.65.

Good cooking, good value. Meals C–M; rooms C. Shut early October; 4 January–6 October; hotel Tuesday from October–May; restaurant Wednesday lunch, Thursday from September–June.

AREA 14

CHAMPAGNE

TAITTINGER · MOËT ET CHANDON
MERCIER · POMMERY

'I have just had a terrible thought,' said the urbane Frenchman as we drank Champagne before lunch at Moët et Chandon. 'If you Protestants had beaten Richelieu at Rochelle, we should never have had Champagne to drink.'

'Why ever not?' I asked.

'You would have closed the monasteries. Dom Pérignon would

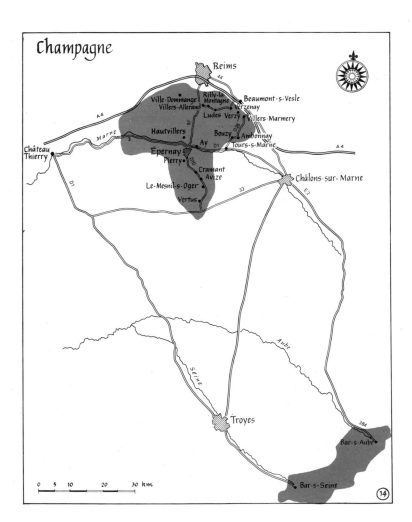

never have had the chance to discover the Champagne method in his Abbey cellars.'

No good telling a man from Champagne that someone else would have discovered the way to 'marry' wines and control the second fermentation. But I wonder if the patient old monk-cellarman of the Abbey of Hautvilliers would have approved of the image his wonderful wine has gained through the centuries? He was surely not seeking the wine of celebration and seduction – the perfect appetiser for food and love.

In the wild days of Versailles, under the Regency of Philippe Duc d'Orléans, Champagne seems to have been a compulsory accompaniment to promiscuity. Strange that we use it now to toast the bride and groom! And Edward VII's affairs prospered under the influence of Champagne Joseph Perrier. More recently Marilyn Monroe blossomed for long on Piper-Heidsieck – a quarter bottle for breakfast, a half bottle for lunch, and a bottle or two with dinner.

I feel genuinely sorry for people who do not like Champagne or think it 'terribly overrated'. But I don't mind having them as guests – it leaves more for us.

There is no room here to go into all the details of the Champagne method of wine making. Some of the big Champagne houses publish excellent booklets in English (Pommery and Moët et Chandon have good ones which they give to British and American visitors). Basically, the first fermentation of the pressed grape juice lasts several weeks. A still wine results. During the winter this is racked several times and thus becomes clear. The wine from each vineyard is then tested and a blend is made to obtain a perfectly balanced wine, with the characteristics of the particular Champagne house. If the wine of a year is exceptional, it is declared a 'vintage' (*Champagne Millésimé*). More often, the wine is mixed with some saved from previous years and becomes 'non-vintage'.

A little cane sugar and fermenting agents are added to the wine,

it is bottled and put in deep cool cellars. The fermenting agents work slowly on the sugar and start a second fermentation. The sugar is turned into alcohol and carbonic gas, which gives the Champagne its fizz. This takes several months.

The bottles stay on their sides in the cellar at a temperature of 10°C (50°F) for three to five years or more. The second fermentation causes a deposit to form.

To remove this, bottles are placed in racks with the necks slightly tilted downwards. Each day, over several months, an expert shakes the bottle gently, gives it a 45 degree turn and gradually increases the tilt until the bottle is nearly vertical, cork down.

Then follows the *dégorgement* (the getting rid of the deposit). This was very tricky until someone thought of freezing the neck of the bottle. A small block of ice forms, containing the deposit. When the cork is removed the ice block shoots out. The empty space in the bottle is then filled with *liqueur* (old Champagne mixed with cane sugar). This is called *dosage*. The amount of sugar depends on the type of Champagne – *brut* (very dry – once called the Englishman's Champagne), *sec* (medium dry), *demi-sec* (more sugary) or *doux* (sweet). Then a new cork is put in, wired, and the bottle is ready to drink. Kept lying down in a cool, dark place, Champagne will last five years or more, but it doesn't improve in the bottle.

Three grapes can be used for Champagne – Pinot Noir black grapes which give the wine body and life, Pinot Meunier black grapes which bring quicker ageing, and Chardonnay white which give it lightness, freshness and elegance. Most wines are a blend of black and white, but Blanc de Blancs is made solely from white grapes, is lighter, and makes a splendid 'elevenses' drink.

Champagne rosé (pink Champagne), popular in the 1920s, is back in fashion in Paris in particular and among the Young Upwardly mobile Professionals (Yuppies) in London. To me the ordinary non-vintage rosés are a poor substitute for white, but we had a 1980 vintage Moët recently which could easily have been drunk with red meat.

Crémant wines are slightly less bubbly than the others. Still white wines are now officially called Coteaux Champenois, and are pleasant and refreshing (and the wine used for cooking) but not up to the standard of Chablis, which is made from the same Chardonnay grapes grown on the same limestone-clay soil of the famous Kimmeridgian clay which runs through many of the Champagne villages to Chablis. This Coteaux Champenois is not a cheap wine, so beware the mistake of an Editor I know who thinks that anyone who drinks anything better than a simple *Vin de Pays* is a wine snob. He walked into a village inn on the N51, brusquely ordered *Vin de Pays* and found himself paying about £10 for a fine vintage Coteaux Champenois. I *did* enjoy drinking it!

Reumage

Not much of Champagne's still red wine, Bouzy, is produced and most of that is drunk locally – although a certain amount sells to passing tourists for its name. It does not suit most British or American tastes. It is much lighter than Côte d'Or Burgundies and when I suggested trying it I got some rude letters from readers saying that it was 'thin'.

The three major Champagne districts are La Montagne de Reims, between Reims and Epernay, with 'mountains' all of 200 feet high, the valley of the Marne, with south-facing slopes, just north of Epernay, and the Côte de Blancs, south of Epernay, where the white Chardonnay grapes are grown. Routes are marked by signs and it is worth driving at least one of them. You can get maps from the Champagne Information Office in Epernay (*see* Further Information).

The proper French way of opening a bottle of Champagne is to take off the wire, hold the bottle at 45 degrees, hold the cork firmly in one hand and turn the *bottle* round with the other hand. You do not put your thumbs under the cork. You are supposed to do all this nonchalantly, preferably making jokes. According to current fashion, you are not supposed to let the cork pop out with a bang. If you do, you are 'English, American or a peasant'. Don't take any notice. Do as you like. It's your Champagne! But don't let the cork fly across the room. I shot a magnum cork right through the stem of a glass one Christmas. Luckily the man drinking from the glass was an army officer just back from fighting in the Malayan jungle. He finished the wine, and tossed the cup of the glass into the wastepaper basket without blinking! To keep the bubbles and the bouquet, do not use those Victorian saucer glasses. Use the traditional *flûte* or better still a tulip-shaped glass. You do not take *un verre* of Champagne but a *coup* or a *flûte*. But, as Jacques Mercier said to me as some amateurs argued: 'Let us not talk about Champagne, let us drink it.'

And I know two good places where you can find many different Champagnes to compare. One is a rather touristy looking café and shop on a corner facing the door of Reims cathedral, which has an enormous choice to drink or take away. I have always been too busy tasting them to notice its name. The other is my friend Jean-Paul Pérardel's 'Aux Armes de Champagne' at L'Epine, near Châlons-sur-Marne. You have a choice of forty-five sparkling Champagnes, twenty still Champagnes and you need not spit any of them out when tasting, so long as you have booked your bedroom first.

Tastings

EPERNAY

In Champagne, perhaps I should call this 'Visits' as most houses which accept visitors do not promise tastings. In most you can buy a bottle (or half) and drink it there – before ordering a case, perhaps!

Moët et Chandon

Where else would you start to learn about Champagne? Founded in 1743 by Möet who took over the very vineyards and cellars of the Abbey of Hautvillers, where Dom Pérignon started it all, after the French Revolution and still own them. The biggest Champagne company, their Champagne is the most popular in France, Britain and the US, and they export to 150 countries. 'Somewhere in the world, a Moët et Chandon cork pops every two seconds' (I do my little bit to help). Unlike some Champagne houses, Moët own vineyards – 1,139 acres in the Champagne and 1,300 acres in the Napa Valley of California (*not* used for making Champagne, of course!). Even 300 acres in Brazil. They also own most of Parfums Christian Dior and are amalgamated with Hennessey cognac. Visits are excellently organised, with tastings at the end. You learn a surprising amount about Champagne making. There are 17½ miles of maturing bottles, but you don't have to go round all of them. A little wine museum includes Napoleon's hat. The Duke of Wellington took his with him – perhaps he drank less Moët.

18 avenue de Champagne, 51200 Epernay, tel.(26) 54.71.11. Visits with tastings Monday–Friday all year 9.30–12.30 hrs; 14–17.30 hrs. 1 April–31 October also Saturday 9.30–12 hrs; 14–17.30 hrs; Sunday 9.30–12 hrs; 14–16.30 hrs. Conducted tours in French, English, German, Spanish, Dutch, Polish or Russian.

Mercier

Since 1970 part of Moët et Chandon, but the Champagne is different. A mere eleven miles of galleries and an electric train to take you round. An interesting museum of wine presses and the largest wine cask in the world, made in 1899 for the Paris Exposition, it is beautifully carved and needed twenty-four oxen to tow it through the streets of Paris. It holds 200,000 bottles – the

75 ave de Champagne, 51200 Epernay, tel.(26) 54.71.11. Visits with tastings Monday–Saturday 9.30–12 hrs; 14–17.30 hrs; Sunday 9.30–12 hrs; 14–16.30 hrs. In English or French.

Hautvillers

perfect wedding present. The caves are so wide that four white horses took a President's carriage through them, and in the 1950s a car rally was held in them. Visits are just as well organised as at Moët (nearly opposite), with tasting at the end.

REIMS

Taittinger

One of the great Champagnes and one of the few old houses still in the same family. They own 600 acres of vineyards in eleven different villages spread around the Champagne. The cellars are superb. Hewn out of chalk between the fourth and thirteenth centuries, they were the cellars of St-Nicaise Abbey. Taittinger keep eight million bottles down there, ageing them for nearly four years, against the one year required by law for Champagne. The result is a delightfully round wine with a rich bouquet and a taste

9 place St-Nicaise, 51100 Reims, tel.(26) 85.45.35.
Tastings usually given on visits but no guarantee! They might be too busy.
Every day, including Sunday 9–12 hrs; 14–18 hrs. English spoken.

that lasts long in your mouth. The family has restored a wonderful thirteenth-century palace of the Counts of Champagne.

Pommery

Another rewarding visit and some of my favourite Champagnes. The huge cellars, reached by 116 steps, are decorated with chiselled bas-reliefs under a nineteenth-century Gothic turreted castle in an English-style park, all created by Veuve Pommery herself. She also pioneered Dry and Brut Champagne when others made only sweet. Most of the production is now Brut Royal. Their vineyards around Champagne cover 750 acres. Look out in the cellars for a cask holding 100,000 bottles beautifully sculpted in 1903 by Gallé.

5 place du Général Giraud, 51100 Reims, tel.(26) 05.05.01. Take boulevard de la Paix, bd Pasteur, bd Henri Vasnier (towards Châlons). Visits (tasting usually given – anyway, you can buy a bottle) Monday–Friday 9–11 hrs; 14–17 hrs. Saturday, Sunday at set times 10, 11, 14.30, 15.30, 16.30. Phoning would help, not necessary. French, English or German.

Piper-Heidsieck

You tour the cellars, containing sixteen million bottles, in an electric train – a very interesting experience. The cellars cover ten miles, and apart from the well-known and much-admired Piper-Heidsieck Champagnes, such as Florens-Louis, some rarer cuvées are produced. One is called 'Champagne Rare', made only in great years from the very best grapes. It was named after a similar wine presented by the founder of the house in 1785 at Petit Trianon to Queen Marie-Antoinette, the girl who lost her head in the Revolution. Then there is a rare Champagne Sauvage. It is absolutely *brut* – dry, with no topping-up sugar at all, and has to be aged in opaque bottles to avoid any light because of its delicacy. Sauvage was produced originally for Claude Terrall, owner of 'La Tour d'Argent' restaurant in Paris – the one with the numbered ducks. Alas, I have not tried either of these rare wines, but Sauvage is said to sandpaper your throat.

Piper-Heidsieck has had quite a history. The family would not

51 boulevard Henry Vasnier, 51100 Reims, tel.(26) 85.01.94. Very near to Pommery. Visits Monday–Friday 9.30–11.30 hrs; 14–17.30 hrs all year; also Saturdays, Sundays from 22 March–11 November. Normally you pay for the wines you taste, but Piper-Heidsieck have kindly said that they will offer a glass to my readers, so show the book! English speaking guides.

collaborate with the occupying Prussians in 1870 so Prince Hohenlowe let his troops pillage the cellars. In 1916 German artillery shelled the caves. In 1943 the boss of Piper-Heidsieck, the Marquis d'Aulan, and his staff hid in the cellars arms dropped by the RAF for the French Resistance. They were betrayed to the Nazis and mostly killed or deported to concentration camps. The Marquis escaped to North Africa, where he was killed as a pilot in the Free French Lafayette squadron. His son, Marquis François d'Aulan, now runs the company. The Queen Mum, it seems, drinks their Champagne rosé with soup, the Queen likes a sweeter Champagne after the meal, and Princess Diana doesn't drink it. That is what Prince Charles told the Marquis, anyway.

CHÂLONS-SUR-MARNE

Joseph Perrier

Cellars in a chalk quarry dug into the hillside by the Romans. The building is eighteenth-century with superb timbered reception room. Non-vintage wine is flowery, delicate and very easy to drink. Vintage wines are of very high standard. Queen Victoria drank it, so did Edward VII, and I am ready to wager which of them drank most. Well worth the phone call.

60 ave de Paris, 51000 Châlons-sur-Marne, tel.(26) 68.29.51. Visits and tastings but phone first. Monday–Friday 9–11 hrs; 16–17 hrs. Shut in August. Ask for secretary. English spoken.

Here are some leading Champagne houses which accept visitors, sell wine direct but do not necessarily offer a tasting glass. Or you may have to pay for it.

Bollinger

16 rue Jules Lobet, 51160 **Ay**, tel.(26) 55.15.11. Phone Monday–Friday office hours. Shut August.

Vineyards near Vertus

Deutz

16 rue Jeanson, 51160 Ay, tel.(26) 55.15.11. Phone Monday–Friday office hours. Shut August.

Canard Duchène

Ludes, 51500 Rilly-la-Montagne, tel.(26) 61.10.96. No need to phone. Monday–Friday 9–11.15 hrs; 14–16 hrs.

Société des Producteurs, Mailly Champagne

51500 **Rilly-la-Montagne**. No need to phone. From 1 May–30 September: Monday–Thursday and Saturday 9–11 hrs; 14–17 hrs; Sunday 15–17 hrs. 30 September–1 May: Monday–Friday 9–11 hrs; 14–17 hrs.

Laurent Perrier

Ave de Champagne, 51500 **Tours-sur-Marne**, tel.(26) 59.91.22. Phone. Monday–Thursday office hours. Shut in August.

G. H. Mumm

34 rue du Champ de Mars, 51100 **Reims**, tel.(26) 40.22.73. No need to phone. Monday–Friday 9–11 hrs; 14–17 hrs.

Veuve-Cliquot-Ponsardin

12 rue du Temple, 51100 Reims, tel.(26) 40.25.42. No need to phone but no tastings. You can buy. Visits 9–11 hrs; 14–17 hrs.

The Sparkling Widow was my first love in Champagne and I knew a Kentish Merry Widow who liked it so much she called her house 'Cliquot Cottage'. The widow Cliquot was only twenty-seven, and the Napoleonic Wars were at their height, when her husband died in 1805 and she took over. When she died in 1866 she had built it into one of the great Champagne houses, and it still is.

Charles Heidsieck

3 place des Droits de l'Homme, 51100 Reims, tel.(26) 85.03.27. Phone. Monday–Friday office hours. Shut August. Heidsieck Monopole, 83 rue Coquebert, 51100 Reims, tel.(26) 07.39.34. Phone. Monday–Friday. Shut August. There are a lot of Heidsiecks in Reims.

Lanson

12 bd Lundy, 51100 Reims, tel.(26) 40.36.26. Phone. Monday–Friday 9–11 hrs; 14–17 hrs. The one with the black label.

BOUZY

Maison E. Barnauto, R. Secondé-Chérier

13 rue Pasteur, 51150 Bouzy, tel.(26) 57.01.54 or (26) 59.01.54. Phone office hours.

A rare chance to try the red wine of the Champagne at the vineyard of the producer. In the same family father to son since 1874.

Further Information

Comité Interprofessionel du Vin de Champagne, 5 rue Henri Martin, 51200 Epernay, tel.(26) 54.47.20.
Office de Tourisme d'Epernay, place Mendès-France, 51200 Epernay, tel.(26) 55.33.00.
Office de Tourisme de Châlons-sur-Marne, place Godard, 51000 Châlons-sur-Marne, tel.(26) 65.17.89.
Office de Tourisme de Reims, 1 rue Jadart, 51100 Reims, tel.(26) 47.25.69.

In London
The Champagne Bureau, Malcolm McIntyre Ltd, Crusader House, 14 Pall Mall, London SW1Y 5LU, tel. 01-839 1416.

Food

The Champagne does not truly have many dishes of its own. It borrows from all the areas around, and the result can be successful. Avoid the tourist restaurants of Reims where gratin of frogs legs is almost compulsory as a starter, everything is cooked in Champagne (or alleged to be) and these days a sorbet of *marc de Champagne* is compulsory at some stage in the meal.

The cooking of the Ile de France is what most people used to regard as 'typically French' and Champagne borrows from it, but takes as much from the Germanic dishes of Alsace and Lorraine (including *potée*), the Flemish sausages and carbonnades of the North and especially from Northern Burgundy (*quenelles of pike*; *gougère* of flaky pastry with lumps of cheese).

There is a very good cured ham in Reims which, unlike the Ardennes ham from the North which is so delicious raw, they bake in pastry. As in the North, pâtés and terrines are wrapped in pastry.

There are several local cheeses. *Cendré de Champagne*, a very nice cheese matured in ash to reduce its fat content, is very rare now as it is made only on a few farms. It is soft with a nutty taste. *Caprice des Dieux* is a soft, mild double cream cheese, factory made. *Carré de l'Est* has a smell of mushrooms but is supple and bland. *Chaumont* is a delightful cheese made by farms and small dairies – a chopped-off cone with a spicy taste and strong smell. *Ervy-le-Châtel*, another truncated cone, is mild with a mushroomy smell. *Langres* is a cone with red-brown rind, strong smell and is nicely tangy. *Trappiste d'Igny*, made by monks of Igny Abbey, is mild and supple. The famous cheese is *chaource*, with its own AOC and fittingly eaten so much in Burgundy with AOC red wines that a lot of people think it comes from there. Some people call it a 'sort of Camembert' but frankly it is not in the same class as a good Camembert to me. It is made from the milk of three types of cow, and has been known since the fourteenth century.

Two other Champagne products are the *andouillette* sausage of Troyes, former capital of the Dukes of Champagne, and *biscuit de Reims*, a sort of macaroon eaten with sweeter Champagnes. And *coq au Bouzy* is *coq au vin* made with red Bouzy wine.

Hotels

Châlons-sur-Marne

Aux Armes de Champagne, L'Epine, 51000 Châlons-sur-Marne, tel.(26) 68.10.43. 8km E of Châlons on N8.

Truly excellent. Very comfortable. Very good traditional cooking loved by my *French Selection* readers, a superb wine list, and a bar where you can taste many Champagnes, including 'Thérèse Pérardel', cuvée of the hotel owner Jean-Paul Pérardel who is also a wine *négociant* and retailer. Next door is his Marché aux Vins with hundreds to choose from. Meals C–E; rooms C–M. Shut 5 January–12 February.

Angleterre et Restaurant Jacky Michel, 13 place
Monseigneur-Tissier, 51000 Châlons-sur-Marne,
tel.(26) 68.21.51.

Another Pérardel hotel, with a restaurant run
by the former chef of 'Armes de Champagne'.
Regional dishes and light modern. Forty-
three sparkling Champagnes and twenty still
Coteaux de Champagne and Bouzy wines.
Meals M–E; rooms C–M. Shut 1–21 July;
20 December–5 January; Saturday lunch,
Sunday.

Epernay

Royal Champagne, Champillon, 51160 Ay, Marne,
tel.(26) 51.11.51. 6km N from Epernay on N51.

Outstanding, attractive eighteenth-century
country hotel in vineyards; Michelin star.
Lovely views. Meals E; rooms M–E.

La Briqueterie, Vinay, 51200 Epernay, tel.(26)
54.11.22. 6km S of Epernay by N51.

Charming. Big garden. Good food. Pricey.
Meals E; rooms M–E. Shut 22 December–
3 January.

Relais de la Diligence, Hameau des Haies, 51160
Germaine-Hay, 51160 Ay, Marne, tel.(26) 52.33.69.
4km E of N51 between Epernay and Reims in heart
of Montagne de Reims.

Simple Logis de France. Good value. Meals
and rooms C. Shut 23 December–15 February. Wednesdays low season.

Reims

Boyer 'Les Crayères', 64 bd Henry Vasnier, 51100
Reims, tel.(26) 82.80.80.

Eugène Boyer moved to this Fin de Siècle
château in a seventeen-acre park overlooking
some of the great Champagne houses and has
taken with him his superb very personalised
cooking and his three Michelin stars. One of
the greatest chefs France has produced. Essential to book. Luxurious bedrooms with
superb service. Meals E; rooms E–VE. Shut
22 December–12 January. Restaurant shut
Monday; Tuesday lunch. His old restaurant,
now called Le Chardonnay, 184 avenue Epernay, Reims, tel.(26) 06.08.60, is still under his
wing, and serves old Burgundian dishes.
Michelin star, excellent value. Meals M. Shut
3 August–2 September; 20 December–13
January; Saturday lunch; Sunday.

Paix et Restaurant Le Drouet, 9 rue Buirette, 51100
Reims, tel.(26) 40.04.08.

Fairly new, largish, comfortable, useful hotel
in the heart of the city. Pool, garden. Meals C;
rooms C–M. Restaurant shut Sunday.

Sept-Saulx (23km SE from Reims by N44, then D8 left)

Cheval Blanc, Sept-Saulx, 51400 Mourmelon-le-
Grand, Marne, tel.(26) 61.60.27.

This country inn has become famous for its
cooking and is popular. Meals M–E; rooms
C–M. Shut mid January–mid February.

AREA 15

ALSACE

GEWÜRZTRAMINER · RIESLING · EDELZWICKER

Many French people take a superior attitude to Alsace. They have no idea of its beauty or its truly delightful old buildings, totally underestimate the wine and think that the cuisine is for German peasants. They know only Strasbourg and foie gras.

With the backcloth of the Vosges mountains, clothed in massed maple, beech and ash trees, and overlooking the vineyards across

the Rhine to the Black Forest, this is one of the loveliest wine areas of France. And although a lot of the beautiful old villages of steep-roofed houses with exposed beams and bright-coloured murals were destroyed in the fierce fighting of 1944, many were not. They are a joy to travellers lured here originally to taste the wine. Poor Ammerschwihr was largely laid waste: sixteenth-century Riquewihr was not and is a stunning village where growers who are also big shippers, like Hugel, have their offices. Here between bottles you can wander narrow cobbled streets lined with half-timbered houses, some with balconies bright with flowers.

The wines and cuisine of Alsace have been described as German materials made beautiful by French flair and know-how. Owner-ship has passed between the two countries many times. It was French from Louis XIV's reign until the end of the Franco-Prussian War in 1871 when the Germans annexed it, and it was French again in 1918, although Hitler took it back from 1940 until 1945. But it was French long before many areas of modern France. Under German rule, the wine makers of the Rhine and Moselle saw to it that Alsace should not compete with them. Noble grapes like Sylvaner and Gewürztraminer were banned. Only lesser grapes like Chasselas could be grown, to make blended plonk and to give extra alcohol to lighter German wines (as France used the vineyards of Languedoc Roussillon for so long). In 1945, to save the vineyards and help the stricken villages, communal wine co-operatives were formed to make the wine and market it. They are still strong and important, with more than 2,500 growers belonging to them. But they had a tough fight to re-establish Alsace wines after 1945. The Germans did not want their wines, and other French wine areas hardly encouraged them. Luckily, however, Britain, Holland, Belgium and Scandinavia were starved of wine and lapped up the dry whites of Alsace avidly.

Though there are some good growers in the north part of Alsace

(Bas Rhin) between Sélestat and Strasbourg, the best of the *Route de Vin* begins at St-Hippolyte and goes down to Thann, ending at lovely old Eguisheim. Partly because of the efforts of local growers to maintain Alsace standards and individuality under German rule, Colmar became the wine capital and still is. In the centre of a modern city it has blessedly kept its old city of timbered houses and narrow streets which is banned to cars.

Alsace wines are nearly all named after the grapes from which they are made, not the commune. Most Britons twin Alsace with the Riesling grape. In fact, only fifteen per cent of the vineyards are planted with it because of the difficulty in making a good Riesling wine with the exquisite fruitiness and delicate bouquet it should have. It is therefore only one of seven main grapes from which Alsace wines are made. Really good Riesling wines should be kept at least three years, up to seven or eight.

A fifth of Alsace wine is made from Sylvaner, a refreshing, light, slightly acidic wine which is easy to make, easy to drink and is drunk young. Sometimes it is *pétillant* (still fermenting a little), so is tingly on the tongue.

Pinot Blanc (often called Klevner locally) covers a bigger area than Riesling. Wines are heavier and more subtle than Sylvaner, but dry and fruity, and go well with any food that is not sweet. They are good value.

I love Muscat d'Alsace for drinking on its own. It is a dry white with a strong musky bouquet, like drinking straight grape juice. Don't mix it up with the sweet Muscat wines of the Midi. Not much is made and it tends to be dear.

Tokay d'Alsace is a fancy name for the Pinot Gris grape, and the wines have no relation to the sweet Hungarian Tokay. It is a heady white wine, full-bodied, rich, and improves in the bottle for three to five years. It lasts on the palate. A superb aperitif, it goes well with rich pâté (such as foie gras), chicken, turkey, duck or even roast beef.

Gewürztraminer is spicy (*Gewürz* means 'spice' in German)

and with its full bouquet is something to give to Auntie Flo who doesn't like wine very much. In my view it should only be drunk as an aperitif, with dessert, or iced for elevenses. It can also be taken with curry.

In hot years the wine gets sweeter and can reach fourteen per cent alcohol against nine per cent for other Alsace wines. That should make Auntie Flo giggle. But I was told when young: 'At first you will like sweeter wines. As your taste matures you will like them drier. Beware when you like sweeter wines again – it is galloping middle age!' It should be drunk when between two and four years old, except in special years when the grapes can be allowed to stay on the vines to become shrivelled and full of sugar (*vendange tardive* – the German *spätlese*). These wines can be kept for many years and are very expensive – quite a different proposition from the usual wines.

Alsace rosé wines are made from the Pinot Noir grape, which is also blended into the sparkling Crémant d'Alsace wines. Almost no red wines are made in Alsace – another reason for neglect by many French people while the strange fashion is to drink young red wines cold as aperitifs.

Alsace also makes a blended dry white wine Edelzwicker which can be lapped easily in litres, as can the simple Vin d'Alsace blend. Both of these usually contain Chasselas grapes or Muller-Thurgau, the Sylvaner-Riesling cross developed in Switzerland and the main grape of Southern England vineyards. But no more of these lesser vines may be planted in Alsace.

Alsace wines are very easy to drink, uncomplicated and deserve more popularity. We used to knock back so much in the 40s and 50s that the first drink on the morning after was called 'the hair of the Alsatian that bit me'.

Tastings

Willy Gisselbrecht

Pretty village with twelfth-century houses and town gates at the foot of the Vosges mountains. An old family business of growers, they also buy-in grapes to make the whole range of wines – Muscat, Pinot, Riesling, Sylvaner, Tokay d'Alsace and an outstanding Gewürztraminer for aperitifs or with desserts. Willy won the Grand Prix at Mâcon for his 1983 Riesling.

67650 **Dambach-la-Ville**, Alsace, tel.(88) 92.41.02. 9–12 hrs; 14–17.30 hrs.

Bott Frères

Vineyards (in same family since 1836) making all the Alsace wines and handling fruit spirits (Kirsch, Framboise Sauvage, etc.) and fruit liqueurs.

13 ave du Gén. de Gaulle, 68150 **Ribeauville**, Alsace, tel.(89) 73.60.48. 9–12 hrs; 14–18 hrs.

Cave Co-opérative de Ribeauville

Very important co-operative making all Alsace wines by modern methods and owners of one of the historic vineyards of France, Clos de Zahnacker, started by Benedictine monks in the ninth century. Later, Louis XIV was addicted to its wine. It covers 300 acres. Opposite the co-operative is their own Auberge zu Zahnacker with wine bar and restaurant serving Alsatian specialities (tel.(89) 47.60.77).

2 route Colmar, 68150 Ribeauville, tel.(89) 73.61.80. Outside the walls of the old town. Visits every day, including weekends 10–12 hrs; 14–17 hrs except January, February, March.

Cave Co-opérative de Hunawihr

Hamlet next to Ribeauville. Attractive tasting room or you can taste at an outside bar converted from a massive barrel. The co-operative produces prestigious wines such as Domaine de Windsbuhl and Rosacker. Also a Crémant sparkling wine by the Champagne method called Cuvée Calixte II.

68150 **Hunawihr**, tel.(89) 73.61.67. 9–12 hrs; 14–17 hrs.

Gustave Lorentz

The family have been in the wine business for 150 years and produce excellent wines from vineyards in the highly reputed Altenberg de Bergheim. Pleasant caves in delightful mediaeval village. Seven wines made. If you can still get '76 Gewürztraminer, buy it. It could convert even me to sweeter wines.

35 Grand'rue, 68750 **Bergheim**, tel.(89) 73.63.08. 8–12 hrs; 14–17 hrs. Phone if possible.

Hugel et Fils

The biggest name in Alsatian wines (growers, makers, shippers, wholesalers) yet still a smallish family firm after twelve generations. They classify some of their own wines according to quality of the vintage. Réserve Personnelle is very high quality, produced only in very great vintages. Vendange Tardive wines are made from special vintages, from grapes which have been allowed to over-ripen and are picked very late. They should be kept for years. For Sélection de Grains Nobles wines just about everything has to be perfect. Small quantities have been produced only in ten years since 1865. All wines are produced as naturally as possible. You'll love Cuvée les Amours – a Pinot Blanc – as delicate and rounded as a love should be. A cask made in 1715 (called Ste-Caterine) is still used for maturing the best wines. It holds nearly 12,000 bottles.

68340 **Riquewihr**, tel.(89) 47.92.15. Visits (30 minutes) with tasting July, August, September. Rest of year, phoning is essential, and visits depend on availability of personnel. But Easter–November a corner shop gives tastings and sells wine direct. Very much for the serious wine-lover. 8–12 hrs; 13.30–17.30 hrs Monday–Thursday; 8–12 hrs Friday. Shut weekends.

Dopff

Founded in 1574 and still run by the Dopff family personally. One of the great wine names of the world. They introduced sparkling wines (Crémant d'Alsace) made by the Champagne method and the long stemmed bottles which distinguish Alsace wines. Truly delicious and reliable wines.

'Au Moulin', 68340 Riquewihr, tel.(89) 47.92.23. 9–12 hrs; 14–18 hrs, including weekends in summer. English spoken.

An old house with exposed beams in Riquewihr

Dopff et Irion

Here, a branch of the Dopff family joined with another wine grower called Irion. They mature their wines in the cellars of the castle, which dates from 1549. Domaines du Château de Riquewihr from good vintages are some of the best wines of Alsace.

Château de Riquewihr, 68340 Riquewihr, tel.(89) 47.92.57. Visits with tasting 1 April–31 October every day 9–19 hrs. English spoken.

Maison Pierre Sparr

The ninth generation of Sparrs now growing grapes and making wine. They are also wine merchants. Some of the best wine of Alsace. Try Riesling Altenbourg and Sylvaner Réserve.

2 rue de la 1ère Armée, 68240 **Sigolsheim**, tel.(89) 78.24.22. Monday–Friday 9–12 hrs; 13.30–18.30 hrs. English spoken.

Caves J. B. Adam

Fourteen generations of Adams, from 1614, have produced wine here. They are known especially for the wine of this district, Le Kaefferkopf, one of the only two AOCs designated for a particular locality in Alsace, where wines are known by their grape type. A fruity wine with a strong bouquet.

5 rue de l'Aigle, 68770 **Ammerschwihr**, tel.(89) 78.23.21. Monday–Saturday 8–12 hrs; 14–18 hrs. English spoken.

Kuehn

Distinguished family who have held high positions locally for generations and have been in the wine business since 1695. Tastings are in seventeenth- and eighteenth-century cellars. The original house above belonged to the Kuehn family until it was destroyed in 1944. Luckily, the cellars and wine were saved, together with the local people who had hidden there, and the church statues. Their Kaefferkopf wines and their late-picked (Tardives) Gewürztraminer are much sought after.

7 Grand'rue, 68770 Ammerschwihr, tel.(89) 78.23.16. Monday–Friday 8–12 hrs; 13.30–17.30 hrs; Saturday in summer 9–12 hrs; 14–18 hrs. English spoken.

Domaine Viticole de la Ville de Colmar

When the Germans annexed Alsace-Lorraine in 1870 and treated the wines as 'plonk', the growers around Colmar formed the *Institut Oberlin* to protect and improve Alsace wines. The French Government has now taken over its research work – the vineyards and caves. All wines are brought-on in oak casks, even the sparkling Crémant. You will find good wines here.

2 rue du Stauffen, 68000 Colmar, tel.(89) 79.11.87. 8–12 hrs; 14–18 hrs.

Léon Beyer

One of the great wine families of Alsace, with vineyards passed from father to son since 1580! Enormous vaulted caves. It's almost impossible to buy their Tokay and Gewürztraminer Tardives (late picked) but the Gewürztraminer Comtes d'Eguisheim is a very nice aperitif or dessert wine and Riesling Cuvée d'Ecaillers is well above average. In a gorgeous little village 6km from Colmar.

2 rue de la 1ère Armée, 68420 **Eguisheim**, tel.(89) 41.41.05. Tasting cave for passing travellers open only office hours July–August; other times professionals or ardent amateurs must ring.

Maison Emile Beyer

Not so famous as the other Beyer but much easier to visit and a fair range of good wines at reasonable prices.

7 place du Château, 68420 Eguisheim, tel.(89) 41.40.45. 8–12 hrs; 13.30–18.30 hrs. No need to phone (except for groups).

Cave Vinicole de Pfaffenheim et Gueberschwihr

Good place for tastings. Two hundred and thirty member wine growers provide the grapes. They produce all Alsace wine-types and a good Crémant d'Alsace sparkler 'Hartenberger'. For Gueberschwihr, *see also* Le Relais du Vignoble under 'Hotels'.

68250 Rouffach, tel.(89) 49.61.08. Monday–Saturday 8–12 hrs; 14–19 hrs. Sunday 10–12 hrs; 14–18 hrs.

Vignobles P. Reinhart

Old-established, much-respected grower and wine maker who produces all Alsace wines.

7 rue Printemps, 68500 **Orschwihr**, tel.(89) 76.95.12. Every day 9–12 hrs; 14–20 hrs for tastings and sales; for visits to caves, phone.

Schlumberger

They make wine only from their own vineyard grapes, which is rare in Alsace, but with 350 acres of vines they are one of the largest owners in the area. The steep slopes and reddish sandy soil produce unusual wines, rather earthy but most attractive. Best wines are kept in bottle for two years before selling. Vineyards are said to date from the year 207AD under the Romans, and were owned by an abbey in the Middle Ages.

100 rue Théodore Deck, 68500 **Guebwiller**, tel.(89) 74.27.00. 8–12 hrs; 14–17 hrs. Phone if possible.

Further Information

Comité Interprofessionel des Vins d'Alsace, 8 place de Lattre-de-Tassigny, 68000 Colmar, Alsace.

Food

Alsatian dishes *are* nearly all hearty and not at all in line with Nouvelle Cuisine, except perhaps the foie gras of Strasbourg, served these days half raw when not in pâté. It is outrageously expensive and not worth the money, even if you can stomach the force-feeding of geese which makes their livers swell up to this size.

And it is no good pretending that the German occupation has not had an influence, either. *Sauerkraut* may be called *choucroute garnie* but it is the same cabbage pickled in layers with salt and cooked in wine for several hours and served with pork, sausages and perhaps a leg of goose. Many people add juniper berries, some use beer instead of wine.

Then there is *backenoffe*, a superb dish of marinaded pork, mutton and beef stewed in wine with potatoes and onions (gorgeously unfashionable), *flammekueche*, now sometimes called *tarte flambée* (open tart filled with bacon, onions, cream cheese and cream), *kassler* (rolled and smoked pork fillet), and *lewerknopfles* (the German *leberknödel* – liver dumplings, served in stews and goulash). Don't worry about Alsatian spellings. They speak and write their own dialect which, they will tell you, is *not* German, any more than Dutch is German. French is almost a 'second' language.

Riesling is used extensively in cooking, of course. *Coq au Riesling* is chicken in white wine and cream sauce with onions and mushrooms – accompanied, of course, by a good bottle of Riesling. *Côtes de porc à la Vosgienne* is pork chops with onions and plums cooked in white wine and wine vinegar.

My favourite pork pie is *Munster tourte*. Alsace is a pig area and the sausages and charcuterie are renowned, such as *saucisse de Strasbourg* (pork and beef), *knackwurst* (small frankfurters, a speciality of Colmar), *cervelas* (white sausage served often cold in a vinaigrette sauce), brawn, called variously *hure*, *kalerei* or *fromage de tête, schinken* (salted loin of pork), *schifela* (smoked pork shoulder, served if you are lucky with *navets confits* – pickled turnips).

With the Rhine and Inn rivers, and the mountain streams of the Vosges mountains, river fish are extremely popular and go well with the Alsatian wines. For example, trout *au bleu* (cooked here in a wine court bouillon with a tablespoon of vinegar, and served with Riesling, which you could not do if you used too much vinegar). Fish stew is made of trout, pike, perch and eel, cooked in Riesling with onions, carrots, leeks, thyme, bay, parsley, nutmeg, then with sour cream, court bouillon, eggs poured in to thicken the sauce and sliced mushrooms cooked for only two minutes. It is made very carefully, and served with – guess what? Riesling!

Munster cheese is so strong, tangy and powerful that it would kill Riesling, surely? Gewürztraminer I suggest.

For perfect accompaniments to Gewürztraminer, try Kirsch soufflé, *birewecke* (fruit bread made with dried pears, apples, plums, figs, orange peel, nuts and cinnamon, and a lot of Kirsch) and *kougelhopf* (cake with almonds and raisins).

The wine information office in Colmar (*see* Further Information) publishes a useful little book of Alsace recipes.

Hotels

Wettolsheim (4.5km SW from Colmar)

Auberge du Père Floranc, 9 rue Herzog, Wettolsheim, 68000 Colmar, tel.(89) 41.39.14.

Comfortable rooms; excellent cooking. Meals C–E; rooms C–M. Shut 1–16 July; mid November–mid December. Restaurant Sunday evening (out of season); Monday.

Rouffach

Château d'Isenbourg, Rouffach, 68250 Haut-Rhin, tel.(89) 49.63.53.

Nineteenth-century castle with views of vineyards. Very comfortable, lots of atmosphere, superb terrace swimming pool. Michelin star. Pricey. Meals and rooms E. Shut early January–8 March.

A La Ville De Lyon, 1 rue Poincaré, Rouffach, 68250 Haut-Rhin, tel.(89) 49.62.49.

Recommended by several *vignerons*. Meals C–E; rooms C. Shut mid January–mid February; restaurant shut Monday.

Ammerschwihr

Aux Armes de France, 1 Grande rue, Ammerschwihr, 68770 Haut-Rhin, tel.(89) 47.10.12.

Alsatian cooking does not seem to appeal much to the Gault-Millau Guide, the bible of 'Nouvelle', but the Gaertners get in with two *toques*. Not surprising. Father Pierre was a pupil of Point at La Pyramide (Vienne), son Philippe was with Bocuse (Collonges) and Boyer (Reims). Two stars in Michelin, too. No place to try traditional Alsatian cooking, but excellent and *very* pricey. Elegant furnishing. Meals E–VE; rooms M. Shut January; Thursday lunch, Wednesday.

L'Arbre Vert, Ammerschwihr, 68770 Haut-Rhin, tel.(89) 47.12.23.

Recommended by *vignerons*. Simple logis with 'good local cooking'. Meals and rooms C–M. Shut 20 November–10 December; 10 February–25 March; Tuesday.

Andolsheim (6km E of Colmar on N415)

Soleil, 1 rue de Colmar, Andolsheim, 68600 Neuf-Brisach, Haut-Rhin, tel.(89) 71.40.53.

Good food, good wine list. Alsatian dishes like pheasant and red cabbage. Meals C–M; rooms C. Shut February; Wednesday.

Ribeauville

Clos St-Vincent, Ribeauville, 68150 Haut-Rhin, tel.(89) 73.67.65; 1.5km NE.

Pricey but gorgeous inn above a hillside of vineyards, with views to Germany. Patron-chef Bertrand Chapotin was manager of the Café de la Paix in Paris. Book ahead; small restaurant. Super service. Splendid place for a weekend with a loving and wine-loving partner. Meals and rooms E. Open early March–mid November. Restaurant shut Tuesday, Wednesday.

Gueberschwihr

Relais du Vignoble (Restaurant Bellevue), 13 rue Forgerons, 68420 Gueberschwihr, tel.(89) 49.22.22. 11km from Colmar.

A discovery. A Logis in a new but attractive building in the vineyards, with views of the Vosges mountains and Black Forest. Pleasantly furnished. Alsatian dishes and wines from the vineyards of the chef-patron. You can also taste wine in his thirteenth-century cellars. Meals and rooms C–M. Excellent value. Shut February; Thursday.

Murbach (5km from Guebwiller)

Hostellerie Saint-Barnabé, Murbach, 68530 Buhl, tel.(89) 76.92.15.

On edge of forest, classical cooking, excellent wine list. Very tempting. Meals C–E; rooms C–M.

Colette, who wrote so convincingly about desire, also wrote passionately and knowledgeably about Loire wines. Many, like the Loire castles built for love and intrigue rather than war, are delicate and seductive. But they vary from year to year, and from place to place in any one year. 1985, for instance, was generally a very good year for white wines and a superb year for Vouvray.

Most of us think of Loire wine as white, but the reds of Chinon and Bourgueil in particular have not only improved but are becoming popular on Paris wine lists. The owner of a Michelin-starred hotel on the Seine told me recently: 'I am buying Chinon. Let the Americans have the Burgundy and the British their Bordeaux – too dear!'

Apart from the remoter Sancerre–Pouilly-sur-Loire area (*see* Area 13), where the Sauvignon grape is used extensively for white wines, the main Loire grape, until you reach the Muscadet area, is Chenin Blanc (also called Pineau de la Loire). From this grape can come wines which are fruitily dry, luscious when *demi-sec*

Below left: statue of Rabelais by the river in Chinon

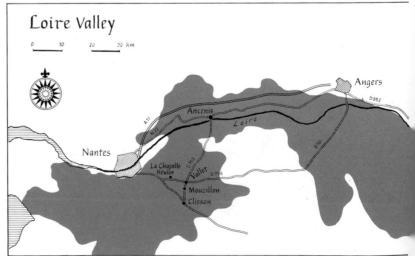

(slightly sweet), richly sweet, or sparkling. When made well, they are delightful. Made badly, they can produce something akin to battery acid. But Sauvignon has strayed successfully to Touraine, and Sauvignon de Touraine is being bought by the knowledgeable to replace dearer Sancerre. Some growers are producing reds from Gamay grapes, strayed from Beaujolais and Sancerre, but most, in my view, are inferior to local wines made from grapes of the Cabernet family – Touraine Mesland from north of the river and Touraine Amboise from around Amboise – AOC wines, with concentrated flavour, though a tiny bit rough when under three years old. These young wines, as with Chinon, are drunk cold but not iced, to preserve the fruit taste.

The good growers in Vouvray make flowery white wines of delicacy and finesse which can be drunk young or kept at least five years and in good years for over ten. The dry and *demi-sec* are lovely as an aperitif, with hors d'oeuvres and with light or subtle fish, especially salmon. The sweeter wines which can be kept thirty or forty years in a good year, can be as luscious as Sauternes

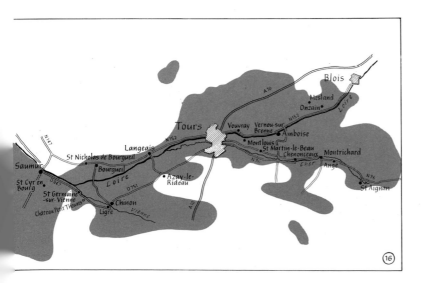

and are superb with strawberries or raspberries. Serve all Vouvray chilled but not iced like Muscadet.

Red, rosé and a few white wines are grown around Chinon on the south bank of the Loire and both banks of the river Vienne. The red is made mostly from the Cabernet Franc grape (called locally Le Breton). A clean, fruity wine, it has a flowery smell of what the trade calls 'violets' and should have a beautiful ruby colour. Smoother than most other Loire reds (and dearer) it is pleasant drunk young at cellar temperature to taste the fruit but can be a revelation in good years when kept for five years or so and drunk at room temperature.

Bourgueil red is made mostly from Cabernet Franc, though some is made from Cabernet Sauvignon on which most of the best Bordeaux wines are based. On different soils, two types of wine are produced – one is light and fruity, with a pleasant smell of raspberries, and the other is heavier and needs time to mature. Often the two are blended, producing a wine which when kept up to ten years produces a most satisfying drink with a clean, no-tannin taste but enough acidity to keep it from collapsing. The kinship to Médoc allowed these wines to be blended into Bordeaux many years back. For years my friends and I drunk Bourgueil as we drunk Cahors, congratulating ourselves on our secret bargain. But a Parisian fashion for the wines a few years back pushed the price up a bit. It is still good value, though. St-Nicolas-de-Bourgueil wines are said to keep best. Some Chinon and Bourgueil producers have cashed in on the Beaujolais Nouveau fashion, selling new 'Primeur' wine in November to get instant cash. Don't fall for it. The Cabernet grape is unsuitable. You will get little but indigestion.

The first fizzy wine to be made by the Champagne method outside Champagne was made in Saumur in 1811. It is still rated as one of the very best substitute Champagnes – if there *is* a substitute.

Muscadet wine is called after its grape, which originated in

Château de Petit
Thouars

Burgundy and is no longer grown there. At its best it is still a delightfully refreshing drink, with grapiness, a lasting flavour and even delicacy. But it has suffered from fashion and over-popularity in France and Britain, and some rough stuff appeared a few years back which suggested that AOC rules were being stretched. Now, trying to get rid of honest acidity, some makers are producing bland, dull wine ('collapsed'). The best comes from around Vallet, Clisson and Le Ballet in Sèvre et Maine. Muscadet-sur-lie means that it has been bottled straight off its lees (pips, skins, etc.) after fermentation and not racked. This gives it more flavour. Muscadet des Coteaux de la Loire is often heavy and uninteresting. Look for Sèvre et Maine wines. Sixty-five million bottles are produced in France each year. Only Beaujolais beats that.

In the Muscadet area, Gros Plant is produced from a grape of the same name. It can be called light, dry, fruity and refreshing or just tart and acidic, which is my verdict. It is a VDQS wine.

Tastings

TOURAINE

Château du Petit-Thouars

The Counts of Petit-Thouars have owned and made wine at this entrancing château with fairy-tale turrets since the sixteenth century. It is in a beautiful position overlooking the river. One Count fought the Moors at the Battle of Aboukir, then went off to fight the English in the American War of Independence. Another kept us out of Tahiti. The present Count, Comte Yves du Petit-Thouars, sells his wine all over France and would like the British to drink more of it. He is also writing a book about Wine and Women in France. His caves cut in the hillside are a delight. His wine is made entirely from Cabernet Franc grapes and matured for a year in old chestnut barrels. It is one of the best of many Touraine AOCs I know, and most years are worth keeping for three years, though they are usually drunk young.

St-Germain-sur-Vienne, 37500 Chinon tel.(47) 95.96.40. Take D751 W from Chinon along S bank of Vienne river for 10km. Petit-Thouars is on the left (marked on yellow Michelin). Ask for Mme Boissinot, wife of the Maître de Chai. 10–12 hrs; 14–18 hrs.

Jacky Charbonnier

A young, enthusiastic small producer, with one and a half hectares of vines and an unprepossessing cave like a big garage, Jacky Charbonnier produces a fruity, not too acidic Cabernet which improves up to three years and is excellent value. The '83 we bought in 1986 to take home cost us £1 a bottle. The '85 is already better. He makes also white, rosé, and a very fair Touraine Mousseux sparkling white, buying in grapes from other growers. I found his Gamay red too sharp. They speak no English but it's all friendly and you can get by.

Le Biard, Angé, 41400 Montrichard tel.(54) 32.10.06. Take N76 E from Chenonceaux, then little D17 on right just before Montrichard. Outside long modern chalet on left at Angé is a small notice 'Jacky Charbonnier – Vins'. 9–18 hrs.

J. P. Monmousseau

Big *négociants* now owned by Taittinger, though a fourth-generation Monmousseau is still President. Cellars are 13km long! Formal tasting room with a range of twenty good wines, from all the Loire. I recommend the sparkling Blanc de Blancs matured in the bottle for eighteen months, made by the Champagne method and called 'Cuvée J.M.93' because the founder, J. M. Monmousseau lived to be ninety-three by drinking it!

Route de Vierzon, BP 25, 41401 Montrichard tel.(54) 32.07.04. Big plant on left going E out of Montrichard to St-Aignan. 9–11.30 hrs; 14–18.30 hrs. Notice needed for groups. Half-hour tour of cellars possible.

Philippe Brossillon

The Brossillon family have produced wine on their thirty hectares for more than two hundred years. The family all speak English. Touraine-Mesland AOC wines have character, and are often fruitier but with more acid than wines of Touraine-Amboise. Philippe Brossillon's wines are well above average. If you like a dry rosé, try his Rosé Sec de Gamay.

Domaine de Lusqueneau, Mesland, 41150 Onzain tel.(54) 70.28.23. Mesland is just N of the Loire, across bridge from Chaumont, 4km NW of Onzain. 8–12 hrs; 14–18 hrs. English spoken.

Dutertre Père et Fils

The family has produced white, red and rosé for generations. Both the AOC Touraine-Amboise and Touraine have won many medals and are some of the best value in the area.

20 rue d'Enfer, place du Tertre, 37400 Limeray tel.(47) 30.10.69. Take N152 NE from Amboise for 5km, then left on D201 (2km). 8–19 hrs. Notice for groups.

J.-C. Poupault

Along the D751 from Amboise beside the Loire, north-east towards Chaumont, is a series of caves cut in the rock where Récoltants offer wines for tasting and sale. Getting drunk within 10km would be no problem. Prices are low but wines not necessarily of the best. This is one of the better caves.

1 rue de la Loire, Chargé, 37530 Amboise tel.(47) 57.53.71.

Clos de St-Fiacre

Orléans used to be a big wine area. The factories increase and vineyards diminish annually. At this *clos* try VDQS de l'Orléannais – Cabernet, Auvernat Noir (Pinot), Auvernat Blanc (Chardonnay) and Gris Meunier (fruity rosé).

560 rue de St-Fiacre, Mareau aux Prés, 45370 Cléry-St-André tel.(38) 45.61.55. 8km SW Orléans; 5km from Cléry. All Saturday, Sunday afternoon, and 15.30–19.30 hrs Monday, Tuesday, Thursday.

James Paget

If you are visiting the fairy-tale castle of Ussé, inspiration for the story of 'The Sleeping Beauty', or the magnificent château at Azay-le-Rideau (both 7km away), take a risk on dropping in, if you cannot phone, and try the Touraine–Azay-le-Rideau AOC white made from Pineau grapes and the rosé made mostly from Groslot – both of them are slightly sweet wines, good for light meals or picnics. Little is produced, and few Britons or Americans know the wine, so take it home and try it on Liebfrau-lovers.

Armentières, Rivarennes, 37190 Azay-le-Rideau tel.(47) 95.54.02. On D7 SW from Tours or over the bridge at Langeais and turn right. 9–20 hrs. Notice preferred. No English spoken (even with a name like this).

Further Information

Comité Interprofessionel des Vins de Touraine, 19 square Prosper Mérimée, 37000 Tours tel.(47) 05.40.01.

Azay le Rideau

VOUVRAY AND MONTLOUIS

Daniel Jarry

Daniel Jarry's 1985 dry and *demi-sec* white wines were so superb in their fruity smell and flowery taste that he knew right away that it was a great vintage which would keep for five, ten or more years. But he had a space problem as so many of his wines were worthy of keeping for at least three–five years. His solution was simply to cut deeper and deeper into the chalk hillside, making his caves bigger. He is one of the great small wine makers of Vouvray whose families have thrived here for centuries. To grow, make, bottle and care for his wines he has just the family and two employees. He is rightly proud of his wines, especially those which keep so superbly. I have tasted his *demi-sec* wines from the '60s and '70s and they are magnificent now. A wonderful contrast of nectar and

La Caillerie, route de la Vallée Coquette, 37210 Vouvray tel.(47) 52.78.75. After the N152 (going E) dips under the motorway at Tours, drive on for 6km watching for a tiny road on the left marked 'Vallée Coquette' (see yellow Michelin). The Jarry caves are 1000 metres up this road on the right. 9–19 hrs. Notice needed for groups.

fruit. The recent wines, with their lovely long-lasting flavour and subtlety, make you wonder where some British wine merchants buy their Vouvray. If you can get any '85 from him, buy it and keep it until at least 1992, or preferably to celebrate the arrival of the twenty-first century! He does not speak English, but his daughter (a student at Tours University) does and is often there.

Cave Co-operative des Producteurs des Grands Vin de Vouvray

Fifty wine growers got together in 1953 to improve their wines. They make their own wine. Then a tasting commission chooses the best for blending and bottling at the co-operative in March. You pay for tasting wine. The selection and value are good.

La Vallée Coquette, 37210 Vouvray tel.(47) 52.75.03. 250 metres before Jarry, on the opposite side of road. Also has a tasting and selling shop on corner of N152 and D47 to Vouvray. 8.30–12 hrs; 14–18 hrs (including Saturday, Sunday). No English spoken, but tasting and ordering are easy because of cards and lists.

Gilles Champion

A truly rural cave in the family for generations. Someone will find you a glass of wine. The dry white I tasted was very pale but deliciously fruity. The *demi-sec* also had a beautifully fruity flavour and a long-lasting taste unusual in a young wine. I look forward to trying some older wines.

Vallée de Cousse, Vernou, 37210 Vouvray tel.(47) 52.02.38. Take D46 from Vouvray through Vernou-sur-Brenne. 3km along take D62 through Vallée des Vaux to Vallée de Cousse. Keep going, despite the road condition – it's a little place on the right. Open every day.

Marc Bredif

A world famous company of *éleveurs* who buy wine to blend, bottle and mature. The wines are blended in glass-lined vats then kept for a month in wood. Known for old wines, they have vintages dating back to the late nineteenth century in their kilometre of caves. Cellar tours. Collection of wine presses and old bottles. Bought in 1980 by Patrick de Ladoucette, producer of Pouilly-Fumé.

87 quai de la Loire, Rochecorbon, 37210 Vouvray tel.(47) 52.50.07. Just outside Tours. Follow N152 under motorway. Rochecorbon is on the left 3km onwards. Bredif are towards Vouvray. Monday–Friday at 10.30 hrs and 16 hrs. English spoken.

Gaston Huet

If you have decided to take home Vouvray, here is a great place to buy it. Old *moelleux* wine has been described as 'like having a bouquet of flowers in your mouth'.

Le Haut Lieu, 37210 Vouvray tel.(47) 52.78.82. Edge of Vouvray. Monday–Saturday 9–12 hrs; 14–18 hrs. Tastings for buyers only.

Cave Co-operative des Producteurs de Vin de Montlouis

A new tasting room above fine old caves. Montlouis is almost opposite Vouvray across the Loire and was sold as Vouvray until 1938. Like Vouvray, it is made only from the Pineau (Chenin) grape. But some dry wines can be acidic when young and neither the dry nor the *demi-sec* becomes so luscious with age. Good wines have a delightful lemon and honeysuckle taste, are soft, and

37270 Montlouis tel.(47) 50.80.98. On the corner of N751 and D40 road to Chenonceaux, just after passing Montlouis on way to Amboise. Every day 8–12 hrs; 14–18 hrs.

Opposite above: *Daniel Jarry's cellar.*

Left: *caves cut into the hillside at the Cave Co-operative des Producteurs de Vin de Montlouis*

can be kept some time. They are cheaper than Vouvray and good value. A fully sweet (*liquoreux*) wine is produced, but much wine goes to making semi-sparkling (*crémant*) and sparkling wines by the Champagne method. Not much reaches Britain.

Berger Frères

Excellent producer of Montlouis wines. Vines get maximum sun exposure by being grown on unobstructed gravel-layered soil. Modern equipment with enamelled stainless steel vats and wooden barrels. One of the few Montlouis wines shipped to Britain. Their Champagne method sparkling wine is recommended.

Caves des Liards, St-Martin-Le-Beau, 37270 Montlouis tel.(47) 50.67.36. Take D751 E from Montlouis then D40. 8–12 hrs; 14–19 hrs. Notice by phone preferred; essential for groups. Ask for Mme Berger. Laurent Berger (son) speaks English.

CHINON, BOURGUEIL AND SAUMUR

Château de Ligré

Gatien Ferrand, who lives in this fine old house with his family, is the dynamic flag-carrier for Chinon wines and his son Pierre an outstanding wine maker. They have modernised the equipment and produce excellent red wines which are vital, full, subtle, well constituted and age superbly. Whites are fine and fruity. A busy place, with many professional visitors, so you will be received politely but not cossetted. Local lad Rabelais, the sixteenth-century writer and devotee of good food and wine, would have approved of these wines.

Ligré, 37500 Chinon tel.(47) 93.16.70. Cross Vienne river at Chinon on D749, follow E for 9km towards Richelieu. Right on D26 for 2km, then left for Château (on left). Monday–Saturday 10–12 hrs; 15–17 hrs.

Paul Dozon

Excellent wines, with fruity tastes of strawberries and red-currants, but normally sold in cases of twelve or multiples, and 32-litre containers for bottling at home (good value, even with duty and VAT paid).

Clos du Saint au Loup, Ligré, 37500 Chinon tel.(47) 93.26.38. D749 across Vienne from Chinon for 3km. Left on D115. Vineyards are both sides of first left turn, caves are along third left turn to Ligré. 9–18 hrs.

Maison Couly-Dutheil

The family owns several vineyards around here, including Clos de l'Echo which once belonged to Rabelais' family. They produce what I think is the best of Chinon – a full-bodied fruity wine which requires long ageing in cask. Greatest vintages produce a superb wine called Baronnie Madeleine. Inevitably pricey, but a new experience. Try also Domaine du Puy but keep it until it's about five years old.

12 rue Diderot, 37502 Chinon tel.(47) 93.05.84. Notify by phone but worth it.

Le Thélème

A very useful place for tasting and buying. Wines of all areas at very reasonable prices but strong, of course, in Chinon and AOC Touraine. For generous glasses or half bottles you pay about 3–9F. I do not mind this. It saves embarrassment if I don't want to buy. You can also taste and buy cheeses and Loire specialities. Little restaurant attached open 12–15 hrs; 19–22.30 hrs (last orders) but closed Monday evening, Tuesday lunch.

7 place Mirabeau, 37500 Chinon tel.(47) 93.49.39. In town. Tastings in wine bar 11–20 hrs.

Cave Touristique de la Dive Bouteille

Maison Audebert et Fils

As well as growing in several vineyards covering twenty-eight hectares in Bourgueil and the neighbouring village of St-Nicolas-de-Bourgueil, this old-established house raises or sells other growers' wines from these appellations, from Chinon, and from Saumur Champigny. Its Domaine de Grand Clos produces a balanced wine, fruity and delicate, strong and full bodied – all that Bourgueil should be. Wines from Les Marquises have just enough tannin to make them keep well and improve with age. All are Cabernet Franc, used for nearly all Bourgueil wines.

Avenue Jean Causeret, 37140 Bourgueil tel.(47) 97.70.06. In town. Preferable to phone, but not essential. 8–12 hrs; 14–18 hrs. English spoken.

Cave Touristique de la Dive Bouteille

A cave set up by dozens of local growers and wholesalers. The ancient cave is charmingly illuminated and includes big wooden wine presses dating back to the fourteenth century. You pay 9F (1986) for the visit and tasting of one glass of good wine.

37140 Bourgueil tel.(47) 97.72.01. At Chevrette, ½km N from Bourgueil village by lane across D35. Open 10–12.30 hrs; 14–18 hrs (or 19.30 hrs from May to end of September); shut December–January.

Ackerman-Laurance

In 1811 Jean Ackerman from Alsace introduced the Champagne method of making sparkling wine – the first time it had been done outside Champagne. The natural caves are almost ideal. You may well have seen Frank Bough quaffing a bottle for the BBC *Holiday* programme when he followed a route of my *Travellers' France*. He is still enthusiastic, although he prefers a vintage Bollinger. (So do I – but look at the price gap!) This Ackerman Brut Royal is a very good wine. Some still Saumur AOC white wines are made, and Ackerman-Laurance deal in good Loire wines from a Muscadet to a Touraine Sauvignon which retired operatic tenor Michael Kehoe (Parma, Covent Garden, Munich, etc.), turned vintner in my neighbouring Kent village, imports for me for the sake of my voice.

St-Hilaire-St-Florent, 49210 Saumur tel.(41) 50.23.33). Suburb of Saumur on south bank of Loire, 3km along D751 towards Angers. Open 1 May–30 September, 9.30–11.30 hrs; 15–17 hrs including weekends. Guided tour.

Bouvet-Ladubay

Impressive galleries in rocks. Started producing Champagne-method wines in 1851. Now owned by Monmousseau of Montrichard, who are owned by Taittinger of Champagne. Cuvée Bouvet Brut Saphir is a smooth, light wine with delicate fruity taste.

Rue Ackerman, St-Hilaire-St-Florent (*see* Ackerman-Laurance above) tel.(41) 50.11.12). Open 1 June–30 September 9–12 hrs; 15–17 hrs. Notice appreciated; essential for groups.

Gratien et Meyer

A veritable underground town, with lovely views across the river when you emerge. House founded in 1864, now tied up with Champagne firm. Lively, interesting sparkling wine by Champagne method made with two parts of white Pineau de Loire grapes to one of black grapes – Cabernet and Groslot. The Crémant de Loire (slightly less sparkling) won a gold medal at the great Mâcon Wine Fair in 1983 – any maker's ambition.

Château de Beaulieu, route de Montsoreau, 49400 Saumur tel.(41) 51.01.54. On D947, S bank of Loire, 3km E of Saumur on Chinon road. Open every day 9–11.30 hrs; 14–17.30 hrs. Highly organised. English-speaking guides.

Cave Co-opérative des Vignerons

This co-operative in vast caves under the hill was created by 230 wine growers in 1957. You go round in cars. They make a very agreeable, fruity sparkling wine, and a good Saumur-Champigny – a charming Cabernet red with a raspberry smell, purple and a bit earthy when young, becoming smooth and deep red with age. A firm finish, as the experts say, which means that it's a bit tannic for some of us. But my favourite among Anjou and Saumur reds.

St-Cyr-en-Bourg, 19260 Montreuil-Bellay tel.(41) 51.61.09. Just off D93, 10km S of Saumur. Open 1 May–30 September.

Further Information

Maison de Vin de Saumur, 25–27 rue Beaurepère, 49400 Saumur; Maison de Vin de l'Anjou, 5 bis place Kennedy, 49000 Angers.

MUSCADET

Finding specific vineyards in villages of the Nantaise has become more difficult since the N249 road east from Nantes through Vallet to Cholet became a dual carriageway, with very few turn-offs. Nearly all local roads are on flyovers. But dozens of little growers offer *Dégustations et Vente Directe* (Tastings and Direct Sales) shown on boards outside. Best roads for these are: D756 Vallet W to Chapelle-Heulin (try Chevallier Frères on left) and N149 from north of Clisson to Le Pallet. Several are around La Haye-Fouassière (just off N149, 9km past Le Pallet). Here also is the official *Maison des Vins du Pays Nantais, Bellevue, 44690 La Haye-Fouassière*, tel.(40) 36.90.10, offering tastings and information.

You can also get information and taste wine in Nantes at Comité Interprofessionel des Vins du Pays Nantais, 17 rue des Etats, 44000 Nantes tel.(40) 47.15.58, across rue des Etats from the Pont Levis of the Château.

Les Vignerons de la Noëlle

A group of producers from the Nantes area (Muscadet, Gros Plant, Coteaux d'Ancenis), Anjou (Cabernet d'Anjou rosé, Rosé d'Anjou and de Loire, Anjou Rouge Cabernet), Chinon, Bourgueil and Touraine, and Sancerre (white) make wines here by the most modern methods with superb equipment. In 1985 they exported 360,000 bottles to Britain. Take a rare chance to try lesser-known, cheaper wines. Crémant de Loire Anjou (AOC Champagne method) is half sparkling and refreshing. Coteaux d'Ancenis is a VDQS wine (can also be white or rosé) which must show the grape type on the label. Light, refreshing, fruity, minimum of ten per cent alcohol. With so many wines to taste, you might dream of a glorious free booze-up. Alas, the Director (M. Dejean) says regretfully: *Dégustations – Quantités Limitées* (tastings limited in number).

BP 102, 44150 Ancenis tel.(40) 98.92.72. Huge building plainly marked in Ancenis, NE of Nantes, with bridge over Loire. It is on the ring-road marked '1' on Michelin yellow map. Coming from N (N923 or A11 motorway) turn left on this *Poids Lourds* deviation road and it is on right near railway bridge. From S (D763) cross bridge and turn right immediately. Caves on left. 8–17 hrs.

Fleurance et Fils

One of the greatest Muscadets, produced by a family who have been *vignerons* since the seventeenth century. Produced in wood, the wines are full bodied, concentrated, fresh on the palate, floral – old-style Muscadet. I would like a cask of Fleurance for Christmas please – one containing 600 litres. Gros Plant well above average, too.

Domaine des Gautronnières, 44330 La Chapelle Heulin tel.(40) 06.74.06. From Vallet on D756; at Chapelle Heulin turn left (or ask). 9–12 hrs; 14.30–19 hrs.

Château de la Noë de Bel Air

Le Comte de Malestroit's family have lived and made good wine here since 1741. Their château was burned down in the Revolution and was replaced in 1836 by an elegant Palladian-style house. In 1960 the present count put his wines on the market and they became famous around the world, especially in the great clubs of Paris.

44330 Vallet tel.(40) 33.92.72. On D756 Vallet to Chapelle Heulin road (marked on yellow Michelin). Phone first.

Pierre Lusseaud

One of the best-loved Muscadets in Britain. Large Domaine producing very top quality wine with character and true flavour by modern methods. Fermentation for three to four weeks. A favourite of mine.

La Galissonnière, Le Pallet, 44330 Vallet tel.(40) 26.42.03. N149 NW from Clisson (7km) or D116 from just S of Vallet (6km). 9–12 hrs; 14–18 hrs. English spoken.

Futeul Frères

The Romans, who introduced wine here, also built a temple to Mercury, hence the name. Wine-making restarted in 1350. Muscadet and a white *Vin de Pays* are made. Normally sold in cases of twelve.

Château de la Mercredière, Le Pallet, 44330 Vallet tel.(40) 54.80.10. For location *see* Pierre Lusseaud above. Monday–Friday 9–12 hrs; 14–18 hrs except 10–25 August.

Sauvion et Fils

Grandpa Sauvion bought this historic château in 1935. Now son Ernest, helped by three of *his* sons, runs it with efficiency, exuberance and flair. Locally, the firm is called '4 S'. Big, bearded Jean-Ernest makes the excellent wine *sur lie* vital, lively, flowery and reliable. The Sauvions are also *négociants* and each year pick their ten *Découvertes* (Discoveries) of outstanding Muscadets, which they market. Then a tasting jury decides which is the wine of the year – called the 'Cardinal Richard', after a previous owner. The château was burned in the Vendéen religious wars. It belonged to the same family as La Noë de Bel Air. The old caves are perfect for keeping wine.

Château du Cléray, BP 3, 44330 Vallet tel.(40) 36.22.55. The new dual carriageway N249 E from Vallet has few turn-offs to villages, so you must make a deviation. Take D756 E from Vallet, then little 'white' road D106 left at Chalbouière over the N249; at first crossroads go left, back over N249. You will soon see the sign of Château du Cléray. 8.30–12 hrs; 14.30–18 hrs. English spoken.

Marcel Martin

A reliable property where wine has been made for 100 years.

La Sablette de Mouzillon, 44330 Vallet tel.(40) 33.94.84. S from Vallet 2km past Mouzillon take D25 left for 4km. Monday–Thursday 8–12 hrs; 14–18 hrs.

Guilbaud Frères

World-renowned blenders, bottlers and *éleveurs* of excellent wines, including Domaine du Grand-Fief and Domaines des Laudières.

Mouzillon, 44330 tel.(40) 36.30.55. On D763, 4km S of Vallet. 8–12 hrs; 14–17 hrs.

Food

Loire cooking tends to be traditional and simple because of the fine fresh food in the markets. When you have superb asparagus, artichokes, young carrots, cabbages, cauliflowers, celery and courgettes, the leeks of the Loire Atlantique, crispy lettuces and plump little shallots, you are not likely to be satisfied with slivers of vegetables as mere décor; when you have Reinette apples and Chasselas and Comice pears piled high on stalls, apricots, peaches, quinces and some of the best raspberries and straw-berries in the world, plus prunes which make nonsense of our shrivelled little midgets, you will settle for featherlight puff pastry tarts filled with these succulent fruits or *tarte tatin*, the caramel-ised upside-down apple pie invented in a Lamotte-Beuvron inn snubbed by modern guide books; forget passion fruit sorbet.

If cream and mushroom sauces come regularly with your fish, chicken or *pintade* (guinea-fowl), it is not lack of 'inventiveness' (that word beloved of fashion food writers). Mushrooms were grown in Loire caves even before wine was matured in them, and Champignons de Paris have long since come from the Loire, not from the caves under the suburban streets of Paris. And the woods of Orléans are rich in delightful fungi – cèpes, girolles and many bolets types. A cèpe omelette is a fine companion for a bottle of dry Vouvray or Touraine Sauvignon. Nantes and the small fishing ports will provide the shellfish for your fruity Muscadet (under three years old, please), the rivers Loire, Cher, Loir and Loiret will provide delicate *sandre* (pike-perch) served with a superb *beurre blanc*, made of shallots and butter; or *quenelles de brochet* (little mousses of pike in a cream sauce) or *fritures de la Loire* (deep fried young river fish). All these are worthy of Vouvray or Sauvignon. But for a younger *demi-sec* Vouvray order some fine fresh salmon. Lamb which comes into the Loire from the salt marshes of the Vendée would rate a young red Chinon, drunk at cellar tempera-

ture; so would the fine ham of Amboise or the *rillons* of Tours (crisp and crunchy squares of fried pork – unlike *rillettes*, cooked pork pounded into a pâté spread). The old wines of Chinon and Bourgueil go best with beef from Charentes, game from the Sologne and the many cheeses of the Loire mild Chavignol goat cheeses such as Crezancy, Selles-sur-Cher, Valençay, Montoire, Tournon, Troo, tangier goat cheeses like Graçay, Ste-Maure (superb when 'fermier', from farm, not factory), Laval cow's milk cheese made by Trappist monks, *Olivet bleu* (excellent cow's milk blue) and *pannes cendré* (low fat strong cow's milk cheese matured in wood ashes). Or you could splash out on a bottle of old, sweet Vouvray for the cheese and finish it with the sweet.

Regional specialities worth trying are *haricot de mouton* (mutton and vegetable stew), *gouguenioche* (chicken and egg pie), *pistoles* (mirabelle plums of Blois turned into prunes), nut oil of Tours or Ste-Maure for salads, *saucisses au Muscadet* (pork sausages made with Muscadet, served with chestnut purée – *purée de marrons*), *gâteau de Pithiviers* (almond cream flavoured with rum in puff pastry), *cotignac* (quince cheese from Orléans – a sweet long believed to be a hangover cure!). Avoid *pâté de Pithiviers* (whole larks in pastry). Soak those big Blois prunes in Vouvray overnight and eat them with cream for breakfast! Or dessert later, of course.

Hotels

Olivet

Le Rivage, 635 rue Reine Blanche, Olivet 45160, Loiret (5km SW of Orléans), tel.(38) 63.48.48.

Typical old Loire restaurant and hotel overlooking Loiret river. I found it when I was young. Now it's famous. Meals E; rooms M. Shut February.

Onzain

Domaine des Hauts de Loire, Onzain 41150, Loir-et-Cher (17km NE of Amboise – cross Loire at Chaumont), tel.(54) 20.72.57.

Superb old turreted hunting lodge in park with lake. Beautiful furniture. Meals E; rooms VE. Open 15 March–1 December.

Pont d'Ouchet, Onzain, Loir-et-Cher (centre of village), tel.(54) 20.70.33.

Simple little auberge. Tasty old-fashioned dishes; clean rooms, shared clean bathrooms. Meals and rooms C. Restaurant shut Sunday evening, Mondays.

Chambord

St-Michel, Chambord, 41250 Bracieux, Loir-et-Cher, tel.(54) 20.31.31.

Opposite the château, peaceful except when Son et Lumière is on. Pleasant cooking. Vouvray, Touraine and Bourgueil wines. Adequate rooms. Meals C (M weekends); rooms C–M.

Montrichard

Bellevue, quai du Cher, Montrichard 41400, Loir-et-Cher, tel.(54) 32.06.17.

Superb view over river and old bridge, grand-mère's cuisine, local Touraine wines. Meals M; rooms C. Shut mid November–mid December; Sunday evening, Monday October–April.

Chenonceaux

Bon Laboureur et Château, Chenonceaux, 37150 Bléré, Indre-et-Loire, tel.(47) 23.90.02.

Almost a cliché. Recommended to me recently by dozens of Touraine *vignerons* – and I have known it thirty years. Still excellent value. Terrace and garden for summer eating, or tasting of good list of fairly priced Loire wines. Regional cooking of local ingredients – a touch of 'modern' creeping in. Meals and rooms M. Shut Wednesday noon, Thursday in winter.

Renaudière, Chenonceaux, 37150 Bléré, Indre-et-Loire, tel.(47) 23.90.04.

Cheap alternative to Bon Laboureur with pleasant garden, good food and wine; excellent value. Meals and rooms C.

St-Martin-le-Beau

La Treille, St-Martin-le-Beau 37270, Indre-et-Loire (9km SE of Amboise by D83), tel.(47) 50.67.17.

Several *vignerons* recommend this for meals, simple rooms and good value. All cheap. I have not tried it.

Amboise

Château de Pray, BP 146, 37400 Amboise, Indre-et-Loire (3km along D751 at Chargé, NE of Amboise), tel.(47) 57.23.67.

Enchanting château on wooded hill overlooking Loire. Old-style cooking of local products. Superb Loire exploring centre. Gets booked up. Meals and rooms M.

Vernou-sur-Brenne

Hostellerie Perce-Neige, rue Anatole France, Vernou, 37210 Vouvray, Indre-et-Loire, tel.(47) 52.10.04.

Family-run hostellerie in old manor set in big charming garden; perfect for summer tasting. Down the road from Vouvray. Bedrooms vary. Pick slightly dearer menus for good meals. Meals and rooms C–M.

Azay-le-Rideau

Grand Monarque, place République, 37190 Azay-le-Rideau, Indre-et-Loire, tel.(47) 45.40.08.

Winningly eccentric old inn in Jacquet family for generations. Renowned as always for good cooking of real Touraine dishes – *sandre*, salmon, duck in local style. Good value. Meals and rooms M. Shut mid November– 1 March.

Chinon

Gargantua, 73 rue Haute Saint-Maurice, 37500 Chinon, Indre-et-Loire, tel.(47) 93.04.71.

In a fifteenth-century palace in the old town. For hearty eaters of fine old-style regional dishes. Meals and rooms M. Shut January, February.

Château de Marçay, Marcay (7km S of Chinon on D749, D116) 37500 Chinon, Indre-et-Loire, tel.(47) 93.03.47.

Expensive but the best place to taste Loire wines. Superb cellar in a fifteenth-century château. Excellent cooking, regional with a touch of modern. Worth every franc. Rabelais himself would have approved. Rooms and meals E. Shut mid January–mid March.

Saumur (at Chênehutte-les-Tuffeaux, 7km W on D751)

Le Prieuré, 49350 Gennes, Maine-et-Loire, tel.(41) 50.15.31.

Lovely hotel made from priory and Renaissance manor house in park in superb position overlooking Loire. Lovely bedrooms; some simpler bungalows in grounds for latecomers. Outstanding cooking with imaginative use of regional ingredients. Since I put it in my *Encore Travellers' France*, readers have given it nothing but praise. Meals VE; rooms E–VE. Shut 3 January–end February.

Gennes (on Loire between Saumur and Angers)

Hostellerie de la Loire, 9 ave des Cadets de Saumur, Gennes 49350, Maine-et-Loire, tel.(41) 51.81.03.

Though the nearby modern Aux Naulets d'Anjou (tel.(41) 51.81.88) is luring many with painting and cooking lessons, I stand by the favourite of my *Travellers' France* readers. An old posting inn with shady terrace overlooking the Loire, it has sun patio, beams inside, very good choice of Loire wines and good cooking of local dishes, especially Loire fish. Meals and rooms C.

Les Rosiers (over Loire bridge from Gennes)

Jeanne de Laval, Les-Rosiers-sur-Loire, 49350 Gennes, Maine-et-Loire, tel.(41) 51.80.17.

Remains one of my favourite places to eat in France. The late great Albert Augereau set a magnificent standard for years with classical cooking of the very best. His son Michel follows the tradition with a touch of Grande Cuisine Moderne. The best Loire wines. Lovely garden. Civilised Old France. Meals M–E; rooms M. Shut Monday; 20 November–28 December.

Ancenis

Val de Loire, Le Jarier (2km along N23 E towards Angers), 44150 Ancenis, Loire-Atlantique, tel.(40) 96.00.03.

Modern Logis de France among vines and meadows. Good Muscadet, Anjou and Saumur wines. Restaurant shut Saturdays. Meals and rooms C.

Near Nantes (11km E on N149)

La Lande St-Martin, Haute-Goulaine, 44115 Basse-Goulaine, Loire-Atlantique, tel.(40) 80.00.80.

Reliable, comfortable modernised hotel in pleasant gardens away from Nantes industrial life and traffic. Useful, with good value menus of traditional cooking and high-quality Loire wines. Good base for finding the Muscadet tastings. Meals C–M; rooms M.

INDEX

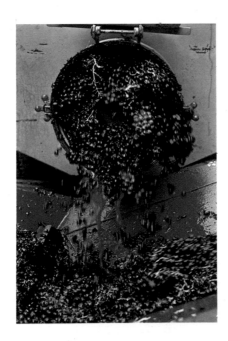